The Principles of New Ethics I

From Descartes to Spinoza, Western philosophers have attempted to propose an axiomatic systemization of ethics. However, without consensus on the contents and objects of ethics, the system remains incomplete. This four-volume set presents a model that highlights a Chinese philosopher's insights on ethics after a 22-year study. Three essential components of ethics are examined: metaethics, normative ethics, and virtue ethics.

This volume mainly studies meta-ethics. The author not only studies the five primitive concepts of ethics—"value," "good," "ought," "right," and "fact"—and reveals their relationship, but also demonstrates the solution to the classic "Hume's guillotine"—whether "ought" can be derived from "fact." His aim is to identify the methods of making excellent moral norms, leading to solutions on how to prove ethical axioms and ethical postulates.

Written by a renowned philosopher, the Chinese version of this set sold more than 60,000 copies and has exerted tremendous influence on the academic scene in China. The English version will be an essential read for students and scholars of ethics and philosophy in general.

Wang Haiming is a professor at the Department at Philosophy at Peking University, China, and a specially appointed professor at Sanya University, China, mainly studying ethics and political philosophy. Email: wanghaimingw@sina.cn

China Perspectives

The *China Perspectives* series focuses on translating and publishing works by leading Chinese scholars, writing about both global topics and China-related themes. It covers Humanities & Social Sciences, Education, Media and Psychology, as well as many interdisciplinary themes.

This is the first time any of these books have been published in English for international readers. The series aims to put forward a Chinese perspective, give insights into cutting-edge academic thinking in China, and inspire researchers globally.

Titles in philosophy currently include:

Leaping Over the Caudine Forks of Capitalism
Zhao Jiaxiang

Theories and Practices of Scientific Socialism
Zhao Jiaxiang

The Principles of New Ethics III
Normative Ethics II
Wang Haiming

The Principles of New Ethics I
Meta-ethics
Wang Haiming

The Principles of New Ethics II
Normative Ethics I
Wang Haiming

The Metaphysics of Philosophical Daoism
Kai ZHENG

For more information, please visit www.routledge.com/series/CPH

The Principles of New Ethics I
Meta-ethics

Wang Haiming

LONDON AND NEW YORK

This book is published with financial support from the Chinese Fund for the Humanities and Social Sciences.

First published in English 2021
by Routledge
2 Park Square, Milton Park, Abingdon, Oxon OX14 4RN

and by Routledge
52 Vanderbilt Avenue, New York, NY 10017

Routledge is an imprint of the Taylor & Francis Group, an informa business

© 2021 Wang Haiming

Translated by Yamin Wu; translation polished by Martin Noble and Matthew Hood and proofread by Yang Aihua.

The right of Wang Haiming to be identified as author of this work has been asserted by him in accordance with sections 77 and 78 of the Copyright, Designs and Patents Act 1988.

All rights reserved. No part of this book may be reprinted or reproduced or utilised in any form or by any electronic, mechanical, or other means, now known or hereafter invented, including photocopying and recording, or in any information storage or retrieval system, without permission in writing from the publishers.

Trademark notice: Product or corporate names may be trademarks or registered trademarks, and are used only for identification and explanation without intent to infringe.

English Version by permission of The Commercial Press.

British Library Cataloguing-in-Publication Data
A catalogue record for this book is available from the British Library

Library of Congress Cataloging-in-Publication Data
A catalog record has been requested for this book

ISBN: 978-1-138-33161-7 (hbk)
ISBN: 978-0-429-44721-1 (ebk)

Typeset in Times New Roman
by Newgen Publishing UK

Printed in the United Kingdom
by Henry Ling Limited

Contents

List of figures	vi
Endorsement	vii
Preface	xi
Introduction to *The Principles of New Ethics*	1
Introduction to this volume	41

PART I
Categories of meta-ethics — 49

1	The starting concept of ethics	51
2	Primitive concept of ethics	75

PART II
The meta-ethical proof — 99

3	The axiom of the existence of value and the postulate of the existence of moral value in ethics	101
4	The deductive axioms and deductive postulates in ethics	139
	Appendix: Contents of The Principles of Ethics	192
	Index	205

Figures

0.1	The objects of ethics	16
2.1	The categories of things in value sciences	95
2.2	The categories of things in non-value sciences	96
3.1	The categories of property	107

Endorsement

Utilitarianism is a most vital field of thinking in contemporary Chinese pluralistic thought. It is rooted in Chinese people's everyday life experience. If we should choose a leading figure of utilitarianism in China, Professor Wang Haiming is undoubtedly the best candidate. He is the first to systematically expound the principles of utilitarianism in contemporary China and the first in China to put forward new principles in what can rightly be called the new utilitarianism. In the past, both in the West and China, utilitarianism has predominantly advocated the principle of "net balance of the maximum interests" or "the greatest interests for the greatest number" as the ultimate goal of morality. The measurement of all actions under the new utilitarianism established by Wang Haiming is, as a crucial point of difference, rather a system of the ultimate standard of morality. The "net balance of maximum interests" is conditional in that is only the ultimate standard of morality in the circumstance of interest conflicts, "increasing the quantum of interests without negatively affecting anyone." The ultimate standard of morality is to be found in the circumstance that the interests do not conflict with one another, therefore "increasing or decreasing everyone's quantum of interests" is the ultimate standard of morality and should be absolutely followed under any circumstance. Obviously, this new utilitarianism can avoid the criticism that "utilitarianism certainly leads to injustice."

Wang Haiming's utilitarian thought, which originates from the profound utilitarian tradition of China, is closely related to the ethical thoughts of Western utilitarianism, and is deeply rooted in the life of the Chinese people whose thinking and behaviors have changed with the process of market economy reform in contemporary China. The formation of his utilitarian thought comes from his frank and sincere personal character, as well as from his discontentment with, and criticism of the hypocrisy surrounding ethical conduct and moral norms prevalent in China when he was a young man. The utilitarian thinking of this work is therefore characterized not only by his understanding of the everyday life experiences of the Chinese people, but also by his own lived experience and acute sense of right or wrong, much of which also reflects his deep immersion in scholarly studies of formal logic. The utilitarian theory he has cultivated completely discards anything that is beyond

viii *Endorsement*

the realities of human nature and society and any kind of ethical thinking that is hypocritical.

Perhaps, for some time, certain hypocritical ethical principles will still prevail with the support of social or political power, but these sorts of principles will never have the universal and eternal values as that of the utilitarian principles and doctrine expounded by Wang Haiming. The blood, sweat and tears of ordinary Chinese people, their honorable conduct and way of thinking, are what weighs on Wang Haiming's mind and motivates his ethical principles. In this way, his work can be seen as both an indictment of specious morals and a call for the return to a world based on true moral conduct. The utilitarianism proffered by Wang Haiming, in its consideration of the concept of self-interest, is by no means a theory for the justification of selfishness, in fact, his criticism of egoism shows that his utilitarianism is based on one of the most fundamental principles of human nature: justice. It is most gratifying that he has inherited and popularized the critical spirit of the May 4th Movement, that his utilitarianism and the theory of justice have "fallen in love" and are integrated into a coherent whole.

There are two points worthy of our attention in this important work by Wang Haiming. First, his efforts to turn "the pursuit of, and attempts at, an axiomatization of ethics, since Spinoza's time, into a science, so that ethics finally becomes an axiom system which is as objective, inevitable, rigorous and operable as physics", and which consequently integrates "meta-ethics, normative ethics and virtue ethics, which have been largely in a mutually exclusive state in the West, as scientific methods to analyze the series of unresolved puzzling problems that reach back to the time of Aristotle."

Second, he has clarified the theories of justice both in China and the West in pointing out the shortcomings of Rawls' theory of justice and constructing a new system of principles of justice. Although I have different understandings and views of Rawls' theory from that of Wang's, his criticism of Rawls is admirable. Despite Rawls' lifelong efforts to construct a theory of justice to replace the popular utilitarianism (still a mainstream trend of thought) in the West, it is hard to say that his efforts have been a success. From his unique utilitarian point of view, Wang Haiming criticizes the deficiency of Rawls' theory of equality, advocating a return from Rawls' second principle of justice to Aristotle's principle of "proportional equality."

Wang Haiming creates the term "equal exchange of interests and harm"—the concepts of "interests" and "harm" being open-ended definitions—and uses it to express the general principle of justice. Then, from this general principle of justice he deduces the fundamental principle of justice: the equal exchange of rights and duties. Based on this fundamental principle of justice he deduces the fundamental principle of social justice, that is, the "principle of contribution": the rights that society distributes to a person should be proportional to his contribution and equal to his duties. And from the principle of contribution, he deduces the general principle of equality: on the one hand, everyone, because of his most basic contribution, is completely equal—everyone is the same, born as a shareholder in the creation and establishment of society—and ought to have fundamental rights and human rights on equal footing ("full equality"); on the other hand, everyone ought to have the corresponding unequal and non-fundamental rights because of the inequality of their contributions; that is to say, the inequality of non-fundamental rights possessed by everyone ought to be completely equal in proportion to the inequality of their contributions ("proportional equality"). Finally, from this general principle of justice, he deduces the "principle of political equality," "principle of economic equality," and "principle of equality of opportunity," and hence establishes a new system of principles of justice, which makes for a valuable contribution of Chinese utilitarianism to the academic fields of the world.

Professor Wang Haiming has devoted himself to the study of ethics for decades, his works have greatly enriched the ethical thinking of utilitarianism in China and have contributed significantly to the Chinese normative theory of ethics. I admire so much his boundless and fruitful thinking. I sincerely hope that in the future, through his new utilitarianism, Wang Haiming, along with his colleagues and students, successfully promotes scientific humanitarianism, liberalism and egalitarianism in far reaching ways, making important contributions to the construction of the new ethics of Chinese academism.

Baogang He
Alfred Deakin Professor
Chair in International Relations
School of Humanities and Social Sciences,
Faculty of Arts & Education
Deakin University
May 5, 2019

Preface

P.1

I was born in 1950 in Zhenlai, Jilin, and grew up in the small town of Tantu, surrounded by farmland, flowers, plants, and chirping insects and birds. My father was a railway worker. His salary of roughly 50 Yuan a month barely covered the expenses of raising six children. To put food on the table, my father resorted to cultivating every plot of barren land he could find. We somehow managed to grow enough produce. My older brother and myself were tasked with turning rock-solid soil with our hoes. Oftentimes, we would toil for hours on end, sweating like waterfalls beneath the scorching sun. We had to soak our shirts in cold water so as not to faint from the heat. On one such day, I asked my brother, "How can I escape this sea of suffering and attain wealth and honor?" I was around 14 at the time. My brother, a few years my senior, replied, "Literacy. Only by persevering through decades of study can one hope to relish in a day of glory." From this point on I devoted myself to my studies. Not long after, i.e. mid-late 1960s, the entire country began to repudiate any efforts towards achieving personal success, and then the altruism movement began. The government pressed vehemently for the "collective," telling people to break from notions of "private" gain and to strive hard against any conceptions of oneself as a personal "I." Although still a relatively young student, I found myself reading up more and more on the subject of ethics. Reading my way through both the classical Western and Chinese texts I was soon transfixed (and have been ever since). The subject matters of altruism and so-called self-interest piqued my curiosity: Can one be truly altruistic? Is it immoral to be self-interested where its purpose is also to benefit others? However, I realized that, without a knowledge of philosophy, without an understanding of the concepts of cause, effect, chance, necessity, essence, and law, I was not intellectually equipped to study ethics. So, I took the necessary steps and immersed myself in the study of philosophy.

On becoming well-versed in philosophy, I then spent many more years writing and revising the manuscripts of a new work titled *New Philosophy*, and by 1983 had finally completed it. It was a work of more than 800,000 Chinese characters in length. In 1984, I was admitted to graduate school.

xii   *Preface*

There I commenced another manuscript called *New Ethics*, which was based on my first foray into moral philosophy in the *New Philosophy*. The new manuscript not only afforded a good opportunity to expand on the matters of moral philosophy raised in that work (a section of just 100,000 or so Chinese characters in length), it was more importantly my first opportunity to focus exclusively on ethics theory.

The work was a result of years spent engrossed in philosophical contemplation. It became a daily preoccupation that had consumed me at almost every moment—as I walked, slept, ate, and even when I was ill—such that nearing its completion, in September 1993, my health began to rapidly deteriorate. On the verge of finishing the manuscript, which I titled *The Essence of New Ethics*, I feared the worst and, in the throes of my illness, said to my wife: "If only this book could be published, I would die without regret." To these words my wife wept. My wife entered my life in 1989 and has accompanied me ever since. Like Sancho followed Don Quixote, despite everyone's doubts, she never left my side as I persevered in my quest to bring this work into fruition. Such was the formidable task of constructing a science-based ethics I often liken it to one man's first attempt at constructing a palace all by himself, since having the knowledge and resources at one's disposal does not ensure its completion. I doubt I could have achieved as much without the companionship of my wife. Unconcerned by my lack of success, in a conventional sense, at forty years of age, she married me, and has been my greatest source of encouragement ever since; even to this day, she tolerates the sort of stubborn pedantry with which I approach my work. I shall never forget the thousands of days we spent under the coconut trees of Hainan merrily discussing and debating the countless issues ethics scholars wrestled with for over 2000 years. The *Essence of New Ethics* was the result of our many happy days together and our enchanting encounters with complex theory. The vision and labor of that work, as of all my works since, have been something we have both shared. By January 1994, still amidst my illness, I rallied enough strength to complete the manuscript, and it was published that same year by Huaxia Publishing House under the altered title *Seeking New Morality: The Establishment of Scientific Ethics*.

Though I was quite pleased with the manuscript as a whole, *Scientific Ethics* was relatively skeletal in its scope. I had decided to write a new manuscript based on this book, and by February 1994 I had begun to systematically revise the core section titled "Scientific ethics." It was then that I resumed an obsessive preoccupation with my work. This was to last another six years. Within the first hour after rising from sleep, work was the first thing on my list. My days generally began with research and note-taking in the morning, and in the afternoon, I did most of my writing at the Summer Palace. There, I would usually have a swim in Tuancheng lake before finding a quiet area near the lake to sit, think, and write. More often than not, however, my afternoons at the Summer Palace were unaccompanied by unbearable fatigue from endless contemplation of philosophical matters. In winter, I routinely

Preface xiii

immersed myself in the icy water of the lake. This relieved me of any mental exhaustion, as well as any kind of physical pain or feelings of despondency. Along with the scenic view to the mountains in the distance, the winter swims always revitalized my body, mind, and spirit, restoring the clarity of my thinking, I repeated this routine every day both in winter and the warmer months until 2000 when I finally finished the manuscript. It was submitted to the Commercial Press of China and titled *The Principles of New Ethics*. To this day, I recount with disbelief that it took an arduous 16 years.

However, when I was proofreading the press proof, reveling in the happiness of "the old cow licking the calf," I suddenly found that the arguments of the book, by and large, were quite rough. This was a defect also noticed by Professor Tang Daixing. In his academic monograph *Theory on Systems of Excellent Morality: A Study of New Ethics*, he commented:

> Despite its theoretical system as a whole it has the rigor of its logical system, though in the particular synthesis and discussion it has the tendency of certain plain thinking which reflects a certain degree of sketchiness.

Starting from the very first page, I set about revising it for a second edition of *New Ethics*. This again, however, took much longer than I had intended. In all, another seven years had passed before I completed it in early 2007. It was submitted again to Commercial Press for publication as a revised edition in 2008. There is good reason for this, however. Its length was three times the first edition (more than 1.5 million Chinese characters in total). It took me an entire 22 years to complete in total. Throughout this time, I had refrained from almost all social activities, abandoning occasions with friends, my wider family, and sometimes even my own family. I had limited my life to writing, lecturing, and physical exercise as a form of release from the mental strain.

My mentor Huanzhang Yang had warned me many years ago that "human beings are social animals, your isolating yourself from society will only bring many difficulties into your life." He was very right, of course. But I did value highly my time and tried to spend my time writing *New Ethics* as much as possible. *New Ethics* is the purpose and meaning of my life, even more important than my own life. Compared to the kind of satisfaction that the completion of this work would bring, I was not worried by the thought turbulence ahead. In 2007, Peking University tallied the citation rates of past published professors in philosophy, and *New Ethics* ranked number 1.

I had never set out to write such a lengthy work. As Darwin had stated, one of the reasons his work *On the Origin of Species* was a success was its short length:

> Another element in the success of the book was its moderate size; and this I owe to the appearance of Mr. Wallace's essay; had I published on the scale in which I began to write in 1856, the book would have been four

xiv   *Preface*

or five times as large as the "Origin," and very few would have had the patience to read it.[1]

Nevertheless, my second edition of *New Ethics* is too lengthy. Thus, from the moment it was published, I began to shorten it. And after two rounds of drastic cuts, I produced another two manuscripts, but neither of them brought me satisfaction. On having finished my other two manuscripts *Stateology* (published in 2012) and *The Economic Characteristics of China: A Comparison of Economic System and Social Formation between China and the West in Five Thousand Years* (publication forthcoming), I dedicated time to completing a third revision because I felt the discourse was lacking thorough argumentation and needed major changes to effect this. However, by the time I completed *The Principles of New Ethics* at the end of 2016, I had managed to scale it down to 650,000 characters or so in total. So, in this respect, at least, I had taken Darwin's advice, and was satisfied with both the substance and length of the work.

P.2

On May 17, 2016, President Xi Jinping repeatedly emphasized innovation in his speech at the Symposium on the Work of Philosophy and Social Sciences: "We should carry out the new innovation project of philosophy and social sciences, build a platform for innovation in philosophy and social sciences, and comprehensively promote innovation in all fields of philosophy and social sciences"; "We should adhere to the use of the past for the present, adapt foreign things for Chinese use, integrate all kinds of resources and constantly promote knowledge innovation, theoretical innovation and method innovation"; "The vitality of theory lies in innovation, which is the eternal theme of the development of philosophy and social science, as well as the inevitable demands of the social development, the deepening of practice and of historical advance to philosophy and social science"; "History shows that the era of great social change must be the era of great development of philosophy and social sciences. Contemporary China is experiencing the most extensive and profound social changes in the history of our country, and is also carrying out the grandest and the most unique practical innovation in human history."[2]

These are impressive statements indeed! In ways, they speak to my own inspirations, innovations, and endeavors, for 22 years and more, to realize the fullest potential of this work. My original intention was for the work to be unconventional, but rather as the outcome of social reality and theoretical speculation. However, just as many things grow in the garden that were never sown there, this work is quite unique in its founding a new ethics. It finds that ethics is essentially a value science concerning the goodness and badness (or the excellence and inferiority) of morality. Furthermore, this work finds that the concept of moral value is fundamentally different from the concept of

Preface xv

morality or the concept of moral norms. The latter concepts are basically the same because they refer to morals that are made or agreed upon by society. Moral values, however, are a kind of fact, so they cannot be made or agreed upon. In other words, moral values are the standard by which we determine the goodness and badness of the moral norms made or agreed upon. In this way, moral values are not dissimilar to nutritional values. For example, the nutritional value of pork is not made by humans; humans can only create conduct norms around eating pork. Whether these norms conform or do not conform to the nutritional value of pork, such as it should only be eaten in moderation, determines whether they are bad or good norms. So, if norms that conform to values are good, and norms that do not conform are bad, how on earth do we make moral norms that conform to moral values?

It turns out that the excellent morality of the behavioral ought can only be derived from the objective nature of the behavioral fact through the ultimate goal of morality—the promotion of everyone's interests. This process is presented in the following deductive formula for moral values.

Premise 1: the behavioral fact (substance of moral value)
Premise 2: the ultimate goal of morality (standard of moral value)
Conclusion 1: the behavioral ought (moral value)
Conclusion 2: the excellent morality is the moral norm that conforms to the moral value of behavior (excellent moral norm)

This deductive formula comprises the ethical axioms. With it, we can deduce all the objects, propositions, and contents of ethics. It is also the answer to the critical question concerning Hume's guillotine, namely whether "ought" can be derived from "fact." Based on the science of the ethical axioms, this work has been divided into four volumes which correspond with the three main disciplines of ethics. Volume I lays the foundation for Meta-ethics as the method for the making of excellent morality. It studies the relationship between "ought" and "is," and thus settles the problem of the justification of moral value judgments—how to make excellent morality that conforms to moral values. In short, meta-ethics is the scientific verification of this ethical axiom.

Volume II and Volume III develop a framework for normative ethics, focusing on the propositions that comprise the ethical axioms: firstly, the deduction of premise 2, namely the concept of morality, the ultimate goal of morality and the ultimate standard of morality; secondly, the deduction of premise 1, namely the 16 types and 4 laws of the behavioral facts; and finally, the consideration of conclusion 1 and 2, using the ultimate standard of morality to measure the good and evil of behavioral facts, so as to deduce the general principle of morality, namely the "moral good," and the moral principles of other-regarding (mainly the value standard of the goodness and badness of state governance and state institutions), which are the principles of "justice," "equality," "humanity," "liberty," and "elimination of alienation," as well as the moral principle of "happiness" which is self-regarding, and from these

xvi *Preface*

seven moral principles we deduce eight moral rules of "honesty," "cherishing-life," "self-respect," "modesty," "continence," "courage," "wisdom," and "the doctrine of the mean." Therefore, mainly through the ultimate goal of morality, normative ethics deduces from the objective nature of the behavioral facts the excellent moral norms of the behavioral ought. In sum, normative ethics is the science concerning the process of making excellent moral norms.

Volume IV arrives at a comprehensive understanding of virtue ethics through an examination of conclusion 2 of the ethical axioms, namely how excellent moral norms are transformed into virtues through "conscience" and "reputation": conscience and reputation are ways to realize excellent morality, and virtue is the realization of excellent morality. Therefore, virtue ethics is the ethics concerning the methods for the realization of excellent morality. In this way, we have not only turned the pursuits of an axiomatization of ethics, since Spinoza, into a science, so that ethics finally becomes an axiom system which is as objective, inevitable, rigorous, and operable as physics, but we have also integrated and necessarily delineated meta-ethics, normative ethics, and virtue ethics; particularly the latter two, which, especially in the West, have largely co-opted and then minimized the relevance of the other as part of their main approach to ethics.

This is a new ethics that my work constructs. One can easily see its originality and value by comparing it with ethical works in the West, although the study of ethics in Western academia is much more developed than the study of ethics in Chinese academia. This is because, on the one hand, meta-ethics, normative ethics, and virtue ethics are not the three major parts of the systematic structure of ethics in the West. Up until the end of the nineteenth century, ethics and the so-called "normative ethics" were almost the same concept. In 1903, when Moore's publication of *Principia Ethica* announced the birth of "Meta-ethics," it dominated Western ethics for more than half a century. In the 1960s, meta-ethics, which deviated from normative ethics and tried to support the edifice of ethics alone, began to decline. Contributing to this decline were the revival of traditional normative ethics epitomized by Rawls' *A Theory of Justice and* the rise of the so-called virtue ethics, which opposed normative ethics. To this day, normative ethicists mistakenly think that ethics is composed of meta-ethics and normative ethics, and that virtue ethics is included in the latter; while virtue ethicists, though they also study moral norms, mistakenly think that the underlying premise of normative ethics is a fallacy and that ethics therefore need only concern itself with meta-ethics and virtue ethics.

On the other hand, since Descartes, great thinkers such as Hobbes, Spinoza, Hume, Helvetius, Moore, and Rawls have actively advocated the axiomatization or geometrization of ethics. But Spinoza was the only one who put this advocacy into practice. Although he made a genuine attempt to construct an axiomatic system, it was undoubtedly a failure: he did not discover an ethical axiom that could deduce all the objects and contents of ethics. After Spinoza, no further attempts were made to build an axiomatic

Preface xvii

system of ethics; the reason being that no one was able to solve Hume's guillotine (and therein discover the ethical axiom). For more than half a century, Moore, Evans-Pritchard, W. D. Ross, Russell, Wittgenstein, Schlick, Carnap, Ayer, Stevenson, Stephen Toulmin, and R. M. Hare and other masters' studies of meta-ethics (as the science of axioms of ethics) not only failed to establish a scientific system of meta-ethics—even a book with the title *Meta-ethics* did not appear—but also mistook meta-ethics as the science of analyzing moral language. As Hare wrongly stated: "Ethics, as I conceive it, is the logical study of the language of morals."[3] Meta-ethics in the West has since been typically defined in the mainstream "as consisting in the analysis of moral language."[4]

In summary, it is understandable why the works on the principles of ethics in the West today are surprisingly incomplete, subjective, arbitrary, and fragmented. Even the most popular works on ethics such as Frankena's *Ethics* (1973), Beauchamp's *Philosophical Ethics* (1982) (and we could include Pojman's *Ethical Theory: Classical and Contemporary Readings* (1995) here as well) are similar in this respect. Frankena's *Ethics* consists of six chapters: the first chapter is "Morality and Moral Philosophy," the second is "Egoistic and Deontological Theories," the third is "Utilitarianism, Justice and Love," the fourth is "Moral Value and Responsibility," the fifth is "Intrinsic Value and the Good Life," and the sixth is "Meaning and Justification."

Beauchamp's *Philosophical Ethics* and Pojman's *Ethical Theory* belong to another type of the prevalent works on ethical principles in the West today: its characteristics is that each disquisition about ethical principles is accompanied by quotations from the original works by masters of ethics. Take Beauchamp's *Philosophical Ethics* for example. The work consists of ten chapters: the first chapter is "Morality and Moral Philosophy," the second is "Objectivity and Diversity in Morals," the third is "Mill and Utilitarian Theories," the fourth is "Kant and Deontological Theories," the fifth is "Aristotle and Virtue Theories," the sixth is "Rights," the seventh is "Justice," the eighth is "Liberty and Law," the ninth is "The Justification of Moral Beliefs," and the tenth is "Facts and Values."

The objects of ethics studied in Frankena's *Ethics* and Beauchamp's *Philosophical Ethics* are incomplete. First of all, the last two chapters of these two books all belong to meta-ethics but only deal with meta-ethics schools without any detailed study of the main objects of meta-ethics such as "value," "good," "ought," "just," "fact," "is," Hume's guillotine (whether "ought" can be derived from "is"), and "axioms and postulates of ethics": in Frankena's *Ethics*, only the "good" is studied, while in Beauchamp's *Philosophical Ethics*, none of these objects is studied.

Secondly, the first three chapters of Frankena's *Ethics* and the first eight chapters of Beauchamp's *Philosophical Ethics* (except the fifth chapter and the introduction) belong to normative ethics, but they are mainly concerned with the main schools of normative ethics, with hardly any analysis on the object of normative ethics: they have not studied the law of "origin and goal of morality," "ultimate standard of morality," "human nature" or "ethical behavior"

xviii *Preface*

and "the degrees of love"; neither have they studied the particular principles of "elimination of alienation," "justice and equality," or "humanity and liberty," nor studied the moral rules of "happiness," "honesty," "cherishing-life," "continence," "courage," "wisdom," "the doctrine of the mean," "modesty," "self-respect," etc.

Finally, the fourth chapter of Frankena's *Ethics* and the fifth chapter of Beauchamp's *Philosophical Ethics* belong to the category of virtue ethics, but there are almost no studies on the objects of virtue ethics: "conscience" and "reputation," which are the main objects of virtue ethics, were completely neglected in both chapters, and neither study the main parts of "virtue," which is the core object of virtue ethics, such as the nature of virtue, the structure of virtue, the types of virtue, the laws of virtue, and the ways to cultivate virtue, namely, the construction of virtuous institutions and moral upbringing.

In short, although these two books are regarded as the authoritative works on the principle of ethics in the West today, they concentrate mostly on the different schools of ethics with little study of particular objects, at least no arguments or proofs thereof. Even the analysis of ethics schools are incomplete: many schools are neglected. There is no intrinsic, necessary, and objective connection between chapters, sections, and ethical problems in either of the works. Both completely discard the axiomatic tradition of western ethics. In particular, the section on meta-ethics in both is placed at or near the end of the work, which is obviously an upside down arrangement, fully exposing the unsystematic feature of Western studies on ethics today.

Despite such great masters as Socrates, Plato, Aristotle, Hume, Smith, Kant, Mill, Sidgwick, Moore, and Rawls, modern works on the principle of ethics, which attempt to synthesize the ethical thoughts of the masters from ancient to present, are unsystematic, incomplete, and lacking in argumentation. The reasons for this are, first, because the ethical problems are discussed without properly addressing Hume's guillotine; second, because the research object of meta-ethics is still not clear; and, third, because a scientific system of ethics is far from being established.

However, as I mentioned at the outset, my intention of comparing *The Principles of New Ethics* with the authoritative works on principles of ethics in the West today was inspired by President Xi's speech on May 17, 2016. The following excerpt from that speech has been lingering in my mind ever since.

> The Chinese culture that has lasted for thousands of years is a profound foundation for the growth and development of philosophy and social sciences with Chinese characteristics. I have said that standing on the vast land of 9.6 million square kilometers, absorbing the cultural nutrients accumulated by the long struggle of the Chinese nation, with the majestic power of the 1.3 billion Chinese people, our taking of own path has an incomparably broad stage and a profound historical heritage, with a unrivaled strong forward force. The Chinese people should have this

Preface   xix

confidence, and every Chinese should have this confidence. We say that we must strengthen the self-confidence in the path, theory, and institution of socialism with Chinese characteristics, but in the end we must strengthen self-confidence in culture.[5]

P.3

This work can be seen as a new ethics principally because it unravels a series of puzzling problems that have troubled ethicists since the times of Aristotle. Below, I have provided key examples:

1. It finds that ethics is fundamentally and most importantly a science concerning the value standards of the goodness or badness of state institutions: "justice and equality" are the fundamental value standards; "humanity and liberty" are the highest value standards; and the "promotion of everyone's interests" is the ultimate value standard. These value standards substantiate Aristotle's statement that "the science of ethics is the science of politics."
2. It finds four major laws of change between the highest and lowest forms of national moral character, and thus further establishes that the construction of institutions (principally economic, political, cultural, and social systems) is the general means for the cultivation of national moral character. The study of the four major laws and the institutions shows that the moral character of the countrymen, on the whole, depends entirely on the goodness or badness of the state institutions. As long as the state institutions are good, the moral character of the vast majority of the countrymen certainly is good; as long as the state institutions are bad, the moral character of the vast majority of the countrymen certainly is bad.
3. It finds that the ultimate moral standard or the so-called utilitarian standard is a system of value standards composed of a general standard and two sub-standards. The general standard is the ultimate standard that ought to be followed under any circumstance: "Increasing or decreasing everyone's quantum of interests." Sub-standard 1 is the ultimate standard under the circumstances when human interests do not conflict with one another or when a compromise can be made, namely the "Pareto Criterion": "Increasing the quantum of interests without negatively affecting anyone." Sub-standard 2 is the ultimate standard under the circumstance when human interests conflict and no compromise can be made, namely "the net balance of maximum interests" or "the greatest interests for the greatest number." All Western utilitarians reduce utilitarian standards to sub-standard 2 and thus make the mistake of taking the part for the whole, triggering the criticisms of utilitarianism.
4. It proves a law of human nature concerning the "degrees of love." Love is the psychological response to the interests and pleasures. Therefore, the

xx *Preface*

less I am the recipient of the interests and pleasure of others, the more I am alienated from others, the less I will love others, and the less I will pursue the interests and pleasure of others; the more I am a recipient of the interests and pleasure of others, the less I am alienated from others, the more I will love others, and the more I will pursue the interests and pleasure of others. Hence, in the final analysis, I love myself the most and most of my actions in life are the pursuit of my own interests, i.e., because I love myself more than I love others, I am more likely to seek interests for myself than I would for others. In sum, self-love is greater than love for others, and self-interest is greater than benefiting others. Likewise, since people pursue their own interests most of the time, it is only some of the time that they behave altruistically to others. This is a law of human nature.

5. It finds three principles of moral good and evil. First of all, *selflessly benefiting others* is the highest principle of moral good. Where it guides our actions, it can only occasionally be observed as a behavioral ought; its function is to enable self-sacrifice or the selfless benefit of others where self-interested actions can otherwise cause harm when they conflict with the interests of others or society. Secondly, *benefiting others out of one's self-interest* is the basic principle of moral good. Where it guides our actions, it is a behavioral ought that can always be observed; its function is to enable benefit to others through self-interested actions, in contrast to harming others through self-interested actions, where self-interest is consistent with others' interests. Finally, *mere self-interest* is the lowest principle of moral good. Where it guides our actions, it can only occasionally be observed as a behavioral ought; its function is to enable self-interest but not self-harm where one's action is not in conflict with the interests of others or society.

6. It finds two principles of equality. On the one hand, everyone ought to enjoy equal basic rights or human rights because everyone is equal in their most basic contribution as a shareholder in the creation of society. This is the principle of the full equality of basic rights, that is, the so-called principle of human rights. On the other hand, people's enjoyment of non-basic rights ought to be unequal and proportional to their contribution, which means people's unequal non-basic rights ought to be equally proportional to their unequal contribution.

For instance, John ought to enjoy one portion of "rights" if he made one portion of contribution, and Jim ought to enjoy three portions of "rights" if he made three portions of contributions. In this way, John's rights are not equal to Jim's rights, but the proportion of the rights John and Jim enjoy is completely equal to the proportion of their contributions. This is the principle of proportional equality, that is, the so-called distribution principle of non-basic human rights.

Preface xxi

The ideological origins of these two principles of equality are Aristotle's two equalities (equality in number and equality in proportion), and Rawls' "two principles of justice."

7. It proves that only free competition can achieve the *exchange of equal values* or justice. Under the conditions of free competition, in order to maximize profits, manufacturers are bound to determine outputs at the level where marginal costs are equal to the price. This means that the price of commodities under the conditions of free competition is equal to the marginal costs, namely that the exchange of equal value is inevitable: the *exchange of equal values* is the law of pricing under free competition. Conversely, the price of commodities under the conditions of a monopoly are bound to be far higher than the marginal costs, which means that non-equal exchange is inevitable: the *exchange of unequal values* is the law of pricing under the conditions of a monopoly.
8. It finds that the root cause of exploitation and economic alienation lies in the monopoly and imbalance of power—both economic power and political power: relying on coercive means such as power, the groups which have monopolistic or excessive power are bound to occupy without compensation the surplus value created by the groups which have no or little power. However, the concentration of capital and economic power that rests with the few as opposed to the distribution of wealth to the masses, ought not to be eliminated by depriving the capital and economic power of capitalists, but ought to be countered only by increasing people's political power. Only when people's political power is greater than that of capitalists can the balance of power between capitalists and the masses be achieved, and can the exploitation and economic alienation be eliminated.

Examples like this are too numerous to enumerate. In short, the reason why this book is a work of new ethics is that it attempts to integrate the most controversial aspects of previous undertakings in ethics into an organized whole. In doing so, we hope to settle the series of ethical problems long debated by different, and even opposing, schools of thought. A work that is not inclusive of competing views is otherwise destined to be a contradictory hodgepodge. To solve the many ethical problems that have triggered so many schools of thought, it is also necessary to put forward new ideas or arguments one by one. This will help unify the different and contradictory theories formed around such puzzling problems. The establishment of new ideas or arguments must be accompanied by corresponding renewal of the many concepts of ethics. As the Chinese saying goes, such is the basic characteristic of an organism that to pull one hair is to affect the whole body. In basing itself on the evolution of ethical thoughts worldwide, the analysis of every problem in this book is at the same time original. Wu Si, the editor-in-chief of *Yan Huang Chunqiu* (《炎黄春秋》), once commented:

xxii *Preface*

> I think Wang Haiming's ...explanations of some of the most abstract questions, such as what justice is, what good is, are very profound, and are quite different from that of some of the great Western philosophers I have ever read.[6]

I think he should say, rather, that although this work on *New Ethics* is different from the works of great western philosophers, it is rooted in them.

The originality of this work lies in part in establishing a new system of discourse in keeping with the accuracy of science. I have renewed and revised many of the older, more familiar concepts, but have also created numerous terms and phrases the reader will be unfamiliar with. So, this work is essentially a mix of old and new terms and phrases to articulate new ethics concepts, such as *benefiting others out of one's self-interest*; *the ultimate standard of morality*; *the general principle of morality*; *the value standard of state institutions*; *the exchange of equal interests or harms*; *excellent morality*; *inferior morality*; *the deductive axiom of excellent norms* and *the deductive postulate of excellent moral norms of ethics*; *the full equality of basic rights* and *the proportional equality of non-basic rights*.

The creation of new discourse systems such as these terms out of pure love of science without the slightest intention of being different and unique, subjective, willful, or catering to the public—this is from the heart. I have always had a strong desire to extricate people from the bondage of the altruistic golden chain of "collectivization," so in ways this is also the result of my intellectual drive to understand the social reality of our country. For some years, I struggled to find the right terminology for *the actions of seeking self-interest by benefiting others and one's society*. It finally came to me 17 years into writing my first manuscript on ethics. I remember the moment vividly. I was in Zhangjiajie at the time, and after having attended a meeting there, I went to a scenic spot that overlooked the mountainous terrain to take in the wilderness the province is renowned for. In deep thought, looking at the sharp ridges and drifting white clouds, a phrase revealed itself to me. It was the perfect expression. It was instant, no more fumbling for words: "benefiting others out of one's self-interest"! That's it, I thought. This conundrum, that had bedeviled me for so long, had finally been solved. The answer it seemed rose from the depths of my soul. It felt it as though a great burden had been lifted. Although I hadn't come close to coining the actual phrase as such when I first took an interest in ethics as a young man, the original intention of all my work on ethics has always been to defend something of the substance of "benefiting others out of one's self-interest."

The other reason for my painstaking endeavor over 22 years for establishing the new ethics and its system of discourse, on the other hand, has much in common with President Xi's advocating "China's learning from foreign countries, its excavation of history and grasping of contemporary times."[7] The most direct source of the important new terms in this work such as "goodness and badness of morality," "excellent morality," and "inferior morality," was

Xun Lu's *A Madman's Diary*. In that work, he summed up the essence of Confucius and the Confucian moral system as "eating people" through the mouth of a madman: "I looked into history, which had no age, and each page was crooked with the words of 'benevolence, justice and morality.' I couldn't fall asleep at all so I read carefully until mid-night before I could see the words between the lines, there are two words written all over the book: 'eating people'!" I closed the book and pondered: doesn't it imply that there are good and bad (excellent and inferior) moralities?

I place so much emphasis now on the new system of discourse created in the these volumes because I was greatly inspired by President Xi's speech a few years back and hope to carry its spirit forward: "To give full play to the role of philosophy and social sciences in China, we should pay attention to strengthening the construction of the discourse system"; "We should be good at refining the concept of identity, and create new concepts, new categories and new expressions that are easily understood and accepted by the international community, and guide the international academic community to carry out research and discussion. This work should start from the discipline of construction, and each discipline must construct a systematic theory and the concepts"; "Only by taking the reality of our country as a starting point of study, can we put forward a theoretical viewpoint with subjectivity and originality, and construct our own disciplines and academic system. Only when Chinese philosophy and social science have a system of discourse in place with its own characteristics can they have an advantage."[8]

I am hugely grateful to Prof. Lu Dan, the chancellor of University of Sanya, who appointed me as a professor of the Institute of National Governance, University of Sanya. In the beautiful "Garden for the Senior Intellectuals" I was able to complete this work amidst the songs of lovely birds and the flowers in full bloom every season.

I am deeply grateful to Professor Baogang He, Fellow of Academy of Social Sciences in Australia, for honoring my book with such a wonderful preface. In 1984 when I was pursuing my master's degree at Renmin University of China, I had the greatest honor of being his classmate and roommate. A true genius, Baogang stunned every one with his straight A record, not by attending classes diligently and working tirelessly for tests, but by ardently reading books of his own choice and passionately writing papers of his own interest; he was privileged to graduate with his master's degree one year ahead of us. He has published numerous academic articles with top journals, a rare accomplishment that earned him a valuable opportunity to collaborate on a book with Professor Li Xiulin, a renowned philosopher in China. As Professor Li acclaims, the best brains of the graduate program at Remin University of China are from Class 1984, and Professor He Baogan, as the then president in charge of academic studies of Class 1984, towers over the whole class with his rare talents and enviable achievements.

xxiv *Preface*

I would like to thank Prof. Lixian Cheng for his suggestion to improve the whole catalogue of this work, and his proofreading *Virtue Ethics*, the fourth volume of this ethical monography. Prof. Cheng was awarded a PhD degree in UK for his doctoral thesis entitled *Western Ideas of Social Justice*. I am so happy that his language abilities and insights in ethics have made this work so much better than expected. By the way, it was just Prof. Cheng who gave the subtitle to one of my books, i.e., *Justice and Humanity: The system of Moral Principles for State Governance*, published by the Commercial Press in 2010. For so many years I have been grateful for his friendly help and I am in admiration of his great capacity and rigorous scholarship.

I wish to express my gratitude and appreciation to Ms. Xiaolu An, the director of the Copyright Office of the Commercial Press, for her careful review and full endorsement; to Lian Sun, who is in charge of the editorial board of the Routledge Press; to Mr. Bo Ding, editor-in-chief of the Wenjin Company of the Commercial Press, who has no care for my humble position other than for encouraging the knowledge and insights of author, and who has also been very kind to me and supported my academic research during the fifteen years I worked with him; to Mr. Qiang Li, the director of the Department of Philosophy Editing of the Commercial Press, who has done everything necessary and in every detail for the publication of this work and its translation into this English version; to Dr. Shuanglong Zhang, the editor-in-charge of the book, who is one of the most knowledgeable and responsible editors I have ever met, every word in this book reflects his hard work.

I would like to express my heartfelt thanks here to the translators and proofreaders of the work, Dr. Peiling Zhao, professor at the Department of English at Central South University, China, who earned her Ph.D in English from the University of South Florida, USA; and Dr. Matthew Hood, who holds a Ph.D in Literature and the Environment from Deakin University, Australia, and who, along with his philosophical background, has strived to make this English version as fluent as that of a native speaker; Aihua Yang, who holds a Master's degree in Law from Minnan Normal University, and who proofread the English version word for word. Thanks also to Martin Noble, who did a substantial amount of amendment to the translation where there were errors in grammar, tenses, plurals, etc.

I especially want to thank Dr. Ying Sun, Dean of the School of Marxism at the Minzu University of China. She not only wrote chapters on happiness, but also discussed structures and ideas regarding my theory. She has been going to the Summer Palace with me for almost ten years to swim, write, and discuss these problems. In 1999, Mr. Wen Xu, who is with the Central Orchestra of China, and who often swims with us in the Summer Palace, wrote a heartfelt poem for us:

A pair of Mandarin ducks swim in the water,
Tackling arduous projects as soon as they arrive onto the bank.

The moon looms over the sea,
As the talented daughter of the Sun family walks down embroidered
stairs.

Both ethics and conscience raise the question:

When will the obscure chaos come to an end?
Picking up the big pen to follow Da Yu's* steps,
And not letting the flood engulf the cosmos.

*Da Yu was a legendary ruler in ancient China, famed for his introduction of flood control and his upright moral character.

And I would like to thank my daughter Jianda Wang, who translated this poem and the first part of the author's preface. She currently attends Macalester College in Minnesota, USA, with an academic concentration on Critical Theory.

Wang Haiming
February 13, 2016
University of Sanya

Notes

1 Charles Darwin, Francis Darwin: *The Autobiography of Charles Darwin: From the Life and Letters of Charles Darwin,* Floating Press, Auckland, New Zealand, 2009, p. 118.
2 Xi Jinping: *Speech at the Symposium on the Work of Philosophy and Social Sciences,* Xinhuanet, May 19, 2016.
3 R. M. Hare: *The Language of Morals,* Oxford University Press, London, 1964, p. 1.
4 Lawrence C. Becker: *Encyclopedia of Ethics,* Volume II, Garland Publishing, Inc., New York, 1992, p. 790.
5 Xi Jinping: *Speech at the Symposium on the Work of Philosophy and Social Sciences,* Xinhuanet, May 19, 2016, p. 10.
6 Wu Si: "Reading is the Main Part in My Life," *Beijing News,* September 5, 2010.
7 Xi Jinping: Speech at the Symposium on the Work of Philosophy and Social Sciences, Xinhuanet, May 19, 2016, p. 15.
8 Xi Jinping: Speech at the Symposium on the Work of Philosophy and Social Sciences, Xinhuanet, May 19, 2016.

Introduction to *The Principles of New Ethics*

0.1 The definition of ethics

0.1.1 Ethics: Science concerning morality

For the importance of morality to mankind, it is enough to point out that society only can exist and develop with morality; that it will collapse and disintegrate without it. This is true of all kinds of societies whether a "society" is as small as a family unit or as big as a country. It is even true for a society of thieves, as Chuang-tzu (庄子) said: "Robbers also have their own morality." Since morality is so important to a society there must be a science to study it. What, then, is the science of morality? No doubt it is ethics! Ethics, many agree, is the science concerned with morality. There is a consensus among many modern Western scholars that ethics "may be defined as the science of morality, or as the science of moral distinctions." Many in the scholarly circle in China also assert: "Ethics is the science concerned with morality."[1]

However, on closer examination, the definition that ethics is the science concerned with morality seems to be superficial and tautological because it implies that ethics is not a special or particular science concerning the morality of certain societies, but rather a science concerning the universality of morality across all societies. Although this definition of ethics is not ideal, it is on one level correct. The word "morality" covers all moralities, including any special or particular moralities, as a generality, abstraction, commonality, or universality. Consequently, ethics is understood as the science of the common, abstract, general, or universal "morality" that is contained in all particular moralities. In other words, it is seen as the science of the universal nature of morality. In the final analysis, it is the same as the concept of "moral philosophy." As H. Gene Blocker claims, ethics attempts to discover and verify the highest order and most general proofs of all human behavior in regard to right and wrong actions.[2]

As the science concerned with morality in its most universal sense, ethics studies neither the different moral norms of different cultures nor the different moral norms of the same culture over time, even opposing special moral norms in both these circumstances. Though, no doubt, suicide occurs frequently, it

2 *Introduction*

is never justified in cultural context as a kind of unspoken "moral norm." In Japan, however, there is an implicit cultural moral norm around acts of suicide where traditionally it was regarded as the honorable thing to do when faced with failure, such that many Japanese today are driven to suicide by the same kind of honorable code or "behavioral ought." Though it sounds even more preposterous when phrased as an "ought" statement, many still approve the historical moral norm that "one ought to commit suicide when faced with failure." Ethics does not study the specific conditions or the specificity of moral norms like "I ought to commit suicide as a matter of honor." Take the example of the different moral norms regarding how women dress. The dress codes of women vary greatly across cultures and have done so across time. In most parts of the world, women cover their breasts and buttocks, but in parts of Africa the exposure of breasts and buttocks conforms to the moral norm. It is the very opposite in Saudi Arabia where the women traditionally cover all parts of their bodies, and some even their eyes. By contrast, in times past, the indigenous women of Tierra del Fuego, despite living a cold climate, exposed all their body parts except their back. Frankena regards cultural particularity, or the specific morality of a culture, as an object of study for the social sciences (such as anthropology). For Frankena, it falls under the rubric of "descriptive and empirical inquiry," the study of which includes the "historical or scientific, such as is done by anthropologists, historians, psychologists and sociologists."[3]

Ethics studies rather universal moral norms such as "good," "justice," "equality," "humanity," "liberty," "happiness," "honesty," "self-respect," "courage," "modesty," "wisdom," and "continence," which are applicable to all societies, at all times. Therefore, ethics, like aesthetics, logic, legal philosophy, political philosophy and economic philosophy, is one of many branches of philosophy. Thus, we return to the point of view that ethics, namely moral philosophy, is the science of the universal nature of morality. This idea, first established by Roman philosopher Cicero (106 BC–43 BC), is still prevalent among leading modern Western ethicists today:

> Ethics, or moral philosophy, as it is sometimes called, is the systematic endeavor to understand moral concepts and justify moral principles and theories.[4]
>
> Ethics is a branch of philosophy; it is moral philosophy or philosophical thinking about morality, moral problems, and moral judgment.[5]

0.1.2 Ethics: Science concerning excellent morality

It is not, however, accurate enough to define ethics as moral philosophy. This is because morality is the norm of behaviors that ought to be, which is made, agreed upon, or accepted by society: morality and the moral norms are the same concept. In this way, morality, as philosophers such as Epicurus and

Hume said, is nothing more than a contract made by humans: "Justice takes its rise from human conventions."[6] *It follows that morality is subjective and arbitrary and, for this reason, cannot distinguish between truths or falsehoods. It can only draw distinctions between goodness and badness, excellence and inferiority, rightness and wrongness.* Take for example the following moral norm of ancient China: a wife upon the death of her husband ought to hang herself and be buried with him as a sign of her fidelity. We cannot say whether the moral norm is true or false. We can only say that it is good, excellent, or right, or that it is bad, inferior, or wrong—which it clearly is. Lu Xun makes a radical allusion to the brutal nature of so-called inferior morality in his *Diary of a Madman*. Seeing things clearly but speaking through the "mouth of a madman," he proclaims that Confucian morality is "eating people."

> I looked into history, which had no age, and each page was crooked with the words of "benevolence, justice and morality." I couldn't fall asleep at all so I read carefully until mid-night before I could see the words between the lines, there are two words written all over the book: "eating people"!

The full extent of Lu Xun's criticism of Confucian morality is debatable, but one thing is certain: morality is comprised of the two extreme types of goodness and badness (namely excellence and inferiority). The purpose of ethics is obviously to avoid bad, inferior, and wrong morality, and make good, excellent, and right morality. In this sense, ethics can be understood as a corrective to morality. Ethics first appeared about 500 BC to 300 BC in the time of Socrates, Aristotle, Laozi, and Confucius; whereas morality had existed well before ethics came into being. In fact, it would not be incorrect to say that as soon as there was a society, there was morality. This is precisely what distinguishes morality and ethics: morality is made at will, so there is inevitably both good and bad morality. Ethics is the need to rationalize morality. As Blocker said:

Moral philosophers reflect on everyday moral assumptions, not just a philosophical restatement of any norms that we already trust, but seek a new understanding and perspective of everyday morality, which will correct some of our moral beliefs and change our daily moral behavior.[7]

To be more precise, ethics is not strictly a factual science of morality. It is chiefly a value science concerned with the goodness and badness, and excellence and inferiority of morality, with a focus on the methods, processes, and realization of excellent morality. So, in a sense, we return to Aristotle. Aristotle saw ethics as both a political science and a study of "excellent political institutions." The latter was the core component of his *Politics*. One can therefore deduce that ethics is essentially a science of excellent morality centered on state institutions.

4   *Introduction*

0.1.3 Ethics: Science concerning moral value

What kind of morality is good and excellent? This is a rather complicated question since it involves three important, inseparable and fundamentally different concepts: "morality" (which belongs to the category of "norms," and thus is the same concept as "moral norms"), "moral value" and "moral value judgment." Almost all ethicists throughout history, both in China and abroad, believe that "morality" or "moral norms" and "moral value" are the same concept. The two are fundamentally different because while morality is that which humans make, this is not the case with moral value. Values are not something humans make. Take non-moral values for instance. How is it possible that we make the nutritional value of corn, eggs, or pork?

Humans only make behavioral norms based around nutritional value for how (or indeed, whether) to eat corn, egg, or pork. When I was a child, my father told me that "pork fat and lard are the most nutritious things, so the more you eat the better." We now know that what my father told me then is a bad behavioral norm. The behavioral norm advocated today by nutrition experts (such as the famous Chinese nutritionist Hong Shaoguang) is that "one ought to eat less lard." The old behavioral norm of "the more lard the better" is not commensurate with the actual nutritional value of lard: it has a negative value, so eating too much lard is not good. The behavioral norm that "one ought to eat lard in moderation" conforms to the nutritional value of lard: it has a positive value, so it is good to eat lard in moderation.

Norms are fundamentally different from values for the simple reason that norms are either good or bad, excellent or inferior: norms that are consistent with values are good norms, and norms that are not consistent with values are bad. Morality belongs to the category of behavioral norms, so good and excellent morality conforms to moral value, and bad and inferior morality does not conform to moral value. The moral norm "a wife upon the death of her husband ought to hang herself and be buried with him as a sign of her fidelity" is certainly inferior morality. Clearly, not only does the moral norm as a whole have negative moral value, so do all the intersecting oughts that constitute the norm. We can easily dissect how the moral norm is completely at odds with moral value. How, then, do we make excellent moral norms that conform to moral values?

No doubt people make moral norms under the direction of a certain "moral value judgment," and it is only under the condition that this judgment is true, that a moral norm can conform to the moral value and thus be a good or excellent moral norm. On the contrary, if the moral value judgment is false, the moral norm made under its direction is certainly bad or inferior since it does not conform to the moral value. For example:

If the moral value judgment that "one ought to benefit others out of one's self-interest" is true, then, as a moral principle, it conforms to the moral value of "benefiting others out of one's self-interest" and is thus an excellent moral principle. Conversely, if the moral value judgment that "one ought to benefit

Introduction 5

others out of one's self-interest" is false, then, as a moral principle, it does not conform to the moral value of "benefiting others out of one's self-interest" and is thus an inferior moral principle.

This leads to a definition that ethics is a science concerned with excellent morality—that excellent morality is a moral norm that conforms to moral value—which actually implies that ethics is also a science aimed at discovering the truth of moral value. Indeed, it is generally accepted among ethicists that ethics is a science of value. For example, it is generally accepted that "Ethics is an organized knowledge system about moral values,"[8] or, in other words, "a science [or] study [of] the value of all activities in life."[9]

However, a definition of ethics as a science concerned with moral value only can be deduced from a definition of "ethics as a science concerned with excellent morality," not from the aforesaid definition of "ethics as the science concerned with morality." This is because excellent morality is not something that can be made and agreed upon at will. The making of excellent morality is certainly connected to moral value: excellent morality is morality that conforms to the moral value, but only morality can be made and agreed upon at will. Furthermore, unlike excellent morality, the making of morality is not necessarily connected to moral value: morality exists irrespective of whether it conforms or does not conform to moral value.

Thence ethics has three definitions: First, "Ethics is both a philosophy and science of morality." Though this definition is true, it still seems superficial and tautological. Second, "Ethics is a science concerned with moral values." As profound as it is, it still seems to be one-sided, that is, it sees only the content (moral value) but not the form (moral norm); Third, "Ethics is a value science concerned with the goodness and badness of morality and making excellent morality." This is the most accurate definition of ethics. In any case, however, it must be asserted that ethics does not claim to be a "science of fact," but rather a "science of norm" or a "science of value," for even though "norms" and "values" are fundamentally different categories, "normative science" and "value science" are the same concept.

0.2 The objects of ethics

0.2.1 Axiomatic method: The scientific method for determining the objects of ethics

From Descartes, Hobbes, and Spinoza to the modern master of justice, Rawls, many thinkers have advocated the scientification and axiomatization of ethics, believing that the axiomatic method is a scientific method to deduce and determine the research object of ethics. Does this hold true? The answer is definitive. First of all, the axiomatic method, known as the axiom system or as the method of the axiom system, belongs to the category of the deductive method to construct a scientific system, though to be sure, the axiomatic method is not exactly the same as the deductive method.

6 *Introduction*

To determine the similarities and differences between the two, let's compare Marx's *Capital* and Euclid's *Elements*: the former is the model of the deductive system, while the latter is the model of the axiom system. The *Elements* first lists 23 terms (definitions), five axioms, and five postulates, then deduces from the axioms and postulates all the propositions of geometry: 417 theorems. The starting point of *Capital* is the concept of "commodity," it then follows an order from the abstract to the concrete, and from the general to the particular, as expressed in the following sequence: commodity–money–capital–profit–interest–land rent.

It is easy to see that the common ground between the deductive method and the axiomatic method is that they all derive the particular concepts and propositions from the abstract concepts and propositions. Thus we can conclude that the axiomatic method is also a deductive method. The difference between the deductive method and the axiomatic method is that the primitive premises of the deductive method of *Elements,* the five axioms and five postulates, are the most general truths, whereas the starting point or primitive premise of the deductive method of *Capital*, namely "Commodities," is the most general concept—absent of truths (or falsehoods). As far as the two different fields of science are concerned, all the propositions derived from the primitive premises in *Elements* are also truths—all truths which potentially lend themselves to other fields, whereas *Capital* is devoid of the axiomatic method—for although all the concepts within its field are derived from the primitive premise it does not sufficiently deduce all the propositions, thus it only adheres to a certain arrangement of concepts.

Therefore, if one starts from abstract concepts that do not contain meanings in terms of truths or falsehoods to deduce the particular concepts, the method employed to construct a scientific system can only be the deductive method; however, if all the propositions of a scientific construct are deduced from some of the most general propositions with truths or falsehoods attached—namely axioms and postulates—it is both a deductive method and an axiomatic method. As Wang Xianjun said, the axiomatic method is a deductive method, but it starts from axioms: "Starting from some axioms to deduce a series of theorems with the deductive method, the deductive system thus established is called the axiom system."[10]

The axiomatic method is a special kind of deductive method. Its particularity lies in the fact that its primitive premise contains the most general propositions, namely its axioms and postulates, from which all the propositions of the science can be deduced. It has then the function of transmitting the truth: it can transfer the truths of axioms and postulates to all the propositions of the science. The deductive method of a non-axiomatic method, as a method of constructing a scientific system, is only the arrangement of the order of the concept system and does not have the function of transmitting truth. A scientific construct must have truths or falsehoods as a conceptual starting point otherwise how is it possible to transmit a truth?

Introduction 7

In short, the fundamental feature of the axiomatic method is to deduce all propositions in a given field by establishing some axioms and postulates: the axiomatic method is then a deductive method that deduces all the propositions of the science from axioms and postulates and transfer the truths of axioms and postulates to all the propositions of the science. Put simply, as Wu Changde(武长德) said, the axiomatic method is the standard form of the deductive method. We might also add that axiomatic method is the most rigorous deductive method, and that the axiomatic system itself is the most rigorous scientific system, which befits Howard Kahane's insistence that "one of the primary motives for constructing axiom systems is *rigor*."[11] How do we then use the axiomatic method to construct a certain science as an axiom system?

The scientific system constructed with an axiomatic method, like other scientific systems, is also composed of three elements, which are *words* (i.e. concepts or symbols), *propositions* (i.e. judgments or formulas) and *derived rules,* just as Kahane points out: "An axiom system has three main elements: symbols (or words), formulas, and inference rules."[12] The difference of the axiomatic system from other scientific systems is that it divides these three elements into primitive and derived parts. It has primitive concepts and the defined concepts, primitive propositions and derived propositions, primitive inference rules and derived inference rules. "Primitive concepts," "primitive propositions" and "primitive inference rules" constitute the axioms and postulates systems of the axiomatic system, and hence are the premises of the axiomatic system, while "defined concepts," "derived propositions" and "derived inference rules" constitute the theorem system of the axiomatic system, and hence are the conclusions of the axiomatic system.[13]

However, as we know, axioms and postulates, are not primitive concepts—concepts do not have a truth or falsehood—but are rather primitive propositions with a truth or falsehood contained in the interrelations of some primitive concepts, and are "sets of primitive propositions" combining "primitive propositions" and "primitive inferences rules" (since primitive inference rules also belong to the category of primitive propositions), which, in the final analysis, are capable of deducing all the propositions and objects of a scientific system. What kinds of primitive propositions though are axioms and postulates? What are the axioms and postulates, as well as their distinctions?

According to Aristotle and Euclid's classic theory of the axiomatic method, a postulate is only valid for a particular science in that it can only deduce the objects and propositions of that science, while an axiom is generally valid for sciences that are alike in that it can deduce all the objects and propositions of these sciences: in this respect, the axioms are the "common truths" of the sciences concerned, whereas the postulates "are only the first principles" of any one of the sciences.[14]

While the above is true, Aristotle and Euclid's view of classical axiomatic theory holds that axioms and postulates are self-evident, intuitive,

8 *Introduction*

and universally acknowledged. The emergence of non-Euclidean geometry, however, shows that this view is one-sided and wrong. Because the Fifth Postulate of non-Euclidean geometry (e.g., through a point outside the line, multiple lines can be made parallel to the original line) is clearly not self-evident and intuitive. On the contrary, it is completely counterintuitive. Therefore, axioms and postulates are not necessarily self-evident and universally acknowledged.

The main feature that distinguishes axioms and postulates from theorem lies in that they can deduce all the propositions of the science, as Karl Popper put it: "The axioms are chosen in such a way that all the other statements belonging to the theoretical system can be derived from the axioms by purely logical or mathematical transformations."[15] Kahane also writes: "Theoretically, any theorems of logic can be axioms, the choice being made to obtain the smallest possible set of axioms from which all theorems can be derived."[16]

Therefore, the so-called "completeness" that epitomizes "the nature of deducing all the propositions of a given science from a number of axioms and postulates" is the fundamental feature of axioms, postulates, and axiomatic systems generally. In short, axioms and postulates are the most general propositions capable of deducing all objects, theorems, or propositions of a given science and related sciences, while the axiomatic system is the deductive system for deducing all objects, propositions, and theorems from a number of axioms and postulates. This definition of the function of axioms, postulates, and axiomatic systems means that completeness—of all the features attributed to the axiomatic system—is the only feature that recognizes an axiom as an axiom, a postulate as a postulate, and an axiom system as an axiom system.

However, it seems that completeness is not the sole requirement or condition of an effective axiomatic system. An effective or correct and good axiomatic system, in Popper's view, must meet four conditions:

> A theoretical system may be said to be axiomatized if a set of statements, the axioms, has been formulated which satisfies the following four fundamental requirements. (a) The system of axioms must be *free from contradiction* (whether self-contradiction or mutual contradiction). This is equivalent to the demand that not every arbitrarily chosen statement is deducible from it. (b) The system must be *independent*, i.e. it must not contain any axiom deducible from the remaining axioms. (In other words, a statement is to be called an axiom only if it is not deducible within the rest of the system.) These two conditions concern the axiom system as such; as regards the relation of the axiom system to the bulk of the theory, the axioms should be (c) *sufficient* for the deduction of all statements belonging to the theory which is to be axiomatized, and (d) *necessary*, for the same purpose; which means that they should contain no superfluous assumptions.[17]

Introduction 9

These four conditions can be summed up as three: *completeness, consistency* and *independence*. First of all, the so-called sufficiency condition is obviously also *completeness*: it is possible to deduce all propositions and all objects of a science from a number of axioms and postulates. Secondly, the so-called condition of non-contradiction is also *consistency*, that is, all the propositions of the axiom system cannot be contradictory: "If there is some formula which cannot be derived as a theorem, then no contradiction can be derived either, and the system must be consistent."[18] Finally, independence means necessity or simplicity: all axioms cannot be derived from each other and must be independent of each other, so they are not redundant, but necessary—or, in other words, simple. In this regard, Einstein makes it very clear:

> We are looking for a system of ideas that can link observed facts together. It will have the greatest possibility of simplicity. The so-called simplicity does not mean that students have the least difficulty in mastering this system, but refers to the least independent assumptions or theories included in this system.[19]

It is widely believed that non-contradiction or consistency is the most important condition for an effective axiomatic system, as Kahane wrote: "The most important requirement for an acceptable axiom system is *consistency*."[20] Actually this is not so. The most important condition is completeness. First of all, completeness is the peculiar condition of an axiomatic system, while non-contradiction, as Popper put it, is the common condition of any system of scientific theory, whether it is an axiomatic or non-axiomatic system.[21] Secondly, completeness already implies or means non-contradiction. If an axiom system is complete, that is to say, all the propositions of a science can be derived from a number of axioms, surely this means there is no contradiction. Conversely, if there is a contradiction, the fact that not all propositions can be derived is unquestionably the failure of the deduction.

Finally, independence, understood as retaining the principle of simplicity, is another common condition of any system of scientific theory. Einstein had made this point repeatedly, as had Newton who stated: "For nature prefers simplicity to boasting about itself for superfluous reasons."[22] The same, of course, holds for the basic theoretical premise of any axiomatic system. Because the premise is an axiom and a postulate it is necessary that the independence of the axioms and postulates that ensue is maintained so that the sets are non-redundant. That is, simplicity largely demands the independence of axioms and postulates. So long as the axiom system is mostly in keeping with the principle of simplification, it is perfectly acceptable for it to contain one, or even several, non-independent axioms and postulates, which enable the construction and deduction of the system. In this respect, Alfred Tarski's incisive exposition of the axiomatic system is helpful.

10   *Introduction*

> We strive to arrive at an axiom system which does not contain a single superfluous statement, that is, a statement which can be arrived from the remaining axioms and which, therefore, might be counted among the theorems of the theory under construction. An axiom system of this kind is called INDEPENDENT (or a SYSTEM OF MUTUALLY INDEPENDENT AXIOMS). We likewise attempt to see to it that the system of primitive terms is INDEPENDENT, that is, that it does not contain any superfluous term which can be defined by means of the others. Often, however, one does not insist on these methodological postulates for practical, dialectical reasons, particularly in cases where the omission of a superfluous axiom or primitive term would bring about great complications in the construction of the theory.[23]

Xianjun Wang, however, is of the view that independence is different from completeness and consistency and is therefore not a necessary condition for an axiom system: "The axioms of an axiom system, even if they are not independent, cannot be regarded as a great drawback."[24] While this is correct insofar as not all the axioms of a system are necessarily independent, it is a limited understanding of independence; that is, the fact that completeness implies not only consistency, but also simplicity, which, we know, is compatible with the meaning of independence in any scientific system. If an axiom system has completeness, that is, if it is possible to deduce all the propositions of a science from a number of axioms, does this not mean that these axioms have the greatest universality and are the most general propositions? Only the most general propositions with the greatest universality make it possible to deduce all the propositions of a given science from them. And the more universal and general the proposition, the simpler the axioms and postulates and the simpler must be the premise, as Einstein said: "The greater the simplicity of the premise of a theory, the more types of things it involves, and the wider its scope of application."[25]

With the simple understanding that an axiom is an axiom, a postulate is a postulate, and an axiom system is an axiom system—that these themselves are in a sense complete for they are consistent, simple, and independent—we can see how completeness emerges as the sole condition for an effective axiom system. Axioms and postulates are the most general propositions from which we deduce all objects, theorems, or propositions of a science, and an axiom system is a deductive system in which all objects, propositions, or theorems of a science can be derived from certain axioms and postulates. Thus, an effective axiom system is an axiom system with completeness: a non-contradictory deductive system in which all objects, propositions, or theorems of a science can be derived from the least number of axioms and postulates.

0.2.2 *Ethical axioms and postulates: Deduction of the objects of ethics*

The study of the axiomatic method shows that whether the ethics system can be axiomatized, as Reichenbach believes, depends entirely on whether axioms

Introduction   11

and postulates of ethics exist, that is to say, it depends on whet7her there are general propositions (i.e., of the most general kind) from which we can deduce all propositions, objects, and contents of ethics.

> Ethics needs moral premises, or moral axioms... When we call them axioms, we consider ethics as an ordered system which is derivable from these axioms, whereas the axioms themselves are not derivable in the system. When we restrict the consideration to a specific argument, we use the more modest term "premise". There must be at least one moral premise for an ethical argument, that is, one ethical rule which is not derived by this argument. This premise may be the conclusion of another argument; but going farther up this way, we remain at every step with a certain set of moral premises. If we succeed in ordering the totality of ethical rules in one consistent system, we thus arrive at the axioms of our ethics.[26]

But are there such axioms in ethics?

Certainly, they do. Ethics has pursued such kinds of scientific reasoning for over two thousand years. As Albert Einstein stated in his *The Laws of Science and Ethics*: "There is not much difference between the establishment and test of ethical axioms and the axioms of science."[27] This system of ethics undoubtedly is the so-called "meta-ethics." Like scientific axioms and postulates systems such as that of geometry, meta-ethics is also an axioms and postulates system composed of three elements: "primitive concepts," "primitive propositions," and "primitive inference rules."

On the one hand, the primitive concepts of ethics, that is, the basic concepts or categories of meta-ethics, are what the meta-ethicists call "moral terms," "ethical terms" and "value terms." These basic concepts or categories, in Moore's view, are "good"; in Russell's view, are "right" and "good"; in Hare's view, are "good," "right" and "ought"; in Ewing's view, are "good" and "ought"; in J. L. Mackie's view, are "good," "ought," and "is"; and in Stevenson's view, are "good," "right," "ought," "values," and "facts." In conclusion, the primitive concepts of ethics can be summed up as five categories: "value," "good," "ought," "right," and "is" or "fact."

On the other hand, the primitive propositions and its inference rules contained in the relationship between these primitive concepts—in particular, the relationship between "ought" and "fact"—can be divided into two serials: "the existence of axioms and postulates of ethics" and "the deductive axioms and postulates of ethics." Together the two serials comprise seven axioms and seven postulates which ultimately make up "the deductive axiom of excellent norms" and "the deductive postulate of excellent moral norms of ethics":

> Excellent (or good) "behavioral norms" conform to "behavioral values," while inferior (or bad) behavioral norms do not conform to behavioral values. In contrast with inferior behavioral norms, excellent behavioral

12 *Introduction*

norms are not made arbitrarily. These can only be made in accordance with behavioral values—namely the utility of "behavioral facts" for "the needs, desires and purposes of the subject." In the final analysis, excellent behavioral norms are derived from the behavioral facts through the needs, desires and purposes of the subject. Therefore, the making of excellent behavioral norms depends directly on the truth or falsehood of the value judgment concerning "behavioral oughts"; fundamentally speaking, it also depends, on the one hand, on the truth or falsehood of the factual judgment in regard to behavioral facts, and it depends, on the other hand, on the truth or falsehood of the subjective judgment concerning the needs, desires and purposes of the subject.

With the deductive axiom of excellent norms we overcome Hume's guillotine; that is to say that "ought" can be derived from "is" through a process of deducing and making "excellent norms" which are directly based on the truth of "value judgments" and are ultimately based on the truth of "factual judgments" and "subjective judgments." In short, the axiom is the most effective method for deducing and making excellent norms. Furthermore, it is universally applicable to all value sciences, not just confined to ethics theory. Two such examples which are integral to our study on ethics are stateology (a value science concerning goodness or badness of state institutions) and Chinaology (a value science concerning the goodness or badness of the state institutions of China). Given the centrality of value, we may refer to the axiom presented below as either the "deductive formula of value" or "deductive formula of excellent norms":

> *Premise 1: the behavioral fact (substance of value)*
> *Premise 2: the needs, desires and purposes of the subject (standard of value)*
> *Conclusion 1: the behavioral ought (value)*
> *Conclusion 2: Norm is good or bad. (whether the norm conforms to value)*

For example, whether it is a good or bad norm that "one ought to drink milk often" undoubtedly directly depends on the truth or falsehood of the value judgment that "one ought to drink milk often" (that is, the fact of drinking milk often has utility in that it conforms to the nutritional needs of the human body). Fundamentally speaking, it depends on whether the factual judgment of "milk is rich in protein" is true or false, and on the judgment regarding the needs of the subject, i.e., whether "the body needs protein" is true or false.

In the field of moral norms, society is the agent who makes moral norms, it is the subject of the moral norms; the purpose for which society makes moral norms (namely the goal of morality) is for the purpose of the subject's activities. The object is all actions that can be morally evaluated, and is regulated by the morality. Moral value is the utility of the behavioral facts to the goal of morality. Thus, if the "deductive axiom of excellent norm" which is universally

Introduction 13

applicable to all fields of norms is applied to the field of moral norms, we can draw the following conclusion:

> Excellent moral norms conform to the "moral values" of behaviors, while inferior moral norms do not conform to the "moral values" of behaviors. Thus, excellent moral norms are made in accordance with the "moral value of behavioral oughts"—that is, they depend on the utility of "behavioral facts" to the "goal of morality." These are not made arbitrarily. In the final analysis, excellent moral norms are derived from the "behavioral facts" through the "goal of morality." Therefore, the making of excellent or inferior moral norms concerning "behavioral oughts" depends directly on the truth or falsehood of the moral value judgments of "behavioral oughts"; fundamentally speaking, this depends, on the one hand, on the truth or falsehood of the factual judgment of the "behavioral facts," and it depends on the other hand on the truth or falsehood of the subjective judgment concerning "the goal of morality."

This process of deducing and making "excellent moral norms" is directly based on the truth of "moral *value judgment*" (and ultimately based on the truth of the "*factual judgment* of action" and "*subjective judgment* concerning the goal of morality"). In short, the method for deducing and making excellent moral norms is the "deductive postulate of excellent moral norms" and is only applicable to ethics. As presented below, it can derive all the objects, propositions, and contents of ethics, and can be termed as either the "deductive formula of moral value" or the "deductive formula of excellent moral norms":

> Premise 1: the behavioral fact (substance of moral value)
> Premise 2: the ultimate goal of morality (standard of moral value)
> Conclusion 1: the behavioral ought (the moral value)
> Conclusion 2: excellent moral norms are the norms that conform to moral values

For instance, whether "benefiting others out of one's self-interest" is a good or bad moral norm depends on the truth or falsehood of the value judgment that benefiting others out of one's self-interest has a positive moral value (that is, that it has a utility that conforms to the goal of morality); on the one hand, it depends on the truth or falsehood of the judgment of behavioral fact that benefiting others out of one's self-interest is a win–win both for oneself and others, and, on the other hand, depends on the truth or falsehood of the subjective judgment that "the goal of morality is to promote everyone's interests."

This "deductive formula of excellent moral norms," along with the four propositions it consists of, can be termed the "deductive postulate of excellent norms of ethics" only because all the objects, propositions, and contents of ethics can be deduced from it. First of all, from this formula we can deduce

14 *Introduction*

that all objects, propositions, and contents of *Normative Ethics* consist of the following three parts:

The first part is the study of premise 2 of the deductive formula, namely, *the ultimate goal of morality (standard of moral value)*. The goal of morality is the moral value standard for the measurement of the behavioral facts; only by this can we deduce the excellent moral norms of the behavioral oughts from the behavioral facts. However, in order to prove what the goal of morality is, it is necessary to prove what morality is: its definition, structure, types, basic nature and so on. This part will study the concept of morality before it then moves on to the origin and goal of morality, and finally, the quantification of the ultimate goal of morality, namely the ultimate standard of moral value.

The second part is the study of premise 1 of the deductive formula, namely *the behavioral fact (substance of moral value)*. From an ethics point of view, we might also call this "the theory of human nature." Human nature that is studied by ethics is confined to that which can be morally evaluated as either good or bad, i.e. the nature of human behavioral facts that can be morally evaluated. It is the substance from which excellent moral norms of behavior that ought to be are derived, namely the substance of moral value. This part studies the structure of behavior (the ends of actions, means of actions and the ultimate motivation of actions), types of behavior (16 types, such as "benefiting others out of one's self-interest"), and the laws of behavior (the four laws of development and change in behavior, such as "everyone is mostly self-interested and only occasionally benefits others").

The third part is the study of conclusion 1 and conclusion 2 of the deductive formula, namely, *the behavioral ought (moral value), and excellent moral norms are the norms that conform to moral values.* Firstly, using the ultimate goal of morality or, rather, in this instance, the ultimate standard of moral value—that is, the increasing or decreasing the quantum of everyone's interests—we measure the 16 types of behavioral facts and the 4 major laws: a behavioral fact that conforms to the standard comes under the general principle of the morality of the "good" guiding all behaviors that ought to be. Secondly, derived from the general principle of the morality of "good," are the excellent moral principles of self-regarding ("happiness") and of other-regarding ("justice," "equality," "humanity," "liberty," and "elimination of alienation"): justice is the fundamental value standard for the goodness or badness of state institutions; equality is the most important justice; humanity, which regards the realization of everyone's creative potential as the highest value so as to make individuals realize their creative potential, is the highest value standard of the state institutions; liberty is the most fundamental humanity; and alienation is the most fundamental inhumanity. Finally, from the seven excellent moral principles of good, justice, equality, humanity, liberty, elimination of alienation and happiness, the eight excellent moral rules of "honesty," "cherishing life," "self-respect," "continence," "modesty," "courage," "wisdom," and the "doctrine of the mean" are derived.

Introduction 15

All three parts comprise all the objects of normative ethics. Emphasizing the key objects, we define normative ethics as essentially a study of how excellent moral norms of "behavioral oughts" can be derived from "behavioral facts" through the "ultimate goal of morality" (namely the "ultimate standard of morality"). In short, normative ethics is concerned with the processes of making excellent moral norms.

Then, how can people be made to comply with excellent morality to realize it? The answer is through conscience, reputation, and virtue. The moral evaluation of conscience and reputation is the way to realize moral norms, whereas virtue is the actual realization of moral norms. The three separate categories, "conscience," "reputation," and "virtue" together constitute all objects of virtue ethics: Virtue ethics is the ethics concerned with the ways of achieving excellent morality and thus is the study of the realization of conclusion 2 of the "deductive formula of excellent moral norms," namely how to realize "excellent moral norms."

The core of meta-ethics is to study how the "deductive formula of excellent moral norms," or, its alternative name, the "deductive formula of moral value," can be established: it is an ethics concerned with the method of deduction of moral value, and with the methods of making excellent moral norms, to be specific, it is an ethics concerned with the methods of making excellent moral norms directly based on the truth of "moral *value judgment*" (and ultimately based on the truth of the "*factual judgment* of action" and "*subjective judgment* concerning the goal of morality"). Therefore, meta-ethics is the method of normative ethics. On the one hand, it studies five primitive concepts of ethics: "value," "good," "ought," "right," and "is" or "fact"; on the other hand, it reveals the primitive propositions and the inference rules contained in the relationships of the primitive concepts—particularly the relationship between "ought" and "fact." The primitive propositions and the inference rules form two serials: "the existence of axioms and postulates of ethics" and "the deductive axioms and postulates of ethics" which are comprised of seven axioms and seven postulates.

Do meta-ethics, normative ethics, and virtue ethics then constitute all the disciplines of ethics? The answer is obviously yes. Ethics is the study of excellent morality so it must necessarily adopt the methods of making it (meta-ethics), the processes of making it (normative ethics), and the ways of realizing it (virtue ethics). Thus, the objects of ethics can be summarized as shown in Figure 0.1.

It can be seen that from the four propositions which consists of the deductive formula of excellent moral norms, all objects, propositions, and contents of ethics can be deduced, so we may term them the ethical postulate: normative ethics is nothing more than a system to demonstrate the "two premises and two conclusions of the ethical postulate"; virtue ethics is just a system to study how to realize the "conclusion of the ethical postulate"; and meta-ethics is a system of argumentation of the "ethical postulate" and the "ethical axiom" from which the "ethical postulate" may be derived. This

16 *Introduction*

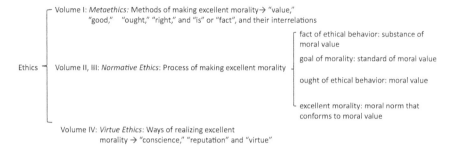

Figure 0.1 The objects of ethics.

means that the system of ethics is a system that can be axiomatized: meta-ethics is the axioms and postulates system of ethics, and is the premise system of the axiomatic system of ethics; normative ethics and virtue ethics are the theorem systems derived from meta-ethics, and the conclusive system of the axiomatic system of ethics.

It is true that the axiomatic system of ethics differs from the axiomatic systems of geometry, mathematics and mechanics. Geometry directly deduces or indirectly deduces through theorems, all the propositions of its field; while ethics directly deduces from a number of axioms and postulates various parts of all the objects and contents of ethics, and indirectly deduces all propositions of ethics, which undoubtedly is a drawback of the axiomatic system of ethics.

Because the axiomatic system of geometry deduces or indirectly deduces through theorems, all the propositions of its field from a number of axioms and postulates, the transmission function of the truth it possesses thus covers all propositions of the science. It can directly or indirectly transmit the truth of the axiom to all its propositions. Therefore, the axiomatic system of geometry is completely rigorous: not only is the system itself rigorous, all propositions contained in it are rigorous also because of its axiomatization.

On the contrary, because ethics directly deduces from a number of axioms and postulates the various parts of all the objects and contents of ethics, and indirectly deduces all propositions of ethics, the transmission function of the truth it possesses can only be extended to the various parts and certain propositions that constitute this science, not to all the propositions of this science. Therefore, the axiomatic system of ethics is only partially rigorous: while the system itself is rigorous because of its axiomatization, not all propositions contained in it are rigorous because of its axiomatization.

However, this is exactly where the axiomatic system of ethics is superior to that of geometry. Because ethics directly deduces from a number of axioms and postulates the various parts of the objects and contents of ethics, and indirectly deduces all propositions of ethics, the axiomatic system of ethics has absolute completeness: no proposition of ethics can avoid the ethics axioms

Introduction 17

and postulates. Still, one might ask: are there any propositions of ethics that can avoid *the deductive formula of excellent moral norms* and the four propositions it contains? Since the formula can deduce all objects of ethics, does this not indicate that there is absolutely no proposition of ethics that can avoid this deductive formula?

On the contrary, the axiomatic system of geometry deduces all propositions of its field directly from the axioms and postulates or indirectly through theorems, so the completeness is always relative and, in this sense, is incomplete. There always exist certain propositions that cannot be deduced from the axioms and postulates of the science. Thus, there is a drift away from the axiomatic system. Kahane makes this very clear:

> Unfortunately, not only has no completeness proof been discovered for arithmetic, but it has been proved that *there cannot be a complete axiom system for all of arithmetic*. No matter how many axioms and theorems such a system contains, we can always find some truth of arithmetic that is not a theorem of that system.[28]

Therefore, to say that mathematics is more rigorous than ethics is relative: only in the terms of each proposition which constitutes the axiomatic system, is this case. In terms of the axiomatic system itself, ethics seems to be more rigorous than mathematics, that is, more complete: the completeness of the axiomatic system of ethics is absolute and there is absolutely no proposition of ethics drifting away from the axioms and postulates of ethics. The completeness of the axiomatic system of mathematics is relative, there are always some mathematical propositions drifting away from the axioms and postulates of mathematics.

0.2.3 Axiomatic system of ethics: Its history and current situation

Like the precision of mathematics ethics can also be axiomatic and therefore a very rigorous science. Since Euclid established it the first axiomatic system has been considered the most rigorous scientific system. While there have been various attempts by scientists in all fields of the natural sciences to adopt the system, only the disciplines of mathematics and physics and some other branches of natural science have been successful. Interestingly, in the humanities and social sciences, no well-known scholars have raised the question of axiomatization, whether it be in economics, law, political science, anthropology, aesthetics, sociology, or linguistics. Ethics is the only exception among them. Since Descartes, some great masters such as Hobbes, Spinoza, Hume, Ayer, and Moore had advocated for establishing an objective, necessary, rigorous, and operable science of ethics, and the axiomatization and geometrization of ethics similar to geometry and physics. Some well-known natural scientists and philosophers of science such as Einstein and Reichenbach had also tried to discover and establish axioms of ethics. In

18   *Introduction*

more contemporary times, Rawls, in his far-reaching masterpiece, *A Theory of Justice*, eagerly advocated that "We should strive for a kind of moral geometry with all the rigor which this name connotes."[29]

However, across history, only Spinoza had put this advocacy into practice in his attempt to establish ethics as an axiomatic system. Unfortunately, he failed. Spinoza was unable to discover and then construct axioms and postulates of ethics from which all the objects and contents of ethics could be derived. He not only clearly understood that the key to the construction of the axiom system lay in the discovery of axioms and postulates, he also scientifically proposed what the conditions for the establishment of axioms and postulates should be, such as non-contradiction, simplicity and completeness (conditions which are so scientifically rigorous they have been inherited by thinkers such as Popper and Einstein). Spinoza pointed out:

> In order to discover such principles, we must ensure the best hypothesis meet the following conditions: (1) the hypothesis ought not to contain any contradictions; (2) the hypothesis ought to be the simplest as far as possible; (3) as a corollary it ought be the easiest to be understood; (4) this hypothesis ought to derive all phenomena observed in nature.[30]

There are no axioms and postulates found to satisfy these conditions in the axiomatic system of Spinoza's *Ethics*. The work itself is divided into five parts, and all propositions therein are derived from what he calls a number of "axioms" and "postulates," but this is not the case for all the objects and other contents of the five parts that constitute the ethics, for no axioms and postulates are established to make such deductions. Only the deduction of some propositions which constitute all the objects and contents of the five parts of *Ethics* can be called the ethical axioms and postulates. The propositions that Spinoza calls "axioms" and "postulates" or "principles" cannot actually be attributed to ethical axioms and postulates because they deduce only some of the contents of each of the five parts, such that they represent only a portion of the external forms and expressions of the geometric axiom system that inhabit his *Ethics*. For example, Spinoza puts forward the definition of the axioms first, then sets about the task of proving and deducing, and so on, but his work in its entirety does not have the essence of the axiomatic system, that is, there is no system of axioms and postulates in it that can deduce all objects of ethics.

Spinoza's failure was historically inevitable without the axioms and postulates of ethics to deduce all the objects and contents of ethics. In fact, not until as late as the eighteenth century was the fundamental issue of the axiom and postulate system of ethics raised by Hume, namely whether "ought" can be derived from "fact" (later to be termed Hume's guillotine). The systematic study of ethical axioms and postulates (meta-ethics) did not begin until the beginning of the twentieth century when Moore's *Principia Ethica*, the foundation of meta-ethics, was published in 1903. Since then, after more than half a century's efforts of Moore, Pritchard, Ross, Russell, Wittgenstein, Schlick,

Introduction   19

Carnap, Ayer, Stevenson, Toulmin, Hare, and others, it became possible to construct the axiom and postulate system of ethics that could deduce all objects and contents of ethics. The starting point of the axiom and postulate system of ethics we are constructing—meta-ethics—is precisely the ethical thought of these great masters.

Therefore, we ought not to ridicule the puerile geometric proof method of Spinoza's ethics, but rather to affirm that in terms of a systematic construction of ethics, Spinoza is the greatest ethicist with no equals. We are Spinoza's disciples in methodology, and our axiom system of ethics is a further development of Spinoza's ethics, which, beyond the axiomatic system itself, was a great achievement in the eighteenth century; ours is but another attempt to construct an axiomatic system of ethics as rigorous as geometry, after Spinoza, in the footsteps of Hobbes, Descartes, Spinoza, Hume, Helvetius, Moore, and Rawls.

0.3 The system structure and discipline classification of ethics: The studies and controversies in contemporary western academia

The axiomatic deduction of the objects of ethics shows that the system of ethics consists of meta-ethics, normative ethics and virtue ethics; normative ethics occupies most of the objects and contents of ethics and thus is undoubtedly the central discipline of the system structure of ethics. In short, ethics is a scientific system that takes normative ethics as its central discipline, and meta-ethics and virtue ethics as its peripheral disciplines. If we were to draw a basic diagram of the overall features of ethics it would be shaped just like a rugby ball with a large middle, which accounts for normative ethics, and smaller two ends, which account for meta-ethics and virtue ethics. Another way of looking at the system of ethics is to liken it to an organism with a head (meta-ethics), a large body (normative ethics), and feet (virtue ethics). On the whole, ethics is a science concerned with excellent moral norms, and, to be specific, it is a science concerned with the methods and processes of making excellent moral norms and with the ways of realizing them, thus is entirely a normative science. So, how can it not be centered on normative ethics?

It is surprising, however, that although Rawls, Reichenbach and the great physicist Einstein advocated the axiomatization of ethics, no one in contemporary times has attempted to construct an axiom system of ethics. Not only this, contemporary western ethics circles even think that normative ethics and virtue ethics are merely two modes of studying the same object, so that one subsumes the other and ethics only has two disciplines—either as meta-ethics and normative ethics or as meta-ethics and virtue ethics.

0.3.1 The misconception of two disciplines: Meta-ethics and normative ethics

Although ethics is divided into two major types, namely "theoretical ethics" and "applied ethics," the term ethics mostly refers to the former, and, as just

20   *Introduction*

mentioned, is further apportioned to meta-ethics, normative ethics, or virtue ethics. Despite Aristotle, Mencius, and Spinoza's study of the concepts of meta-ethics such as the study of "good," and Hume's study of the fundamental problems of "is-ought," none of these disciplines existed as such before 1903. Prior to this, ethics and so-called "normative ethics" theory were almost one and the same the same.

When, in 1903, Moore published his *Principia Ethica*, declaring the birth of another kind of theoretical ethics—meta-ethics—it dominated Western ethics for more than half a century afterward. Its representatives, besides Moore, include Pritchard, Ross, Russell, Wittgenstein, Schlick, Carnap, Ayer, Stevenson, Toulmin, and Hare. Ethics, or theoretical ethics, had come to be seen as comprising two main disciplines: meta-ethics and normative ethics. One finds this, for instance, in the works of Joseph P. Hester and David Copp, both claiming that ethics or the "philosophical study of ethics" can be divided into two these broad categories or areas.

The authoritative definition of the objects of the meta-ethics comes from Frankena. Hester notes:

> Metaethics, observes William K. Frankena, asks the following questions: "(1) What is the meaning or definition of ethical terms like *right, wrong, good, or bad*? That is, what is the nature, meaning, or function of judgments in which these and similar terms occur? What are the rules for the use of such terms and sentences? (2) How are moral uses of such terms to be distinguished from non-moral ones, or moral judgments from other normative ones? What is the meaning of *moral* as contrasted with *non-moral*? (3) what is the analysis or meaning of related terms or concepts like *action, conscience, free will, intention, promising, excusing, motive, responsibility, reason*, and *voluntary*? Finally, (4) Can ethical and value judgments be proved, justified, or shown valid? If so, how and in what sense? Or, what is the logic of moral reasoning and of reasoning about values?"[31]

For these four questions, Mark Timmons further summarized: "The first set of three questions is concerned with the meaning of ethical terms; the fourth set is concerned with the justification of moral judgments."[32]

Douglass Geiveit also divides the objects of meta-ethics into "ethical terms" and the "justification of moral judgments" as the proof method of the truth or falsehood of moral value judgments:

> Metaethics differs from both normative and applied ethics in that it explores conceptual and epistemological questions that arise for those who use moral discourse and who devise and apply normative theories of right and wrong. Conceptual questions are posed for moral terms and statements; epistemological questions are raised about the possibility and character of moral reasoning. Conceptual Questions...terms such

Introduction 21

as "good", "evil", "right", or "wrong" are examined directly. This sort of analysis is supposed to clarify what it means to use a moral predicate within a sentence of the form "X is right" or "X is wrong"…How does one go about determining which moral judgments are true and which are false?[33]

How true this last statement is! Geiveit's question goes to the heart of the problem concerning the function of meta-ethics, which I will come to shortly. First, however, it should be noted that most contemporary Western ethicists divided the objects of meta-ethics into "ethics terms" and the "justification of moral judgments." In short, the former is mainly the categories of "good" and "right" and so on, while the latter concentrates on the proof method of the truth and falsehood of moral value judgments, namely the "logic of moral reasoning and of value reasoning." Importantly, the proof method, Frankena points out, is the fundamental problem of meta-ethics. Discussing the four objects of meta-ethics, he writes that while "(1) and (4) are the more standard problems of meta-ethics…Of these two problems, it is (4) that is primary."[34]

Lacking the rigorousness of science, however, ethicist still fail to see that "the logic of moral reasoning and of value reasoning," in the final analysis, rests on solving Hume's guillotine: whether "value" and "ought" can be derived from "is" or "fact." Where meta-ethics need only concern itself with the five categories—"value," "good," "ought," "right," and "is" or "fact"— that have direct relevance for the proof method, ethicists "extend the scope to include other related terms or concepts such as 'action,' 'conscience,' 'free will,' 'intention,' 'promising,' 'excusing,' 'motive,' 'responsibility,' 'reason,' 'voluntary,' etc." Does this not mean that meta-ethics is potentially the study of all ethical terms or usages, hence mistakenly equating meta-ethics with ethics?

Put simply, ethicists are not equipped with the means, despite efforts to solve Hume's guillotine, to determine which moral value judgments are true or false, for the "truth or falsehood of value judgments" depends on whether "value judgments" conform to "moral values"; fundamentally speaking, this depends, on the one hand, on the truth or falsehood of the "factual judgment," and, on the other, on the truth or falsehood of "the judgment regarding the needs of the subject." Without the "deductive axiom of excellent norms of ethics and the deductive postulate of excellent moral norms" that "can deduce all objects of ethics" any attempt to construct an axiom system of ethics is not be possible. Meta-ethics is an ethics primarily concerned with the deductive methods of excellent moral norms, which, in the final analysis, is the axiom and postulate system of ethics that is missing in contemporary ethics theory.

The broad but basically correct viewpoint above, namely that the object of meta-ethics is to study both the meaning of ethical terms and the logic of moral reasoning or value reasoning, is the reason why the contemporary Western ethicists drew the vague and grotesque conclusion that meta-ethics is the science of analyzing moral language. The master of contemporary

22   *Introduction*

meta-ethics, Hare, wrote: "Ethics, as I conceive it, is the logical study of the language of morals."[35] This appears to have been the definition of meta-ethics adopted by most contemporary mainstream ethicists in the West. As has been documented, it was "typical to define meta-ethics as consisting in the analysis of moral language."[36]

This definition of meta-ethics was not only vague and grotesque, but also untenable for it implied that the study of "moral language" belonged to the category of "language" study or to one of the branches of linguistics. In practice, however, not all the analyses of "moral language," the study of the meanings of "ethical terms" and the justifications of "moral judgment" belong to meta-ethics. Take for example the term "continence," which is an ethical term, and the statement "continence ought to be observed," which is a moral judgment. Although the analysis of both belongs to an "analysis of moral language," the analysis and justification of "continence" and "continence is what ought to be" is obviously the object of normative ethics not the object of study of meta-ethics.

Indeed, contemporary Western ethicists do see that meta-ethics is about the proof method of the truth and falsehood of moral value judgments, and thus is the scientific method to guide the study of normative ethics. As Oliver A. Johnson elaborates:

> What process do ethicists reach their conclusions? When they state a theory, say, of the good life for the mankind, to what they appeal to support it? Are their theories based on empirical evidence, as scientific theories are, or are they based on authority, or, on intuition or moral insight, or perhaps on established social practice? Furthermore, what kind of arguments will they use in defense of their theories? Will these be deductive, inductive, or of some other kind particular to ethics? Or are ethical theories defensible at all? This last question leads to the most important set of problems with which meta-ethics have been concerned, those of knowledge.[37]

Douglas Gewitt quite rightly points out that the question studied by meta-ethics is logically prior to the question studied by normative ethics.[38] Michael Smith also writes: "Philosophers have surely been right to give meta-ethical questions a certain priority over questions in normative ethics."[39] But Moore's view is still the most accurate. For Moore, meta-ethics is the "prolegomena to any future Ethics that can possibly pretend to be scientific."[40] Nevertheless, the "is-ought" question remains unsolved. Where there is much discourse on the proof of the scientific method concerning the truth or falsehood of moral value judgments, crucial questions are overlooked as to just how these the truth or falsehood of moral value judgments emerge. As this work demonstrates, the truth or falsehood of moral value judgments are directly dependent on whether it conforms to the moral values of behavioral oughts, and fundamentally dependent on the truth or falsehood of the factual judgment of behavioral facts, as well as on the truth or falsehood of the subjective judgment concerning the goal of morality.

Though meta-ethics in the contemporary West is seen as a scientific method to guide normative ethics, precisely how the scientific method guides normative ethics is found wanting in much of the literature. This is in some measure evidenced by the inadequate and unsystematic integration of meta-ethics in major works on ethics, such that Frankena's *Ethics* and Beauchamp's *Philosophical Ethics*, both highly influential, place their sections on meta-ethics not at the start but towards the end of their work. If meta-ethics is the method of normative ethics, why not put it before normative ethics, instead of after it? An explanation for this is that meta-ethics is not recognized, or rather not distinguished, as principally a science that specializes in methods for making excellent moral norms—which, this work establishes, are based on the truth of moral value judgments that are themselves based on the truth of the judgments of the behavioral fact and of the subject concerning the ultimate goal of morality.

This is not, however, the main problem of contemporary Western ethics. Its greatest error, as alluded to earlier, concerns the classifications of the objects of study of normative ethics and virtue ethics, namely that the objects of study in both are the same—when, in fact, they are different. So, ethics became predominantly seen as composed of two disciplines, that is, as meta-ethics and normative ethics or as meta-ethics and virtue ethics, depending on where allegiances lie. As this work demonstrates, the three distinct disciplines, meta-ethics, normative ethics, and virtue ethics, compose the structure of the axiom system of ethics. Without first clarifying and then examining the objects of study in each the system would be incomplete. But first let's examine why ethics has been reduced to just two disciplines.

0.3.2 Two modes of studying the same object: Normative ethics and virtue ethics

In the 1960s, meta-ethics began to decline because it had broken away from normative ethics and tried to support the edifice of ethics alone. Instead, the decade saw the revival of both traditional normative ethics, as represented by Rawls' *A Theory of Justice*, and so-called virtue ethics, which opposed to normative ethics. According to Gregory Velazco Y. Trianosky, the rise of virtue ethics started from an essay published in 1958: "The debate which inaugurated much of the renewed interest in the virtues began in Anscombe's well-known article, 'Modern Moral Philosophy' (1958)."[41] As time went on, the voice of virtue ethics grew louder. To this day, however, despite its classic roots, it has not been able to establish or construct its own scientific system, or even publish an influential theoretical monograph on contemporary virtue theory under the title "virtue ethics."

Most scholars are familiar with virtue ethics, but its modern-day representative figures, except for perhaps Alasdair MacIntyre, are not well-known.

24   *Introduction*

Other representatives of virtue ethics may include the likes of Peter Geach, Philippa Foot, Michael Slote, G. H. Von Wright, Gary Watson, Gregory Velazco Y. Trianosky, Wallace, Taylor, and Warnock.

However, virtue ethics today still looks to its ancient masters, namely Aristotle and Aquinas. Foot, for instance, writes: "Virtues and vices, often neglected in analytic philosophy, are discussed here, drawing on the works of Aristotle, St. Thomas Aquinas, and Immanuel Kant."[42] Slote also makes reference to its antiquity: "Philosophical interest in virtue and the (particular) virtues has had a long and—though the term is inadequate—distinguished history."[43] So then, what precisely is virtue ethics?

A key problem in this regard is that western scholars treat meta-ethics, normative ethics and virtue ethics as two disciplines of ethics rather than as three:

With the birth of meta-ethics in 1903, ethicists were largely divided between meta-ethics and normative ethics and virtue theory was seen to be a part of normative ethics: "normative ethical theory focuses upon a comparative study of such general ethical theories as utilitarianism, egoism, Kantian formalism, virtue ethics, and so forth."[44] With the revival of virtue ethics in the 1960s, the virtue ethicists started to assert ethics is not composed of meta-ethics and normative ethics but of meta-ethics and virtue ethics.

Though they dispute the importance of each other's work, it turns out that both virtue ethicists and normative ethicists regard the "objects" of their study identically. This is because the ethics in each of their fields is composed of same two parts: one part is "morality, norms, and action," and the other is "virtue, moral character, and agent." In other words, one part is seen to explain the other: for normative ethicists, the center of the ethics system is morality, norms and action rather than moral character, virtue, and actor; for virtue ethicists, the center of the ethical system is morality, virtue, and actor instead of morality, norms, and action.

In defining virtue ethics, Nathan R. Kollar writes, "Much of contemporary ethics (normative ethics) focuses on specific acts that are justified by rules or consequences. Virtue ethics focuses on good judgment as a consequence of good character."[45] Barbara MacKinnon also says that in normative ethics, "Virtues are secondary. The primary goal is to *do* good and *act* rightly rather than to *be* good. In virtue ethics, the primary goal is to be good."[46] On the one hand, MacIntyre advocating the revival of Aristotle's virtue ethics in opposition to the prevailing normative ethics, argues: "Normative ethics' rejection of Aristotle's tradition is a rejection of a rather unique morality. In this morality, norms, which dominate modern moral theories—are but part of a larger system subordinate to the centrality of virtue."[47]

Neither normative ethics nor virtue ethics excludes or replaces the objects of study of the other, rather, they are subordinate or secondary concerns: normative ethics studies moral character, virtue, and agents, but these are already "determined" or prescribed seeing that they are based on morality, norms, and actions; and virtue ethics studies morality, norms, and actions, but these are "to be determined" given that virtue or agents is the foundation of its

Introduction 25

study. In a nutshell: "The place [normative ethics] has for virtue and/or vice is….different from that accorded them by an ethics of virtue."[48]

It is easy to see that the definitions of normative ethics and virtue ethics by Western ethicists are untenable. The fundamental cause of this error is undoubtedly their taking the part for the whole, thus exaggerating the objects of study. However, while the two parts—"morality, norms, and actions" and "moral character, virtue, and agents"—are fundamentally different, it is also true that we can deal with them as one discipline as the contemporary western ethicists do. We could even put the object of meta-ethics together with these two parts and treat all three as one discipline. Indeed, for more than two thousand years—from the time of Aristotle to the publication of Moore's *Principia Ethica*—had not ethicist considered such "objects" indiscriminately as one discipline?

But in present times, these older ways of studying ethics are considered unscientific because the nature of scientific development demands categorization: on the one hand, science divides the world we face into fundamentally different parts and studies them accordingly through different sciences such as "philosophy," "social sciences," and "natural sciences"; on the other hand, the objects of one science field are often further divided into several different sciences and disciplines, for instance, the objects of philosophy are divided into "ethics," "logic," "aesthetics," etc., and further still, are divided into sub-disciplines of other fields, such as "ethics," which is divided into "meta-ethics," "normative ethics" and other specialized disciplines, e.g., applied ethics and its various fields. Exactly how many disciplines ethics can be divided into depends on how many different parts the objects of ethics are divided into.

So, to recap, after Aristotle, ethics persevered as just one discipline, namely the science of morality, and though clearly its objects of study had changed with the tide of history it wasn't until Moore's *Principia Ethica* (1903) that ethics split into two distinct disciplines, meta-ethics, and normative ethics. With the rise of virtue ethics in the 1960s, normative ethics and virtue ethics came to be seen not as two sciences with different objects of study but as two modes of studying the same objects, an error which reveals an important truth about fundamental differences between "virtue, moral character" and "morality, norms," showing that ethics, as formerly the "science of morality," is originally made up of three fundamentally different but inseparable parts: the deductive methods of excellent morality (i.e., the object of meta-ethics), the deductive processes of excellent morality (i.e., the object of normative ethics) and the ways of realizing excellent morality (i.e., object of virtue ethics). And so it is that these three parts necessitate different approaches that we assert ethics consists of the three disciplines: meta-ethics, normative ethics, and virtue ethics. Furthermore, the controversies arising between moral-centrism and virtue-centrism also raise an extremely complicated and important question: what is the central discipline of the construction of the ethics system and of the classification of disciplines?

26 *Introduction*

0.3.3 The central discipline of ethics: Moral-centrism and virtue-centrism

It is very puzzling examining the works of contemporary Western virtue ethicists, as there are no rigorous theoretical arguments for why ethics should be virtue-centered—namely that "moral character," "virtue," and "what kind of person one is" are said to be more fundamental, important, and decisive than "morality," "norms," and "what one does." Such an argument is absent even from MacIntyre's great work *Whose Justice? Which Is Rationality?*—which he claims is centrally preoccupied with "the nature of connection between virtue and law."[49] As a result, we may well say that the conclusion of virtue-centrism is based more on intuitive perception than on theoretical argument.

Their main perception is that *being a virtuous person* is more important and decisive than *doing something that conforms to moral norms*, so virtue is more important and decisive than norms. If people are without virtue, moral norms, no matter how good they are, would not be observed, rendering them meaningless; conversely, if people have virtue, moral norms would be observed. According to Macintyre, the master of virtue-centrism, "In any case, there is another extremely important link between virtue and rule, that is, only those who have virtue and justice may know how to enforce the rules."[50] Similarly, Gilbert C. Meilaender states that "one can only distinguish 'is' correctly before he can do it correctly."[51]

It is true that if people are without virtue, then even the best moral norms will not be observed; moral norms only can be observed if people have virtue. However, does it lead to the conclusion that virtue is more important and more decisive than moral norms? The answer is no. On the contrary, the goodness or badness of the moral character of the vast majority of a country's population depends entirely on the goodness or badness of the country's state institutions, which, in the final analysis, depends on the goodness or badness of the moral norms the country pursues. This is because an institution is a system of behavioral norms, as Rawls and Ross point out:

> by an institution I shall understand a public system of rules...We have seen that these principles are to govern the assignment of rights and duties in these institutions and they are to determine the appropriate distribution and burdens of social life.[52]

John R. Commons speaks more vividly:

> The institution seems to be likened to a building, a structure of laws and regulations, like the occupants of a house, individuals move within the structure.[53]

It goes without saying that all behavioral norms established or recognized by society are only two categories: power norms and non-power norms. The so-called power norms are laws (including statute, policy, etc.). Relying on power for their enforcement, these are the behavioral norms that ought to and must be observed, such as the prohibition of killing, looting, and theft, while the so-called non-power norms are moralities which are realized merely relying on non-power forces of public opinion, reputation and conscience, and are the norms that merely ought to be observed, such as helping others, tolerance, continence, beneficence, and humility.

When the force on which certain behavioral norms depend is put aside, and only the norm itself is thus considered, the relationship between morality and law is the relationship between the general and the particular. On the one hand, not all moralities are laws, for instance, *selflessly benefiting others*, pleasure in helping others, compassion, and repayment for gratitude; on the other hand, all laws are also moralities, for example, ranging from the prohibitions of killing, violence, abuse, harm, or theft, concerning wider society, to more private affairs, concerning the welfare of our children or elderly parents.

Therefore, if the force on which a norm depends is put aside and only the norm itself is considered, then law is just as a part of morality. Then, what part of morality is law? It is undoubtedly a particular type of morality, one which we may characterize as the "minimum" type of morality. This principle is well summarized by the philosopher and jurist Georg Jellinek (1851–1911) in a well-known saying: "Law is the minimum of morality." Thus, *law* and *the minimum types of morality* are the same norms; the only difference between them lies not in their norms, but in the force in which the norms are to be realized: The same norm, if it is realized by power, it is law, and, if it is not realized by power but merely by some form of public consensus, it is morality.

The force of the norms aside, all laws can be seen as particular types of moralities derived from the general principles of morality. In this sense, law itself has no principles other than what can be described as particular, trivial, and fragmentary rules. That said to be the principles of law or legal principles such as justice, equality, liberty, truly speaking, do not belong to the category of law but to the category of morality and moral principles.

This is self-evident, for who would say that justice is a law? Who would say equality is a law? Who would say liberty is a law? Is it not the case we can only say justice, equality, and liberty are moralities and therefore are the moral principles of national governance? Do they not then become principles of law, namely principles of politics (since politics is the realization of law)? The only reason why justice, equality, and liberty are the core issues of jurisprudence and political philosophy is precisely because they are principles of law and politics.

Thus, on the one hand, although state institutions include economic, political, cultural, and social systems, that is, in terms of the "institutions" belonging to the category of a "system of behavioral norms," there are only two normative systems: law and morality. On the other hand, if the factor of force is put aside and only the norm itself is considered, given that law is a particular type of morality, what we call the "minimum" type of morality,

28   *Introduction*

all state institutions, in the final analysis, belong to the category of "moral norms."

The study of virtue ethics shows that state institutions are decisive and fundamental factors, while people's moral character in general is a subordinate and non-fundamental factor. The goodness or badness of a people's moral character depends on the goodness or badness of the state institutions. As long as the state institutions are good, the moral character of the vast majority of a country's population certainly will be good; if the state institutions are bad, the moral character of the vast majority certainly will be bad. As Deng Xiaoping said:

> Good institutions can prevent bad people from doing anything evil at will, and bad institutions can inhibit good people from doing enough good, or even vice versa. Even a great man like comrade Mao Zedong was so badly affected by some bad institutions that he had caused great misfortunes to the Party and to the state, including to himself—this by no means, means that he himself is not responsible for that, but rather to say that the system of leadership, the system of the organization is more fundamental, overall and long-term.[54]

The crux of the problem lies in the fact that a state institution is only a normative system of law and morality, which, we know, belongs to the category of moral norms. Therefore, somewhat different from the virtue ethics view above, the goodness or badness of moral norms a country pursues is the cardinal principle; it is the decisive and fundamental factor, while the moral character of a people is the non-fundamental and "to be-determined" factor. The goodness or badness of the moral character of the people on the whole depends on the goodness or badness of the moral norms they pursue. As long as the moral norms a country's state institutions pursue are good, the moral character of the vast majority of the people certainly is good; if the moral norms the country pursues are bad, the moral character of the vast majority certainly is bad. Let's demonstrate with three good moral norms of the system of state institutions, namely the three principles of liberty:

- The principle of political liberty: the politics of a country ought to be directly or indirectly with the consent of every citizen; ought to be conducted directly or indirectly according to each citizen's own will; and, in the final analysis, ought to be conducted according to the will of the governed.
- The principle of economic freedom: economic activities ought to be adjusted by market mechanisms and not controlled by government; the management of government ought to be limited to the establishment and safeguard of economic rules; within the scope of these economic rules, everyone ought to have the freedom to conduct their economic activities in full accordance with their own will, enjoying the freedom of economic

Introduction 29

activities of production, distribution, exchange, and consumption in full accordance with their own will.

- The principle of freedom of thought: every member of society ought to have the freedom to receive and impart any thought; in the final analysis, speech and publication ought to be completely free and ought not to be subject to any restrictions.

It is easy to see that if a country pursues such excellent moral norms, its politics certainly is fair and transparent, its economic development certainly is rapid, its distribution of wealth certainly is fair, its culture certainly flourishes, and everyone certainly is able to fully realize their creative potential. Consequently, the people certainly cleave to their virtue and happiness, the degree of satisfaction of material needs certainly is sufficient, the moral desire, moral awareness and moral will of being a virtuous person certainly is strong, and the moral character of the vast majority of the people certainly is noble. Conversely, if a country pursues bad moral norms, the country's politics certainly is corruptive, the economy certainly stands stagnant, the distribution of wealth certainly is unfair, culture certainly is bleak, and everyone's creative potential certainly is difficult to realize. Consequently, people certainly deviate from virtue and happiness, the satisfaction of material needs certainly is insufficient, the moral desire, moral awareness, and moral will of being a virtuous person certainly is weak, and the moral character of the vast majority of the people certainly is inferior.

It can thus be seen that the moral character of countrymen depends on the country's institutions, and ultimately on the moral norms the country pursues. Although, it is more important to be a virtuous person than to act according to moral norms, whether the vast majority of countrymen can be virtuous depends entirely on the moral norms their country follows. In the final analysis, moral norms are more critical than virtue.

Virtue-centrism mistakenly believes that virtue is more fundamental than moral norms, not only obviously because it only perceives that *being a virtuous person is more important and decisive than doing something that conforms to moral norms,* but fails to see that *whether it is possible to be a virtuous person depends on the goodness or badness of the moral norms that are followed;* it neither understands that there is a distinction between the goodness and badness of moral norms, nor that state institutions are a system of moral norms, the goodness or badness of which determine the moral character of the vast majority of the people in the country.

Another reason why virtue-centrism is untenable lies in the fact that so-called virtue, as Aristotle pointed out, is nothing more than one's "psychological self" formed and expressed by the long-term behavior of following moral norms:

In the case of the virtues....we acquire them as a result of prior activities; and this is like the case of the arts, for that which we are to perform by

30   *Introduction*

art after learning, we first learn by performing, e.g., we become builders by building, and lyre players by playing the lyre. Similarly, we become just by doing what is just, temperate by doing what is temperate, and brave by doing brave deeds.[55]

Everyone's moral character is the outcome of their long-term compliance with or violation of moral norms: "morality," "norms," and "what one does" are the cause, "moral character," "virtue," and "what kind of person one is" are the outcome. Does not this mean that moral norms are more fundamental, and more important and decisive than virtue? This is the reason why, in terms of the structure of its system, the primary and fundamental contents of ethics are "morality," "norms," "actions," or "what one does," which we may also take to be "reasons," "causes," or "premises," while its secondary and non-fundamental features are "moral character," "virtue," or "what kind of person one is," which we may take to be "outcomes" or "conclusions" of the main contents of the system.

Should ethics first study, or indeed can it directly study, the problem that "I ought to be a person who selflessly benefits others"? The answer is no. Whether one ought to be or not be an unselfish person is obviously based on the premise that there exist unselfish actions: if there are such selfless actions as altruism, such as Comte, Kant, Confucius, Mozi, and others advocated, then "selflessly benefiting others" can be established as a moral norm, and "I ought to be a person who selflessly benefits others" is tenable, but, if what Claude Helvetius, Horbach, Feuerbach and others said are right and there are no such selfless actions at all, then "selflessly benefiting others" ought not be established as a moral norm, and "I ought to be a person who selflessly benefits others" is totally nonsense.

Even if there actually are selfless actions, "I ought to be a person who selflessly benefits others" is still not necessarily tenable, for its tenability requires a series of other prerequisites such as the study of the ultimate goal of morality. If, as Nietzsche, Sartre, Yangzhu, Chuang Tzu, and other individualist thinkers believed, the ultimate goal of morality is self-interest, then selflessly benefiting others and self-sacrifice would not conform to the ultimate goal of morality and therefore ought not to be regarded as moral norms, and it follows that I ought not be a person who selflessly benefits others. If, as stated by Confucius, Kant, and Christianity, the ultimate goal of morality is to perfect one's moral character, then selflessly benefiting others and self-sacrifice conform to the ultimate goal of morality, and thus are moral norms that ought to be. Therefore, I ought to be a person who selflessly benefits others.

This is the reason why, from the perspective of the structure of the system of ethics, "morality," "norms," "actions," and "what one does" occupy most of the content of ethics as the primary and most fundamental premises, causes, and reasons, and why "moral character," "virtue," and "what kind of person one is" occupy only some of the content of ethics as secondary or non-fundamental conclusions and outcomes. This structure makes common sense, because, generally speaking, the premise is always more complex and more important than the conclusion; and the cause is always more fundamental and more decisive than the outcome. Therefore "norms" and "what one does" are more decisive than "virtue" and "what kind of person one is."

Questions concerning "What ought I do?" are extremely complicated and is something ethicists have been debating for more than two thousand years. Consider the following: Under what circumstances are self-interested actions more important than unselfish actions or vice versa? Is virtue wholly acquired through the selfless actions that benefit others not oneself? When is it wrong that one benefits others for one's own benefit? Should one act in ways that contribute to the greatest happiness of the greatest number? Or should one act out of a sense of duty to others? Is it virtuous to be honest in all situations no matter how bad the consequences? Conversely, the question "what kind of person ought I be?" is not a primary and fundamental issue: this can be achieved just by acting in accordance with the moral norm of "what one ought to do."

In light of this, it is understandable that Aristotle's ethics is so-called virtue ethics. Despite setting the agenda for ethics for centuries to come, it was still in its embryonic stage of development as a system of thought. It is no surprise that almost all the contents of ethics back then were confined to "virtue," "moral character," and "what kind of person one ought to be." As we know, the production of knowledge goes from observing outcomes to tracing the cause, from intuitive particularity to speculative abstraction, from simple external phenomena to complicated intrinsic essences. With the development of human cognition, the center of ethics gradually shifted from the simple, intuitive, and specific problems of "virtue," "moral character," and "what kind of person one ought to be" to more complicated, abstract, or profound problems of "morality," "norms," "actions," and "what one ought to do," and then further shifted to meta-ethics problems concerning the method of making excellent moral norms. The ethics of Kant's deontology and Mill's ethics of utilitarianism are transmissions of Aristotle's virtue-centered theory to moral-centrism; and Moore's meta-ethics marks the transition of moral-centrism to meta-ethics concerning the methods of deduction and the making of excellent moral norms. In short, modern ethics is the complete form of these two transformations and thus the advanced stage of ethics.

However, irrespective of how it has evolved, ethics has throughout its long history always been a so-called "normative" science concerned with moral norms and making excellent moral norms. In the final analysis, the methods and the processes of deducing and making excellent moral norms, and ways of realizing them belonged as much to ethics past as they do to modern ethics today—the difference is that we can classify the methods as the objects of meta-ethics, the processes as the objects of normative ethics, and the ways of realizing excellent moral norms as the objects of virtue ethics. Judging from this scientific definition of ethics, virtue ethics neither diverges from nor is

32   *Introduction*

independent of normative ethics, for it undoubtedly is an ethics concerned with moral norms, namely with the ways of realizing excellent moral norms.

In terms of the above definition, morality, and norms—taken together as the same concept—are complete and independent, forming the whole object of ethics, whereas virtue and moral character are incomplete and entirely dependent on and subordinate to morality and norms, for they occupy only part of the object of ethics, that is, as the realization of moral norms. James Rachel makes a similar observation in his detailed account of virtue ethics, concluding that "it seems best to regard the virtue theory as part of overall theory of ethics rather than as a complete ethics in itself."[56] Therefore, in any research of scientific ethics "morality," "norms," and "actions" should be primary considerations, while "moral character," "virtue," and "agents" should only be secondary considerations, meaning that former categories ought to occupy the central, decisive, and primary position, and that the latter categories ought to occupy the subordinate, secondary, and determined position.

Interestingly, virtue-centrism also has an argument that is different from its typical line that *being a virtuous person is more important and decisive than doing something that conforms to moral norms*, which, namely, can generally be taken to mean that virtue is the ultimate moral standard for evaluating the rightness or wrongness of all actions. This, however, not only fails to prove that virtue is at the center of ethics, on the contrary, it also shows that virtue is subordinate to morality. The authoritative elaborator of this argument is the contemporary virtue-centered ethicist Gregory Velazco Y. Trianosky, who writes:

> Formulated more precisely, rigorously, a pure ethics of virtue makes two claims. First it claims that at least some judgments about virtue can be validated independently of any appeal to judgments about the rightness of actions... Second, according to a pure ethics of virtue, it is this antecedent goodness of traits which ultimately makes any right act right.[57]

Daniel Statman, Gerasimos X Santas and a number of other virtue ethicists have all quoted this passage when discussing the fundamental features of virtue ethics. Santas also quoted G. Watson as a further explanation:

> 1. Living a characteristically human life (functioning well as a human being) requires possessing and exemplifying certain traits, T. 2. T are therefore human excellences and render their possessors to that extent good human beings. 3. Acting in a way W is in accordance with T (exemplifies or is contrary to T). 4. Therefore, W is right (good, or wrong).[58]

In the end, Santas concludes that "in a virtue ethics right conduct is defined in terms of, or derived from, or validated, or explained, by reference to the virtues."[59]

Introduction 33

These arguments imply that virtue is the ultimate standard of morality for evaluating the rightness or wrongness of all actions. Let's first assume that this assertion of virtue-centrism is true. Does this not clearly suggest that virtue is the ultimate standard of morality belonging to the category of "moral standard," "moral norms," and "morality"—that the three are the same concepts—thence is subordinate to moral norms? Furthermore, the implied proposition that virtue is the ultimate standard of morality for evaluating the rightness and wrongness of all actions, we know, is the core of Kant's ethics of deontology, but not of the virtue ethics that opposes it.

To sum up, virtue-centrism is a kind of specious sophistry, while moral-centrism is truth. If it is not virtue that is the core structure of the ethics system but morality, does this not mean that the core structure of the ethics system is normative ethics? Clearly it is. As we have argued, meta-ethics and virtue ethics, merely round out normative ethics as two smaller ends of the ethics system. In that it is one of two smaller ends, virtue ethics complements what meta-ethics sets out to achieve with its methods of making excellent morality, for its contents are the conclusions and outcomes of normative ethics concerning its processes of excellent morality. As the other smaller end of the ethics system, meta-ethics is only the method of normative ethics for normative ethics is the purpose of meta-ethics. Neither meta-ethics nor virtue ethics then, without normative ethics at the center, are a valid from a scientific perspective. Therefore, we can come to the conclusion that the system of ethics is composed of meta-ethics, normative ethics, and virtue ethics, and that the core of its structure is normative ethics. With this understanding, we see that the disciplines of ethics are necessarily divided into not two but the three distinctive and interrelated areas of meta-ethics, normative ethics, and virtue ethics, and that the central discipline is normative ethics.

0.4 The position of ethics in sciences

0.4.1 Theoretical status: The most complicated science

Ethics is more complicated than natural sciences such as physics. This can be accounted for in the following two aspects. On the one hand, what constitutes the ethical behaviors of human beings is more complex than physical phenomena and the sorts of behaviors we typically associate with psychology. As a Chinese saying goes: "One is able to draw the skin of a tiger but never the bones, just as one can know a person on the surface but never the heart." Like other sorts of human behavior, ethical behavior can be classed as a particular expression of human psychology, but the self-conscious activity of ethical behavior deviates from standard psychology for its arbitrary and ever-changing nature can camouflage or be a façade for other motivations, which can make it extremely difficult to understand the laws and nature of ethical behavior. More precisely, it is motivation of ethical behavior or, rather, what motivates one to be ethical, that makes ethical behavior more complicated and

34 *Introduction*

abstruse than behavior. The motivation of behavior, as the object of psychology, can be measured and verified through observation and experimentation, but the same cannot be said of the motivation of ethical behavior. Love, for instance, is a motivation for ethical behavior. How can we measure "love"? "Love" cannot be measured, as the well-known Chinese pop lyric goes, "You ask how much I love you? The moon represents my heart."

On the other hand, a natural science, such as physics, is a science of facts made up of only factual judgments, and thus theoretical divergence is simpler: it only has one divergence, that is, the cognition of facts. Conversely, ethics is a value science made up of value judgments (whether a behavioral ought is what *is*), factual judgments (whether the behavioral fact is what *is*), and the judgments of subjects (whether the goal of morality is what *is*), thence is at least three-fold more complicated in terms of theoretical divergence. For this reason, almost no school within the field of the natural sciences (physics, biology, geology, etc.) negates another school; however, in the field of ethics, there are many schools with different and competing views. Is ethics, then, not the most complicated and abstruse science?

Undoubtedly, the more abstract and general a science is, the more complicated and abstruse it is. The question "What is this table?" is a simple question for one often need only look at it to ascertain its general purpose (e.g. a kitchen table, coffee table, card table, picnic table, etc.). It does not need the use of science. However, the question "What is a table?" is not so easily answered. It is more conceptual because it concerns the form and substance of a table. Has it four legs or two legs? Is it round or square, wooden or iron? If we go even further past the concept of a table itself to ask the abstruse and abstract question "What is substance/matter?" we then encounter the age-old puzzle that led to the two major philosophical schools of materialism and idealism. The number of schools based around a problem is undoubtedly proportional to the abstraction, generality, abstruseness, and complexity of the problem: the more abstract, general, complicated, and abstruse, the more difficult to understand and explain, thence the easier it is to form different schools.

The schools of academic studies will never be established around such simple questions. Who would argue endlessly about a table to form different schools? Philosophy, we know, is the most abstract and universal science, and hence is the most complicated and abstruse science, which is well proven by its many schools, disciplines (metaphysics, natural philosophy, social philosophy, spiritual philosophy, axiology, logic, ethics, aesthetics, philosophy of science, etc.), and competing schools of thought within those disciplines. What, one may ask, is philosophy's most complicated and abstruse discipline? In the view of Marx W. Wartofski, it is axiology, as he put: "value theory constitutes the domain of one of the most difficult and rigorous of the philosophical disciplines."[60]

We can further assert that ethics is the most complicated and the most abstruse of the value sciences because it has more schools than any other

Introduction   35

value science. What has given rise to so many different schools and debates is simply that ethics has almost no simple problems; and this, moreover, explains why debates that span more than 2,000 years have never been [properly] settled. Even the question "What is morality?"—seemingly the simplest or most elementary question given that it has the least cognitive divergence—has six schools of thought: "moral subjectivism," "moral objectivism," "moral skepticism," "moral realism," "ethical relativism," and "ethical absolutism."

We might declare that ethics is too abstruse and difficult to answer; that despite all the great masters up to present, as Russell conceded, "there is no consensus in the field of ethics."[61] Since Confucius and Socrates, generation after generation has sought answers to ethical dilemmas. What, then, has compelled humankind to resolve this most intractable of sciences? Could it be that of all the sciences ethics has the greatest value for human beings?

0.4.2 Practical status: The most valuable science

The research object, system structure, and discipline classification of ethics show that the center of ethics is moral norms. In other words, normative ethics is the central discipline of ethics. Moral norms are divided into moral principles and moral rules: moral rules are only the extension and realization of moral principles, and moral principles are undoubtedly far more important and complex than moral rules. Therefore, ethics is mainly the science concerning moral principles. As mentioned earlier, the moral principles that ethics studies can be summed up as seven principles in total, namely good, justice, equality, humanity, liberty, elimination of alienation and happiness: good is the general principle of the morality of behaviors that ought to be; happiness is the moral principle of self-regarding; and the other five (justice, equality, humanity, liberty, and elimination of alienation) are mainly the value standard of the goodness and badness of state institutions.

Consequently, from a quantitative point of view, most of the moral principles studied by ethics belong to the category of the value standard of the goodness and badness of state institutions; from a qualitative point of view, the value standard of the goodness and badness of state institutions in terms of justice, equality, humanity, liberty, and elimination of alienation are undoubtedly far more important than goodness, benevolence, or other such moral principles. This is why Aristotle repeatedly stated that "In all kinds of virtues, people think that justice is the most important."[62] Smith also wrote:

> Beneficence, therefore, is less essential to the existence of society than justice. Society may subsist, though not in the most comfortable state, without beneficence; but the prevalence of injustice must utterly destroy it... [Beneficence] is the ornament which embellishes, not the foundation which supports the building, and which it was, therefore, sufficient to recommend, but by no means necessary to impose. Justice, on the contrary, is the main pillar that upholds the whole edifice. If it is removed, the

36   *Introduction*

great, the immense fabric of human society, that fabric which to raise and support seems in this world, if I may say so, to have been the peculiar and darling care of Nature, must in a moment crumble into atoms.[63]

Rawls put it in a nutshell: "One may think of a public conception of justice as constituting the fundamental charter of a well-ordered human association."[64]

The most important and substantive part of ethics, namely the core and foundation of ethics, therefore, is the study of the value standard of the goodness and badness of state institutions. Insofar as all its objects of study are concerned, ethics studies not only the *value standard* of both the "good" and the "bad" of state institutions, but also whether the state institutions themselves are good or bad. As we know, the state institution is the normative system of behavior and the normative system of law and morality. We also know that if the force on which the norms depend is put aside and only the norms themselves are considered, "law" and the "minimum" particular form of morality are the same norms, and thus all state institutions fall into the category of "moral norms." This is why there is a saying in China that "one can govern a country efficiently with just half volume of *Analects of Confucius*." And it is why Aristotle said that "The science of ethics itself is political science," and that "Political science examines nobleness and justice."[65]

Therefore, ethics is not only a rigorous science that can be axiomatized, and the most abstruse science, it can also be called the most valuable science. As the goodness or badness of the state institutions in a country relate closely to the greatest interests of everyone in it, it has the greatest value for everyone. In particular, the state institution is undoubtedly made by people under the guidance of the value standard of the state institutions, which implies that the goodness or badness of the state institution directly depends on the goodness or badness of the value standard of the state institution people pursue in a country: if the value standard is good, the state institution made under its guidance certainly is good, and hence has positive value for everyone; if the value standard is bad, the state institution made under its guidance will be bad, and hence has negative value for everyone. Ethics is a science mainly concerned with the value standard of the goodness and badness of state institutions. The reason why we characterize ethics as the science with the greatest value is much clearer when we compare the similarities and differences between the social developments in China and the West.

Why did ancient China and ancient Greek civilization both flourish around the same period (i.e. the Spring and Autumn Period and the Warring States Period in China)? Wasn't it because, basically speaking, both civilizations advocated the principle of freedom of thought? In the West, thinkers like Protagoras, Socrates, Plato, and Aristotle played important roles in the flourishing of Western philosophy, while in China, thinkers like Confucius, Mencius, Laozi, Chuang Tzu, Mozi, Han Feizi, and Gong Sunlongwere the masters of One Hundred Schools of Thought. Why did both civilizations stagnate during the middle ages? Wasn't it because people in both China and the West had lost their liberty under the rule of despotism? Why in modern times did the West make rapid progress and China fall behind? Isn't it because the West rid itself of despotism, aspiring again to the principle of liberty, while China stayed with its autocratic tradition, moving even further into despotism?

In the late 1770s, when the United States had attained independence from Great Britain, it was a small, largely agrarian nation, occupying only a narrow strip of North America along the Atlantic coast, with a territory of merely 400,000 square miles and a population of only 2.4 million. How, in a relatively short space of time, did it become the strongest nation in the world? Is not because it laid the foundations for the principle of liberty and ever since has fervently endorsed it as a mainstream ideology? Is America not the freest nation in world?

This is why, in a 1916 article for the *New Youth*, titled the *Ultimate Consciousness of Our Youth*, Chen Duxiu (陈独秀) writes:

> When Western civilization became increasingly known to people throughout the whole of our country its first influence impressed on the consciousness of our people a very different kind of scholarship, and its second influence a different kind of politics. This is evidenced by current political trends in our own form of governance in its attempt to break from the past. Where our people are doubtful and indecisive it is clearly a problem of our ethical tradition: no consciousness past or present is ever complete without the continual development of an ethical consciousness; the people will be lost in a state of confusion between new models and the old ways. I dare to assert that a new ethical consciousness is the ultimate enlightenment of the final consciousness.[66]

In the same year, Chen Duxiu further elaborated in his *Constitution and Confucianism* (published in the *New Youth*) that

> If ethical problems are not solved, politics and academic problems are merely the branches and leaves, not the trunk, so even a momentary thought of getting rid of the old and starting new, without changing any fundamental ideas, a return to old concepts is inevitable.[67]

Chen's statements are of profound insight! The ethical consciousness of the Chinese people—the abandonment of inferior morality and pursuit of *excellent morality*—is the ultimate consciousness. In the final analysis, a country's prosperity fundamentally depends on instilling the spirit of excellent morality in state institutions so that they maximize the interests of everyone, while a country's stagnation is the result of the inferior morality of bad state institutions which minimalize the interests of everyone. Ethics is a science concerned with not only the excellent morality, but also the value standard

38   *Introduction*

of the state institutions and the study of the goodness and badness of state institutions themselves, and thereby has the greatest value of all sciences.

Notes

1 Luo Guojie, ed. *Encyclopedia of Ethics of China. Volume of Principles of Ethics.* Jilin People's Publishing House, 1993, p. 1.
2 H. Gene Blocker: *Ethics: An Introduction*, Haven Publications, 1988, p. 10.
3 William K. Frankena: *Ethics*, Prentice-Hall, Inc., Englewood Cliffs, N.J., 1973, p. 4.
4 Louis P. Pojman: *Ethical Theory: Classical and Contemporary Readings*, Wadsworth Publishing Company, Belmont, CA, 1995, p. 1.
5 William K. Frankena: *Ethics*, Prentice-Hall, Inc., Englewood Cliffs, N.J., 1973, p. 4.
6 David Hume: *A Treatise of Human Nature,* The Clarendon Press, Oxford, 1949, p. 199.
7 H. Gene Blocker: *Ethics: An Introduction*, Haven Publications, 1988, p. 22.
8 Luther J. Binkley: *Ethics in the 20th Century*. Hebei People's Publishing House, 1988, p. 214.
9 Huang Jianzhong: *Comparative Ethics*, National Academic Press Inc., 1974, p. 34.
10 Wang Xianjun: *Introduction to Mathematical Logic*. Peking University Press, p. 35.
11 Howard Kahane: *Logic and Philosophy: A Modern Introduction*, Wadsworth Publishing Company, Belmont, CA, 1986, p. 42.
12 Howard Kahane: *Logic and Philosophy: A Modern Introduction*, Wadsworth Publishing Company Belmont, CA, 1986, p. 422.
13 Howard Kahane: *Logic and Philosophy: A Modern Introduction*, Wadsworth Publishing Company Belmont, CA, 1986, p. 423.
14 Also see: Felix Christian Klein: *The Thought of Mathematics, Ancient and Modern.* Vol. 1, Shanghai Science and Technology Press, 1979. (*Complete Works of Aristotle*, Vol. 1, Renmin University of China Press, 1990, p. 266.)
15 Karl R. Popper: *The Logic of Scientific Discovery*, Harper Torchbooks, Harper & Row, New York, 1959, p. 71.
16 Howard Kahane: *Logic and Philosophy: A Modern Introduction*, Wadsworth Publishing Company, Belmont, CA, 1986, p. 423.
17 Karl R. Popper: *The Logic of Scientific Discovery*, Harper Torchbooks, Harper & Row, New York 1959, p. 71.
18 Howard Kahane: *Logic and Philosophy: A Modern Introduction.* Wadworth Publishing Company, Belmont, CA, 1986, p. 424.
19 Albert Einstein: *Collection of Einstein*, Volume 1, Commercial Press, Beijing, 1976, p. 299.
20 Howard Kahane: *Logic and Philosophy: A Modern Introduction*, Wadsworth Publishing Company, Belmont, CA, 1986, p. 424.
21 Karl R. Popper: *The Logic of Scientific Discovery*, Harper Torchbooks, Harper & Row, New York, 1959, p. 101.
22 Sir Isaac Newton: *Selected Works on Philosophy of Nature.* Shanghai Translation Press, 2001, p. 3.
23 Alfred Tarski: *Introduction to Logic and to the Methodology of Deductive Sciences*, trans. Olaf Helmer, Dover Publications Inc., New York, 1996 [unabridged translation of the 9th edition, 1961, of the original published work in 1941, pp. 131–132].

Introduction 39

24 Wang Xianjun: *Introduction to Mathematical Logic.* Peking University Press, p. 102.

25 Albert Einstein: *Collection of Einstein*, Volume 1, Commercial Press, Beijing, 1976, p. 345.

26 Hans Reichenbach: *The Rise of Scientific Philosophy*, University of California Press, Berkeley and Los Angeles, CA, 1954, p. 279.

27 Albert Einstein: *Collection of Einstein*, Volume 1, Commercial Press, Beijing, 1976, p. 280.

28 Howard Kahane: *Logic and Philosophy: A Modern Introduction*, Wadsworth Publishing Company Belmont, CA, 1986, p. 436.

29 John Rawls: *A Theory of Justice (Revised Edition)*, The Belknap Press of Harvard University Press Cambridge, MA, 2000, p. 105.

30 Baruch Spinoza: *Descartes Principles of Philosophy.* Commercial Press, Beijing, 1997, p. 125.

31 Joseph P. Hester: *Encyclopedia of Values and Ethics*, ABC-CLIO, Santa Barbara, CA, 1996, p. 260.

32 Mark Timmons: *Morality without Foundations*, Oxford University Press, New York, 1999, p. 16.

33 John K. Roth: *International Encyclopedia of Ethics*, Braun-Brumfield Inc., U.C., 1995, pp. 554–555.

34 William K. Frankena: *Ethics*, Prentice-Hall, Englewood Cliffs, N.J., 1973, p. 96.

35 R. M. Hare: *The Language of Morals*, Oxford University Press, London, 1964, p. 1.

36 Lawrence C. Becker: *Encyclopedia of Ethics* Volume II, Garland Publishing, New York, 1992, p. 790.

37 Oliver A. Johnson: *Ethics: Selections from Classical and Contemporary Writers*, 4th Edition. Holt, Rinehart and Winston, New York, 1978, p. 12.

38 John K. Roth: *International Encyclopedia of Ethics,* Braun-Brumfield, U.C., 1995, p. 554.

39 Michael Smith: *The Moral Problem*, Blackwell, Oxford, U.K. and Cambridge, U.S.A., 1995, p. 2.

40 G. E. Moore: *Principla Ethica*, China Social Sciences Publishing House, Chengcheng Books, 1999, p. 35.

41 Daniel Statman: *Virtue Ethics*, Edinburgh University Press, 1997, p. 44.

42 Philippa Foot: *Virtues and Vices and Other Essays in Moral Philosophy*, University of California Press, Berkeley and Los Angeles, CA, 1978, p. 1.

43 Michael Slote: *From Morality to Virtue*, Oxford University Press, New York, Oxford, 1992, p. 87.

44 John K. Roth: *International Encyclopedia of Ethics,* Braun-Brumfield Inc., U.C., 1995, p. 554.

45 John K. Roth: *International Encyclopedia of Ethics*, Braun-Brumfield Inc., U.C., 1995, p. 915.

46 Barbara MacKinnon: *Ethics*, Wadsworth Publishing Company, San Francisco, CA, 1995, p. 90.

47 Alasdair Macintyre: *After Virtue*, China Social Sciences Publishing House, Chengcheng Books Ltd, 1999, p. 239.

48 William K. Frankena: *Ethics*, Prentice-Hall, Inc., Englewood Cliffs, N.J., 1973, p. 66.

49 Alsdair MacIntyre: *Whose Justice? Which Is Rationality?* University of Notre Dame Press, 1989.

40 *Introduction*

50 Alasdair Macintyre: *After Virtue*, China Social Sciences Publishing House, Chengcheng Books Ltd, 1999, p 14.
51 Gilbert C. Meilaender: *The Theory and Practice of Virtue*, University of Notre Dame Press, 1984, p. x.
52 Jon Rawls: *A Theory of Justice* (Revised Edition, the Belknap Press of Harvard University Press, 2000, p. 47.
53 Commons: *Institutional Economics,* Volume 1, Commercial Press, Beijing, 1997, p. 86.
54 Deng Xiaoping, *Selected Works of Deng Xiaoping*, vol. 2, People's Press, 1994, p. 333.
55 Aristotle: *Nicomachean Ethics*, translated with commentaries and glossary by Hippocrates G. Apostle, Peripatetic Press, Grinnell, Iowa, 1984, p. 21.
56 Steven M. Cahn and Peter Markie: *Ethics: History, Theory, and Contemporary Issues*, Oxford University Press, New York, Oxford, 1998, p. 681.
57 Daniel Statman: *Virtue Ethics,* Edinburgh University Press, 1997, p. 43.
58 Daniel Statman: *Virtue Ethics*, Edinburgh University Press, 1997, p. 261.
59 Daniel Statman: *Virtue Ethics*, Edinburgh University Press, 1997, p. 262.
60 M. W. Wartofsky: *Conceptual Foundations of Scientific Thought*, The Macmillan Company, New York, Collier-Macmillan Limited, London, 1968, p. 404.
61 Bertrand Russell: *Religion and Science*. Commercial Press, Beijing, 1982, p. 119.
62 Aristotle: *Complete Works of Aristotle*. Vol. 8, Renmin University of China Press, p. 96.
63 Adam Smith: *The Theory of Moral Sentiments*, China Sciences Publishing House, Chengcheng Books Ltd, Beijing, 1979, p. 86.
64 John Rawls: *A Theory of Justice (Revised Edition),* The Belknap Press of Harvard University Press, Cambridge, MA, 2000, p. 5.
65 Aristotle: *Complete Works of Aristotle*. Vol. 8, Renmin University of China Press, pp. 4–5.
66 Chen Duxiu: *Selected Works of Chen Duxiu*. Lin Wenguang ed., Sichuan Literature and Art Publishing House, 2009, p. 25.
67 Chen Duxiu: *Selected Works of Chen Duxiu*. Lin Wenguang ed., Sichuan Literature and Art Publishing House, 2009, p. 37.

Introduction to this volume

I.1 Ethics: Etymology and definition

In English, "ethics" originates from the Latin word *Ethica,* and *Ethica* originates from the Greek word *Ethos*, and means moral character, temperament, customs and mores. Morality originates from the Latin word *Mos*, and also refers to moral character, temperament customs and mores. Because they have the same etymology, ethics, and morality both refer to behavioral norms that ought to be, which are externalized into customs and mores and internalized into moral character and virtue. The ancient Roman philosopher Cicero (106 BC–43 BC) thus translated *Ethos*, Aristotle's work, into Latin as *Mores* (morality).

The etymological meaning of ethics is somewhat different in China. The Chinese term for ethics is *lún lǐ* 伦理. The character 伦 (pronounced *lún*) originally means "family generations." According to the *ShuoWenJieZie* (《说文解字》), the first character dictionary in China, a variation of the meaning of *lún* is "Ethics; the generations in family," which has been extended to mean "interpersonal relationships." For instance, the "Five ethics" are five different interpersonal relationships: that between monarch and subjects, father and son, husband and wife, the elderly and the young, and between friends. In other words, as Huang Jianzhong said, "Ethics is the interdependence of human relations."[1] The character 理 (pronounced "lǐ") originally means to carve jade stone. In the *ShuoWenJieZie*, "the un-carved jade is called unprocessed jade stone" (璞, pronounced *pú*), so the carving of jade is extended to mean other processes such as the renovation or restoration of things, as well as to the texture, character, or feature of intrinsic matter such as the grains of wood, veins under the surface of skin, etc., but, for our purposes here, it also refers to processes such as laws and rules. In other words, *li* is the factual laws. "It is nothing else but nature.... the *never-changing law* of the nature of heaven, earth, human beings and all matters."[2] In terms of rules, *li* refers to the necessary rules for human action that ought to be, as Jianzhong Huang said: "only the necessary rules of matters are law."[3] Therefore, so-called ethics, in terms of its Chinese etymological meaning, concerns the

42 *Introduction to this volume*

"factual laws" of interpersonal relationships and the norms of interpersonal relationships that ought to be.

The different etymological meaning of ethics between China and the West can be put thus: in the West ethics only refers to the norms of what interpersonal behavior ought to be, while in China it refers not only to the norms of interpersonal behavior that ought to be, but also to the laws of the facts of interpersonal behaviors (hereon referred to as the "law of behavioral facts"). Conceptually, although the definition of ethics is consistent in both, the difference resides in the different languages. To return to the concept of the "Five Ethics," for instance, we can assert that the relationships between monarch and subjects, father and son, husband and wife, the elderly and the young, and friends are five different kinds of ethical relationships, not five different kinds of moralities. For example, ethics concerns the relationship between the monarch and subjects, as well as the "righteousness" of monarch and subjects, while morality only considers the righteousness of the monarch–subject relationship, not the relationship itself. More exactly, the relationship between monarch and subjects is the fact of the interpersonal relationship, while the "righteousness" of monarch and subjects is the norm of the interpersonal relationship that ought to be. As to the basis of all five relationships, morality only considers the different kinds of interpersonal relationships that ought to be (the norms), while ethics considers both the different kinds of interpersonal relationships that ought to be (the norms) and the facts of the different kinds of interpersonal relationships.

Then, can we define ethics as "the laws of the facts of interpersonal behavior and the norms of interpersonal behavior that ought to be"? The answer is no. Because, on the one hand, the laws of the facts of interpersonal behavior and the norms of interpersonal behavior that ought to be are not necessarily ethics. Let's take dining habits as an example. While Westerners are accustomed to using knives and forks, many educated Indians are getting used to using their fingers which is the traditional cultural custom. These two different habits are undoubtedly the norms of two kinds of interpersonal behaviors that ought to be, but they bear no relation to ethics. On the other hand, there are of course also the laws of the facts of non-interpersonal behavior and the norms of non-interpersonal behavior that ought to be which undoubtedly also belong to ethics but do not necessarily relate to society or others, such as continence, cherishing life, and self-regarding. Then, what exactly is ethics?

In answer to that, ethics concerns the laws of the facts of behaviors with social utility and the norms of the oughts of behaviors with social utility. Why is it that the dining habits of using chopsticks, or knife and fork, or fingers do not come under the category of ethics? Isn't it because neither are an advantage or disadvantage to the existence and/or development of society, and hence do not have social utility? Why does ethics include behaviors unrelated to others or society such as those mentioned above or self-restraint self-indulgence, self-preservation or self-harm? Isn't it because these norms, in the final analysis, are either an advantage or disadvantage to society? For

Introduction to this volume 43

this reason, many Western thinkers more or less agree that our definition of ethics here, namely that it is a science or study of the laws of the facts of behaviors with social utility and of the norms of the oughts of behaviors with social utility. Dewey stated that "Ethics is the science which studies human actions and distinguishes their right and wrong, good and bad."[4] And Spencer said: "Ethics studies the most evolved human behaviors among general behaviors which directly or indirectly promote or impede the welfare of society and oneself."[5] Wilhelm Wundt also commented that "Ethics, established as a normative science, ought to first examine the facts of moral life, then the norms can be transformed from facts to laws."[6]

I.2 Meta-ethics and the science of meta-ethics: Etymology and definition

In the English language, meta-ethics adopt the prefix "meta-," which comes from the Greek prefix μετά-, and means "after," "beyond." If, in the contexts above, meta-ethics etymologically means "beyond-ethics" and "beyond ethics study," then what is "beyond-ethics" or "beyond ethics study"?

In its original sense, so-called "beyond-ethics" is "ethics that goes beyond ethics." In other words, it is not ethics, but includes ethics (just like animals are not humans, but the term includes humans), which is similar to David E. Cooper's notion that meta-ethics engages "questions *about* morality, not *of* morality."[7] In the final analysis, then, meta-ethics is the superordinate concept of "ethics": the relationship between the two is the relationship between the general and the particular. Therefore, by definition, if "ethics are the laws of facts of behaviors with social utility and the norms of oughts of behaviors with social utility," it follows that meta-ethics more generally concerns "the laws of facts of behaviors and the norms of oughts of behaviors" and broader still, concerns "the laws of facts and the norms of oughts," which, in the final analysis, are "the laws and rules *of 'ought' derived from 'fact'.*"

Furthermore, "ought" is subordinate to "good"; and "good" is subordinate to "value"; while the opposing concept of "ought," "good," and "value" is "fact": the four are inextricably connected. Therefore, in a nutshell, meta-ethics, which is beyond-ethics, on the one hand, concerns the laws and rules of "ought," "good," "value," and "fact," and, on the other hand, concerns the laws and rules of the relationship between "value, good, and ought" and "is or fact," or, to be more exact, the laws and rules deriving "value, good, and ought" from "is or fact." With this, we arrive at the proper definition of meta-ethics extended from its etymon.

We can affirm that meta-ethics is the ethics concerning the laws and rules of the relationship between "ought," "good," "value," and "fact," that is, it is concerns with the derived process of "ought," "good," and "value" from "facts." Where meta-ethics, for instance, deals with the fundamental problems of "Hume's guillotine," ethics only deals with the problems of whether moral ought, moral good, moral value, and excellent moral norms conform to moral

44   *Introduction to this volume*

values. Therefore, we say that meta-ethics is "beyond-ethics" because it is the ethics that transcends moral ought, moral good, and moral values, that is, it is the kind of ethics that contends with ought, good and value, but, in the final analysis, is still ethics in that it directly applies to excellent moral norms— namely the rules that conform to values.

Nevertheless, the reason that meta-ethics is not *ethics* because the study of ought, good and value is different from the study of moral ought, moral good, and moral value, or, because the study of excellent norms is different from the study of excellent moral norms. On the contrary, it is precisely because meta-ethics transcends ethics that the study of ought, good, and value is *also* the study of moral ought, moral good, and moral values, and that the study of excellent norms *also* belongs to the study of excellent moral norms. In other words, it transcends ethics because it serves as the method for ethics.

One cannot understand particularity without understanding generality: the understanding of generality is the method of understanding of particularity. One cannot understand what salmon is without understanding fish: understanding fish is the method of understanding salmon. Therefore, before knowing where "moral ought," "moral good," and "moral value" exist and how they emerge and are derived we should first know where "ought," "good," and "value" exist and how they emerge and are derived: The understanding of "ought," "good," and "value" is the method of understanding "moral ought," "moral good," and "moral value." And, before knowing how to make "excellent moral norms" we should first know how to make "excellent norms": the understanding of "excellent norms" is the method of understanding "excellent moral norms."

Therefore, the study of "ought, good, and value" in meta-ethics is also part of the study of "moral ought, moral good, and moral value" in ethics. Thus, insofar as meta-ethics is concerned with moral value, it is the deductive method of moral values. Similarly, the study of "excellent norms" in meta-ethics is also part of the study of "excellent moral norms" in ethics. Furthermore, while both are concerned with excellent moral norms, meta-ethics is the ethics concerning the method of making excellent moral norms.

In sum, meta-ethics (understood as "beyond ethics") concerns the factual laws and the norms of the oughts, and, by further extension, the laws and rules of "ought," "good," "value" and "fact." Ethics, on the other hand, concerns the factual laws of behaviors with social utility and the norms of the oughts of behaviors with social utility. More specifically, ethics is the science concerned with moral ought, moral good, and moral value, and "excellent moral norms," while meta-ethics (understood as beyond-ethics) is the science concerned with ought, good and value, and "excellent norms." The etymology and definition of meta-ethics is similar to Cooper's view that meta-ethics engages "questions *about* morality, not *of* morality."[8] Meta-ethics is, then, the most abstract, most general and most essential discipline of ethics for the reason that ought, good and value are more abstract, general, and basic or essential than moral ought,

Introduction to this volume 45

moral good and moral value; and because excellent norms are more abstract, more general, and more basic or essential than excellent moral norms. In this respect, the Chinese translation of "meta-ethics" (yuan lunli 元伦理) seems much closer to a proper definition of the concept, as "yuan" (元) means "basic," "original," "first," "primary," "principle," etc.

I.3 The objects of meta-ethics

Can the objects of meta-ethics studies be summed up as "ought," "good," "value," and "fact"? The answer is yes but not exactly. As stated in the *Introduction*, meta-ethics is an axiom and postulates system of ethics composed of three elements—the primitive concept, the primitive proposition, and the primitive inference rules, just like the axiom and postulates system of geometry and mechanics. We can properly divide the three elements into two parts, namely Part I and Part II. Part I is the study of the primitive concepts of ethics such as "value," "good," "ought," and "fact," which are what the meta-ethicists call "ethics terminology" or "moral terms," "ethics terms," and "value terms." As these terms also cover the categories of normative ethics and virtue ethics they are obviously too broad, so we would rather put them under the "category of meta-ethics," that is, as "primitive concepts of ethics."

Part II is the study of the primitive proposition and the primitive inference rules of ethics, which is the proof of the primitive propositions and their inference rules contained in the interrelations of the primitive concepts, especially that of "ought" and "facts," and also the proof of the axioms and postulates of ethics, which are ultimately the proof of the seven axioms and seven postulates of the two series of "the existential axiom and postulate of ethics" and the "deductive axiom and postulate of ethics": these are what the meta-ethicists call the "justification of moral judgments" or "moral justification." Not only are these terms too broad, they tend to be specious, completely lacking the essence of justification, that is, is a scientifically grounded basis for it, namely the analysis and proof of the ethical axioms and postulates; hence the terms fail to fully understand or appreciate the complexity of the concepts of ought and fact, especially as a potential solution to Hume's guillotine. So, we would rather call any kind of moral justification "meta-ethical proof: the ethical axioms and postulates."

The arrangement order of the two parts of *Meta-ethics* obviously ought to be the same as the order of all axiomatic systems, from the primitive concept to the primitive proposition and the primitive inference rules, namely from the "category of meta-ethics: the primitive concepts of ethics" to the "meta-ethical proof: the ethical axioms and postulates." Then, what are the primitive concepts of ethics or categories of meta-ethics? The study of meta-ethics shows what the premise of solving this problem is: which category or categories are at the core of the meta-ethics categories or the primitive concepts system of ethics?

46   *Introduction to this volume*

The core categories of meta-ethics vary widely: they are "good" in Moore's view, "right," and "good" in Ross's view, "good," "right," and "ought" in Hare's view, "good" and "ought" in Ewing's view, "good," "ought," and "is" in Mackie's view, and "good," "right," "ought," "value," "fact" in Stevenson's view. Then what are exactly the core categories of meta-ethics? At first sight it is "good," because almost all categories of meta-ethics can be summed up as "good": "ought" is the action of good; "right" is moral good; "value" is the nearest genus to good; "is" or "fact" is the source and substance of all good and value. Therefore, Moore believed that "good" is the most important category in the category system of ethics, and that "how 'good' is to be defined is the most fundamental question in all Ethics."[9]

However, the core category of meta-ethics is undoubtedly determined by the fundamental problem of meta-ethics, which, as Frankena and other ethicists point out, is the justification of moral judgment or value judgment, namely the logic of the moral reasoning or value reasoning, which is also the problem of the source and basis of "ought" and "value," and thus is the problem of the relationships between "ought, value" and "is" or "fact," which, in the final analysis, is the so-called "guillotine": whether "ought" can be derived from "is"?

In view of this, the most basic category of meta-ethics undoubtedly is "ought" instead of "good" no matter how important and complicated "good" is. The system of meta-ethics categories developed around "ought" includes not only the basis and source of "ought" or the opposite concepts of "is" and "fact," as well as "good" which is the superior concept of "ought," and "right" which is the lower concept of "ought," but also includes, as Charles L. Reid says, "value" and "evaluation," for the latter is the prerequisite of analyzing the former: "as we review the study of good and bad, of course, the main problems discussed always go deep into the nature of value and its recognition."[10] Ross also writes in the opening of his meta-ethics masterpiece *The Right and the Good*:

> The purpose of this inquiry is to examine the nature, relations, and implications of three conceptions which appear to be fundamental in ethics—those of "right," "good" in general, and "morally good." The inquiry will have much in common with the inquiries, of which there have been many in recent years, into the nature of value.[11]

Therefore, the category system of meta-ethics—the primitive concept system of ethics—can also be named as the category system of "ought." According to the principle of the conceptual arrangement of the scientific system—moving from the "abstract to concrete"—the starting concepts of this primitive concept system are "value" and "evaluation," then "good" that is particular to value (good is also "positive value"), followed by the good of action: "ought"; in the second place is the moral good of action: "right"; and finally the opposite concept of these concepts: "is" or "fact." However, in this primitive conceptual system of ethics, though "ought" is a core concept, it is not the most complicated and most important concept: the most complicated and most important concept, as it is known, is "value."

If we understand what value is, it is then clear that other categories of meta-ethics such as "good," "ought" and "right" are all special values. The analysis of "value," which is the most complicated concept created by human beings, not only unlocks other categories of meta-ethics but is also of great significance for the whole of ethics. Only under its guidance can we scientifically study the particular value, namely "good," which is the "positive value" as opposed to the "negative value." And only under the guidance of "value" and "good" can we scientifically study "ought" which is the core category of meta-ethics, for "ought" is the action with positive value and is the good of action. Only under the guidance of "ought" can we scientifically study "moral ought" and construct the system of normative ethics, then construct the system of virtue ethics system. In a nutshell: The analysis of the concept of value is the cornerstone of the entire edifice of ethics.

If we understand what value is, it is then clear that other categories of meta-ethics such as "good," "ought," and "right" are all special values. The analysis of "value," which is the most complicated concept created by human beings, not only unlocks other categories of meta-ethics but is also of great significance for the whole of ethics. Only under its guidance can we scientifically study particular value, namely "good," which is the "positive value" as opposed to the "negative value." And only under the guidance of "value" and "good" can we scientifically study "ought," which is the core category of meta-ethics, for "ought" is the action with positive value and is the good of action. Only under the guidance of "ought" can we scientifically study "moral ought" and construct the system of normative ethics, then construct the system of the virtue ethics system. In brief: the analysis of the concept of value is the cornerstone of the entire edifice of ethics.

Therefore, we separate the primitive concept of "value" (including "evaluation") from other primitive concepts as one independent chapter titled as "The Starting Concept of Ethics," and put the other four primitive concepts—"good," "ought," "right," and "fact" into another chapter titled as "The Primitive Concepts of Ethics." Since only the primitive concept that is ranked first can be called "the starting concept," and since in any axiomatic system there can be several or even dozens of primitive concepts, we call the rest of the concepts "primitive concepts."

Notes

1 Huang Jianzhong: *Comparative Ethics*, National Academic Press Inc., 1974, p. 27.
2 Huang Jianzhong: *Comparative Ethics*, National Academic Press Inc., 1974, p. 28.
3 Huang Jianzhong: *Comparative Ethics*, National Academic Press Inc., 1974, p. 27.
4 Cited from Huang Jianzhong: *Comparative Ethics*. National Academic Press Inc., 1974, p. 32.

48   *Introduction to this volume*

5 Cited from Huang Jianzhong: *Comparative Ethics*. National Academic Press Inc., 1974, p. 32.
6 Cited from Huang Jianzhong: *Comparative Ethics*. National Academic Press Inc., 1974, p. 36.
7 David E. Cooper: *Ethics: The Classic Reading*. Blackwell Publishers, 1998, p. 3.
8 David E. Cooper: *Ethics: The Classic Reading*. Blackwell Publishers, 1998, p. 3.
9 G. E. Moore: *Principia Ethica*. China Social Sciences Publishing House, Chengcheng Books, 1999, p. 57.
10 Charles L. Reid: *Choice and Action: An Introduction to Ethics,* Macmillan Publishing Co. Inc., New York, 1981, p. 200.
11 W. D. Ross: *The Right and Good,* Clarendon Press, Oxford, 1930, p. 1.

Part I

Categories of meta-ethics

1 The starting concept of ethics

1.1 The concept of value: Utility theory of value

Roughly speaking, *value* seems to be a self-evident concept: isn't value *good* or *bad*? Who does not know what good or bad is? Indeed, value and *good* or *bad* are the same concept. Value is *good* or *bad*: *good* is positive value, *bad* is negative value. However, as Pojman puts it, value is an extremely vague and ambiguous concept.[1] Bryan Wilsons even says that "among all concepts, there is hardly any concept as difficult to define as value."[2] This difficulty, I'm afraid, first of all, is that to define value, we must use "object" and "subject"— concepts that are themselves quite complicated and have long been debated. Nevertheless, since value is something that has to do with other things, it can be considered as a relational category. When we say, for instance, that a stone is valuable and a good thing, it must be for something else. Without these other things the stone itself is nothing of value. Therefore, as a matter of relationships, value is always a question of "What has value?" and "To whom (or to what) it has value?." The former is a question of the so-called object of value, while the latter is a question of the so-called subject of value. Therefore, to define value, we must define "object" and "subject" first.

1.1.1 Subject and object: Subjectivity is also autonomy

The subject is firstly a category of relations: only when one thing is relative to another can it be the subject, thus, without a certain relationship, as far as a thing itself is concerned, there is no subject. Is then the subject only relative to the object? Not the case. The subject is also relative to "property." Furthermore, it can be the noumenon and bearer of the property (the thing that the property depends on and is subordinated to), that is, the "substance," which is an extension of the etymology of "subject," and so has the same meaning as it. The term subject originates from the Latin word *subjectus*, which means to put beneath, as the foundation, then is extended to mean noumenon, substance, and material carrier of certain properties. Therefore, Aristotle says: "The reason that the primary substance is most legitimately called the primary substance is because it is the foundation and subject of

52 *Categories of meta-ethics*

all other things."[3] Marx and Engels also wrote: "Substance is the subject of all changes."[4] The subject can also be relative to the "object," and can still be termed the subject and narrated: "Everything that can express the object can also be used to describe the subject."[5] The subject can also refer to the main component as relative to the secondary component, as we say "the subject project in architecture" and "the students are the subject of the May Fourth Movement, etc." These meanings of the subject are obviously not the definition of the subject as a category in a value science such as ethics, because the "subject" as a category of value science is the subject relative to the "object." What exactly is then this subject that is relative to the object?

It is not difficult to see that the subject relative to the object is the agent and the initiator: the subject is the agent and the initiator while the object is the object of activity and the passive receiver. But this is not the definition of subject and object, because, reversely, not all agents and the initiators are subjects and not all the objects of activity and passive receivers are objects. For example, volcanoes have active periods, and an active volcano in the state of activity is then is an agent. When the active volcano engulfs a village, the village then becomes the object of volcanic activity, making the volcano the initiator and the village the passive receiver. However, we obviously cannot say that the volcano is the subject and the village that is engulfed by the volcano is the object. Despite the subject being the agent and the initiator, the agent and the initiator is not necessarily always the subject. Then, what kind of agent or initiator is the subject?

A subject is something that can be autonomous. It can be an autonomous initiator and agent. So-called autonomy means autonomy of selection and autonomous selection. This selection is different from Darwin's "natural selection," which is a kind of automatic selection that is mechanical, that has no capacity to distinguish between goodness and badness, advantage and disadvantage, and no objective, thus no capacity to make good use of advantage and avoid disadvantage. On the contrary, autonomous selection has the capacity to distinguish between goodness and badness, advantage and disadvantage, and it has objective, thus the capacity to make good use of advantage and avoid disadvantage. Therefore, saying that the subject is as an autonomous agent means that the subject is an agent that can select independently and has the capacity to distinguish between goodness and badness, advantage and disadvantage, that is, possess the objective or capacity to make good use of advantage and avoid disadvantage to maintain its own existence.

Just think, why is it that the volcano that engulfs a village is not a subject, but bandits who ransack a village are a subject? Isn't this because the bandits have autonomous capacities and the volcano does not? Isn't this because bandits are autonomous agents and the volcano is not an autonomous agent? Isn't this because bandits have the capacity to distinguish between goodness and badness, advantage and disadvantage, and the volcano has no such capacity? Isn't this because bandits have objectives and can therefore make good use of advantage and avoid disadvantage to maintain their own existence, while the

The starting concept of ethics   53

volcano has no such capacity? Therefore, autonomy is the feature of the subject as subject, and is so-called subjectivity: on the one hand it expresses "the ability of distinguishing between goodness and badness, advantage and disadvantage," and on the other hand it expresses "the capacity to seek advantage and avoid disadvantage to maintain the subject's own existence." Therefore, the subject that is relative to the object still has all the connotations of the substance and noumenon, because as the autonomous agent it undoubtedly belongs to the category of substance and noumenon. However, there is a separate kind of relationship of belonging between the subject and the substance and noumenon: the substance and noumenon are the material bearer of all properties, while the subject is only the material bearer of the "autonomous" properties, as well as the material bearer of the property concerning its "capacity to distinguish between goodness and badness, advantage and disadvantage" and its "selective capacity to seek advantage and to avoid disadvantages to maintain its own existence."

With the definition of the subject, the definition of the object is settled. The so-called object is obviously the object of activity of the subject, namely, the object of activity of the autonomous agent and the object the agent of autonomous activity is directed to. This is also the meaning from the etymology of "object." The object originates from Latin *objicio*, which means "throw or put to, towards, in front of or before," and is extended to mean the object of activity of the agent and the object of activity of the subject. Thus the category of object is more extensive and simpler than that of the subject, as everything—the sun, the moon, the planets, mountains, lakes, birds, animals, humans, society, thoughts, ideas, substance, property, etc.—can all be the objects of the activity of subject, and therefore can all be objects: the object can be either a substance or a property. Even the subject itself can be the object of the activity of the subject, and therefore can be both the subject and the object at the same time, because a subject's own activities can also be directed to itself, such as self-knowledge and self-transformation—the self of the knower and the self of one that transforms is the subject, while the self of the object of knowledge and transformation is the object.

1.1.2 Value: The utility of the object to the need of the subject

Given the basic meanings of the subject and the object—the subject is an independent agent that can distinguish between goodness and badness, advantage and disadvantage, the object is the object that the activity of the subject is directed to—the reason why the subject's activity is directed to the object obviously is that the object possesses a certain property that has effect on the subject, thus cause the activity of the subject directed to it, in its pursuit of things that are good and avoidance of things that are bad. However, what is the exact meaning of good and bad?

Li Deshun says: "The combination of 'good' and 'bad' is a fundamental expression of both positive and negative possibilities of general 'values'."[6] He

54 *Categories of meta-ethics*

is right: the combination of good and bad constitutes the so-called concept of value. In its broadest sense, value is undoubtedly an interaction and relationship between subject and object.[7] Value is not, however, the relationship of the subject to the object or the effect of the subject on the object, but rather the relationship of the object to the subject or the effect of the object on the subject, just as Ralph Barton Perry states: "Value can be defined as the relationship between the object and the evaluation of subject."[8]

However, value is not the effect or relationship of the object to everything of the subject: Which parts of the subject then does the object have an effect on or relationship to? Perry's famous "theory of interest" provides a very incisive answer to this, as he put it: "It can be admitted that the value of the object lies in its relationship to interest"[9] and that because of this "value can be defined as a function of interest."[10] Perry's concept of interest has a broad extension, as he said: "Interest is a series of events that are determined by the expectations of the results,"[11] "it includes desire, will or objective"[12] and "and it ought to also be a category for terms such as 'like-dislike, love-hate, hope-fear, desire-avoidance'."[13] Defining value in terms of interest, Perry concludes that for the present perspective value must ultimately be seen as a function of will or like.[14]

It can be seen that the essence of Perry's "interest" are various forms of transformations of "needs" in a subject's consciousness, to be more exact, are "needs" and their ideological forms, such as desire, will, objective, interest, and like. Therefore, we can further say that value is the utility of the object to the subject's needs (and its various transformational forms in consciousness such as desires, purposes, and interests). For it is self-evident that when the object can satisfy the needs of the subject it is good or is thought have positive value; when it obstructs the satisfaction of the needs of the subject it is called bad or is thought have negative value; when the object is irrelevant to the needs of the subject, it is neither good nor bad, hence is valueless. The goodness or badness of the object for the subject is undoubtedly a certain effect of the object on the needs of the subject, which is the so-called utility: utility obviously belongs to the category of effect, and it is an effect on needs. Therefore, Makiguchi Saburo says: "Value can be defined as the relationship between [a] human life and [an] object, which [is] no [different] from the terms 'utility' and 'effectiveness' used by economists."[15]

Thus, value, in short, is the utility of the object to the *needs* of the subject (which can take various forms of transformation in the subject's consciousness such as desire, purpose, interest). This can also be seen from the etymology of "value," which, as Marx pointed out, comes from the Sanskrit of "Wer" (meaning cover, protect) and "Wal" (meaning cover and reinforce), Latin "vallo" (meaning to surround with embankment, reinforce, and protect) and "valeo" (meaning powerful, robust, healthy), and it is extended to mean "useful." Therefore Marx said,

> Bailey and others have pointed out that the words 'value, valeur' used together represent a kind of property of things. Indeed, they were

The starting concept of ethics 55

originally nothing more than to indicate an object's value in its use to humans, to indicate the usefulness of objects or properties for the pleasure of people. In fact, the words "value, valeur" and "Wer" cannot have other sources in etymology.[16]

Then, is value the utility of all the properties of the object to the needs of the subject? The answer is definitive. All properties of an object are nothing more than intrinsic properties and relational properties. Intrinsic properties are the properties such as the quantity of matter and the length of electromagnetic wave. Relational properties are divided into properties of factual relationship (such as color and sound) and properties of value relationships (such as good, bad, use). It is true that value can be the effect of intrinsic properties and the factual properties of the object on the subject, and it can also be the utility of the object's value or utility to the subject. For example, the use value of commodities is the marginal utility of the factual properties of commodities to the needs of use and consumption, while the exchange value of commodity is the utility of the use value of commodities to the needs of exchange. In the final analysis, it is the utility of the marginal utility of commodity to the needs of exchange.

Therefore, value is the utility of all properties of the object to the subject's needs (desire, purpose, and interest, etc.), namely the utility of the object to the subject's needs (desire, purpose, and interest, etc.), or, more simply, the utility of the object to the needs of subject. This definition can be termed as the "definition of utility theory of value," which is not only consistent with common sense, but also has been widely acknowledged in academic circles.[17] Even the definitions opposed to the utility theory of value, when carefully examined, are in fact no different from the utility theory of value. Let's analyze some representative definitions:

The first is the so-called "theory of relationship." Li Lianke writes: "The so-called value is a particular (affirmative and negative) relationship between the object and the needs of the subject."[18] Then is not the relationship between the affirmation or negation of the object and the needs of the subject certain sorts of the utility of the object for the needs of subject? Let's see the definition by Li Deshun:

> The most general meaning of the category of "value" is the expression of a special content of the subject–object relationship. The peculiarity of this content lies in whether the effect of the object is consistent or conforming to the structure, scale or needs of the subjects: if it is "yes," it belongs to the positive value that people refer to with all kinds of commendatory words, and if it is "no" it belongs to the negative value that people refer to in various derogatory terms.[19]

However, isn't the "conformity," "consistency" or "proximity" of the object to the needs of subject also the utility of object for the needs of the subject?

56 *Categories of meta-ethics*

The second is the so-called "theory of meaning." Yuan Guiren contends: "Value is the positive or negative meaning of the object to the subject."[20] The meaning has two connotations: one is the meaning and denotation of language; the other is the effect and utility of the object on the needs of the subject. When meaning is used to define value it obviously is the latter connotation of meaning. Therefore, saying that value is the meaning of the object to the subject is no different from saying that value is the utility of the object on the needs of the subject. Thence Yuan Guiren also admits that "value relation is a kind of meaning relationship or utility relationship which is equivalent. Value is the meaning of the object to the subject, which is the effect of the utility of the object on the subject."[21]

The third is the "theory of property." Li Jianfeng writes: "Value refers to the functions and properties of the object that can meets the needs of the subject."[22] Without the needs of the subject, the functions and properties of the object that can meets the needs of the subject would have no meaning of value; the functions and properties of the object rather only have a value relative to the needs of the subject. However, for the needs of the subject, aren't the functions and properties of the object the properties of the object that have utilities to the needs of the subject? Are they not then the certain utilities of the object to the needs of the subject?

In short, just as Lai Jinliang states:

> From the perspective of domestic studies on the theory of value, although scholars have slightly different definitions of the category of 'value,' for example, some define value as the satisfaction or affirmation of the object for the needs of the subject, and some define value as the conformity, proximity, or consistency of the object to the needs of the subject, etc., the utilitarian orientation of these definitions is quite obvious, or, they can all be categorized as the definitions of the theory of utility about 'value'.[23]

1.1.3 Value: Can only be defined by "object" and "subject"

Interestingly, the definition of "utility theory of value" has been challenged by scholars such as Lai Jinliang from the perspective of methodology: a central concern is what is the basis for defining value by the model of the relationship between subject and object?[24] Indeed, why do we have to say that "value is the utility of the object to the needs of the subject"? Why must we define the value with the model of the subject–object relationship which still needs to be explained? Isn't it clearer to say that "value is the utility of a thing to the needs of another thing?" Or isn't it easier to equate *value* with *utility* like David Gautier does?[25] Shu Hong also opposes the use of the subject–object relationship model to define value: "According to this idea, it seems that value can be defined as the significance and effect of something on the existence and development of something connected to it."[26] However, value definitions such as

The starting concept of ethics 57

these which evade the concept of subject and object are untenable: Value only can be defined by the model of the relationship between subject and object.

It turns out that anything, whether living or non-living, has needs, because the so-called needs, as is well known, are the dependency of things on something else for their existence and development. A living thing needs sunlight means that its existence and development depend on sunlight. The existence and development of good things have certain dependence on bad things, therefore the existence and development of good things needs bad things: there is a need to fight against and overcome bad things. The existence of stones depends on the balance between internal and external environment, so the existence of stones needs the balance between internal and external environment. It can be seen that "need" is the universal property shared by all things, both organic and inorganic.

Then, can it be said that what guarantees the existence and development of a thing and thus meets its "needs" is good or has positive value? Reversely, does it mean that what prevents, threatens or contributes to the demise of the existence and development of a thing and which is therefore contrary to its "needs," is bad or has negative value? The answer is no. Although everything has "needs," to say that "things that *satisfy* the needs of other things are good or have positive value" obviously should be based on the premise that the thing it satisfies has some capacity to distinguish between goodness and badness, advantage and disadvantage, and that it is able to make good use of advantage and avoid disadvantage. Only things that at least have the capacity to distinguish between goodness and badness, can be said good or bad; for things that do not at least have the capacity to distinguish between goodness and badness, there is no issue of good or bad.

Clearly, for a block of iron, nothing is good or bad, valuable nor valueless. We can't even say that melting down a block of iron such that the block no longer exists in this state is a bad thing for the iron. Why is it that the existence or non-existence of a *block* of iron in-itself not positive value or negative value? Obviously, in contrast to humans or organisms, it has no identity and capacity in and of itself to evaluate or select. For human beings, everything (whether animate or inanimate), more or less, is good or bad, in other words, has value. Isn't it that things have value because human beings are able evaluate: that we distinguish between goodness and badness, and make complex selections regarding whether a thing is to our advantage or disadvantage?

Obviously, it is inaccurate to say that "value is the utility of a thing to the needs of another" because not all the utility of one thing to the needs of another have value; only the utility of one thing to the needs of another that has the capacity to evaluate goodness and badness, advantage and disadvantage, and to make a selection based on the best option, is value. Because the subject is the agent that has the capacity to evaluate and make a selection it necessarily follows that only the utility of one thing to the needs of the subject can be called value. The thing that has utility to the needs of the subject, which *exists* relative to the needs of the subject, is the so-called object.

58 *Categories of meta-ethics*

Therefore, value can only be defined as the utility of the object to the needs of the subject, and can only be defined by the subject–object model. This is also echoed by Makiguchi, as he says: "As far as the concept of value is concerned, it can only be explained by the relationship between subject and object."[27]

1.2 The concept of value: The theory of marginal utility and labor theory of value

As we have covered, value is the utility of the object to the subject's needs (and its various transformational forms in consciousness such as desire and purpose), which, in the final analysis, is the utility of the object to the needs, desires and purposes of the subject, in short, it is the utility of the object to the needs of subject. This definition of value is common sense, and is generally accepted in the contemporary academic community. However, whether the definition of value in the "utility theory of value" is tenable still faces challenges. This is understandable because in the science of economics the question as to whether the value of a commodity is the utility of a commodity, just as Wicksell says, "has been debated for more than a century."[28] Ricardo even contends that "in [economic] science, no other word than 'value' has caused so much controversy."[29] If the value of a commodity is indeed not the utility of a commodity to human needs, but the general human labor congealed in a commodity, as stated in the labor theory of value, then the proposition that "value is utility" is untenable and the utility theory of value is a falsehood. This is why, even though value defined by its utility has actually been accepted, many scholars still try to avoid using "utility" to define value. Yet the truth or falsehood of the definition of value in utility theory is a crucial question. Let's revisit it: is the value of a commodity the utility of a commodity?

1.2.1 Value of a commodity: The utility of commodity to human needs

There are "two kinds of concepts of value" that are quite popular in academic circles in China. One is the concept of value from a philosophy perspective, which regards value, more or less as I render it, as the utility of the object to the needs of subject; the other is the concept of value from an economics perspective, which holds that the value of a commodity is not the utility of a commodity to human needs, but the general human labor congealed in the commodity. It is obvious that the theory of the two concepts of value cannot be tenable, such is the law of logic that two contradictory judgments cannot be the same truth, as demonstrated by the following assertions: "all values are the utility of the object to the needs of the subject" and "the value of the commodity is not the utility of the commodity to human needs." It seems that one must be true and the other false. Clearly, we hold the former to be true, but why do we say the latter is false? If the value of a commodity is not the general

The starting concept of ethics 59

human labor congealed in the commodity, but the utility of a commodity to human needs, then what exactly do we mean by this?

The economist Yan Zhijie says:

> The concept of value in economics ought to be a general concept of value, that is, the concretion of the relationship between subject and object. That is to say, the value of a commodity refers to the relationship between wealth and commodity and human needs. The value and the size of value depend on whether they can satisfy the needs as well as the degree of satisfaction.[30]

He is quite right. So-called value, as mentioned earlier, is the utility of the object to the needs of the subject, which obviously implies that the value of commodity is the utility that the commodity possesses to satisfy human needs: the utility of satisfying the needs of the owner's direct usage is called the use value of a commodity, while the utility of satisfying the needs of the owner in exchange with other commodities is called the exchange value of a commodity, which is the definition and classification of the so-called value of a commodity in the utility theory of value that has existed since the time of Aristotle—excluding the historical stages represented by Smith, Ricardo, and Marx.

Aristotle not only discovered that the value of a commodity is the utility of a commodity, but also divided the value of a commodity into use value and exchange value, holding that both are the utility and use of commodity on human needs. But he regarded the use value as the "appropriate use" and exchange value as "inappropriate or exchangeable use" of a commodity:

> Everything we have has two uses and both belong to the object itself but in a different way. One is the appropriate use and the other is inappropriate or secondary use. For example, shoes can be worn or exchanged, and both are the uses of the shoes.[31]

But the clearest definition of the value of a commodity in utility theory is that by the British mercantilist Nicholas Barbon: "The values of all commodities come from the use of the commodities; what is not useful has no value, as an English idiom says, they are worthless. The use of the commodity is to satisfy human needs."[32]

The theory of marginal utility inherits the value theory of utility of commodity, which has been around since Aristotle, and further discovers that the use value of a commodity is the marginal utility of a commodity to people's needs of consumption. The so-called marginal utility of a commodity is the utility of the last added unit of commodity, as Samuelson and Nordhaus said: "The word 'marginal' is used throughout economics to mean extra or additional. For example, 'marginal cost' means the additional cost of producing an extra unit of output."[33] "We use the term 'marginal utility' to mean

60 *Categories of meta-ethics*

'the utility added by adding the last unit of items'."[34] Therefore, the use value of a commodity is the marginal utility of a commodity to human consumption needs, which means that the use value of each commodity is the utility of the unit of a commodity that is last added.

It turns out that the use value of a commodity is the marginal utility of a commodity to satisfy human consumption needs or desires, that is, the use value of commodities is the utility of commodities to human consumption needs or desires that have not yet been satisfied, not to the consumption needs or desires that are already satisfied. This is because once the needs or desires are satisfied, they are no longer needs or desires. The use value of a commodity is the utility of a commodity to a subject's needs that have not yet been satisfied, instead of to the needs that have already been satisfied, it implies that the use value of a commodity is the utility of a commodity to human surplus needs, which, in the final analysis, is the satisfaction of human surplus needs.

Therefore, the use value of each unit commodity is also the satisfaction of the surplus needs after "deducting the needs already satisfied by other commodities," hence it is the utility of "surplus needs" after deducting the needs already satisfied by other commodities, thus is also the utility of the satisfaction of the last added *unit commodity* to human needs, which is also the marginal utility of the unit commodity: The marginal utility is the utility of the last added unit commodity. The use value of the unit commodity then is the marginal utility of the unit commodity, and the total use value of the commodity is the sum of the marginal utility of each unit commodity. That is why Samuelson and Nordhaus said that "The total utility of consuming a certain quantity of commodity is equal to the sum of the marginal utilities of each commodity that is consumed."[35]

For example, suppose there are ten thermos bottles. The use value of each is the utility to people's unsatisfied needs, and is the utility to the people's surplus needs. In the final analysis, it is also the utility of the surplus needs subtracting the needs which the other nine thermos bottles have satisfied. It is then utility of the last thermos bottle (i.e. the tenth bottle) that is the marginal utility of each thermos bottle. The sum of the marginal utilities of each of the ten thermoses constitutes the total use value of them.

Then, what is the exchange value of a commodity? The reason that commodities can be exchanged, and thus have exchange value, just as Ricardo says, is only because a commodity has use value; anything that has no use value does not possesses exchange value:

> If a commodity is in no way useful,—in other words, if it could in no way contribute to our gratification,—it would be destitute of exchangeable value, however scarce it might be, or whatever quantity of labour might be necessary to procure it.[36]

Therefore, the so-called "exchange value" of a commodity is nothing more than the utility of the *use value* of the commodity to "exchange needs," and

The starting concept of ethics 61

the use value of commodity is the cause, substance, and material bearer of "exchange value."

In this way, the use value of a commodity is the marginal utility of the commodity, which implies that the exchange value of a commodity is the utility of the marginal utility of the commodity in exchange for another commodity. Therefore, the amount of marginal utility of a commodity determines the magnitude of exchange value it has: The amount of exchange value of a commodity is equal to its amount of marginal utility. This formula, as Boehm-Bawerk says, is the law that determines the amount of the exchange value of commodity: "The law which governs amount of value, then, may be put in the following very simple formula: The value of a good is determined by the amount of its Marginal Utility."[37]

Therefore, the value of a commodity—the use value and exchange value—certainly decreases with the increases in the amount of commodities. The more commodities, the more people's needs and desires are satisfied, the less people's unsatisfied needs and desires, the less important people's unsatisfied needs and desires. In this way, the needs and desires that the last unit increment can satisfy are the least and the least important, the marginal utility of a commodity is the least, and the use value and the exchange value of the unit commodity are also the least. It is termed the law of diminishing marginal utility: "The law of diminishing marginal utility states that as the amount of a good consumed increases, the marginal utility of that good tends to decrease."[38]

1.2.2 The solution of the "paradox of value": Use Value is the marginal utility of commodity

"Value" or the "value of a commodity" in economics generally often refers to the "exchange value of a commodity" or "exchange value," as Mill pointed out: "The word 'value,' when used in the political economy with no additional words, usually means exchange value."[39] The view that value of a commodity or exchange value is not a commodity utility mainly stems from what came to be called the "paradox of value," the fact that water has great utility but typically little exchange value, contrary to diamonds which have little utility but great exchange value. This has puzzled economists such as Adam Smith:

> The things which have the greatest value in use have frequently little or no value in exchange; and, on the contrary, those which have the greatest value in exchange have frequently little or no value in use. Nothing is more useful than water: but it will purchase scarce anything; scarce anything can be had in exchange for it. A diamond, on the contrary, has scarce any value in use; but a very great quantity of other commodity may frequently be had in exchange for it.[40]

This means that the definition of value in the utility theory of value must itself contain a paradox. This is because, according to the definition of value

62   Categories of meta-ethics

in the utility theory of value, commodity value or exchange value is the utility of the commodity that satisfies human needs. In this sense, in saying that "the utility of water is great, but its exchange value is small," is no different from saying that "the exchange value of water is great, but the exchange value is small," that is, that "the exchange value of water is both great and small," which is obviously a paradox. This is the so-called "paradox of value," namely the "paradox of the definition of value," in the final analysis, is also the "paradox of the definition of value in the utility theory." The definition of value in the utility theory of value contains a paradox which implies that the definition itself is a fallacy. This is the reason why economists such as Smith, Ricardo, and Marx, when faced with the "paradox of value"—a two thousand year old problem—had rejected the idea that commodity value or exchange value is the utility of commodity, stating instead that commodity value or exchange value is the labor congealed in commodities: "All commodities as value are just crystallized human labor."[41]

After perplexing thinkers for more than two thousand years, the problem of the "paradox of value" was scientifically solved by the theory of marginal utility. The theory of marginal utility discovered that the use value of a commodity is the marginal utility of the commodity, and that it is the utility of the last unit increment of the commodity; the marginal utility of the commodity decreases with the increases in the amount of the commodity, and thus the use value of the commodity decreases. In this way, the exchange value of diamonds is large, not because of its small utility, but only because of its scarceness, which make its marginal utility or use value large. The exchange value of water is small, not because of its great utility, but because of its large quantity, which make its marginal utility or use value small. In a nutshell, marginal utility discovered that the exchange value of water or diamonds is proportional to the use value, and thus makes the paradox of value untenable.

Let's explain it in popular language. The theory of marginal utility discovers that water has great utility, which is only in terms of the utility of the sum of water (or the utility of all water or the utility of the general water or the utility of the abstract water). Specifically and practically speaking, each unit of water has its different utility: the more water a person has, the less utility each unit of water has for him; after a certain amount its utility will be equal to zero, and may even become negative: Value must be zero value twice throughout its development, first, where one has nothing, and, second, where one has everything.[42] Therefore, the lack of exchange value of water is not due to the great utility of the sum of all water, but, because when it exceeds a certain amount, its unit utility is zero. On the contrary, the exchange value of a diamond is great not because of the small utility of its sum, but because of its extreme rarity, thence the great utility of each unit.

Therefore, in fact, there is no "paradox of value" and "paradox of the definition of value in the utility theory of value," and no so-called "fact" that contradicts the definition of commodity value in the utility theory of value—the value of a commodity is the utility of the commodity to human needs.

The starting concept of ethics   63

In the final analysis, the statement that "water is of great utility but has no exchange value, while a useless diamond has great exchange value" is not a fact but an illusion: it does not falsify but instead only proves the validity of the definition of value in the utility theory of value. Harking back to this illusion shows that the use value and exchange value of all commodities such as water and diamond are a certain utility of the commodity. In sum, the use value is the marginal utility of the commodity to consumption needs; and the exchange value is the utility of use value—namely the marginal utility—to "exchange needs."

1.2.3 The misunderstanding of "paradox of value": Commodity value is the congealed human labor in commodity

The so-called labor theory of value, as it is known, is that labor is the only source and substance for creating and determining commodity value or exchange value. Its main representatives are Smith, Ricardo, and Marx.[43] However, the labor theory of value does not deny—and no economists deny—that labor and land are two sources and the substance of creating use value, they only deny that they are the two sources and the substance of creating value and exchange value. Then, why does the labor theory of value hold that labor and land are only two sources and the substance of use value, but not that of exchange value or value?

The works of Smith, Ricardo, and Marx show that the theoretical premise or epistemological root of labor theory of value can be summed up as a "paradox of value" such that the degree of exchange value is often opposite to that of use value or completely unrelated.[44] Is it possible that, as Smith, Ricardo, and Marx contended, the labor theory of value can be deduced from the "paradox of value"? The answer is yes.

It is an indisputable fact and is indeed common sense that labor and land are two sources and the substance of creating use value. However, the "paradox of value"—namely, that the degree of exchange value is often opposite to that of use value or completely unrelated—means that the source and the substance of use value (labor and land) cannot be the source and substance of exchange value; otherwise, how could the magnitude of exchange value be opposite to or completely unrelated to use value? What is the source and substance of exchange value, one might ask? Obviously, it can only be labor. Therefore, Meek had summed up the premise of the labor theory of value (which denies that land is the source of creating exchange value and believes that labor is the sole source of creating exchange value) as the fundamental difference between "value (exchange value)" and "wealth (use value)," which also is a "paradox of value":

> It was not until the vital distinction between wealth and value had been properly established that it was possible to clarify the problem of the role of land. It had, of course, been appreciated from a fairly early date that

64 *Categories of meta-ethics*

the use value of a commodity was something different from its exchange value: the famous water-and-diamonds illustration had been used by several writers before Smith, and there had been economists before Hutcheson who had pointed out that the exchange values of commodities often bore little relation to their utility. But it was some time before the distinction which Ricardo always emphasized between wealth (a sum of use values to the creation of which both land and labour contributed) and value (which was determined by labour alone) was accurately formulated, although several early economists had employed the distinction without being fully aware of what they were doing. Once land had been got rid of in this way as a determinant of value, it remained only to make it clear that labour contributed value to commodities, not per medium of the reward paid to it but per medium of the expenditure of the labour itself.[45]

It is well-stated indeed. If "labor is the sole source of creation of exchange value," it is then understandable why the exchange value and use value—that labor and land are two sources and the substance of the creation of use value—are often opposite.[46] Therefore, the controversies on whether labor is the sole source of the creation of value or exchange value (namely, whether the labor theory of value is tenable) are centered on whether the so-called "paradox of value" is tenable. The mistaken belief that the "paradox of value" is tenable is the theoretical premise or epistemological source of the labor theory of value. Where exchange value is directly proportional to use value, use value is the source and entity of exchange value, labor, and land are undoubtedly the two sources of creating value or exchange value, thus the labor theory of value is untenable.

The labor theory of value is untenable not only because its theoretical premise (the "paradox of value") is false but also because the existence of human labor congealed in a commodity does not depend on human needs, or even on human beings. The human labor congealed in a piece of gold jewelry would still exist even if human beings ceased to exist. We can see that human labor congealed in a commodity therefore is the intrinsic property of the commodity which is independent of human needs.

Since, according to the labor theory of value, the commodity value is the human labor congealed in the commodity, doesn't this also mean that commodity value is the intrinsic property of commodity? Marx indeed believed that value is the intrinsic property of a commodity and stood for the realism of commodity value, so he repeatedly stated:

> The labor expended in the production of a used commodity is manifested in the inherent nature of this thing, namely its value,[47]

and

> If we say that all commodities are only a value crystallized by human labor, then our analysis is to transform a commodity into value abstraction, but

The starting concept of ethics   65

they still have only one form, that is, the natural form of useful things. But, when the value of a commodity is related to that of another commodity, the situation is completely different; from this point onward, the nature of its value reveals itself as an intrinsic property that determines its relationship with another commodity.[48]

However, isn't it absurd to think that commodity value is the intrinsic property of commodity? Undoubtedly, a value cannot be the intrinsic property of the object; it can only be the relational property of the object, just as Yan Zhijie states, "Regardless of the original meaning of value or of people's common sense conceptions of it, the word value never implies the intrinsic property of commodity."[49] Value is a category of relations, not a category of substance.[50]

Furthermore, the absurdity of the definition that "value is the labor congealed in a commodity" also lies in that: If the value of a commodity is the labor congealed in it, things without congealed labor such as land and so on, would then have no commodity value or exchange value. Marx actually admits that this is indeed the case: "If a use value can be created without labor, it has no exchange value."[51] "Land is not a product of labor and therefore has no value."[52] "A waterfall, just like land and all natural forces, has no value, because there is no objectified labor in it."[53]

This kind of assertion is not only untenable but also absurd, because anything, as long as it can be traded and exchanged for other things, certainly has an exchange value; otherwise, if a thing does not have exchange value, it certainly cannot be traded and exchanged, and cannot be exchanged for other things. Then, what are the conditions for having exchange value? It is obvious that one of them is its usefulness, namely the use value, since things without use value obviously cannot be traded. Another condition is its scarcity, for if something with use value is not scarce but in limitless abundance, such as water, sunlight and air, it obviously cannot be traded and thus has no exchange value. Anything, whether it contains or congeals labor, as long as it has use value and is scarce, obviously can be exchanged or traded thus certainly has exchange value: use value and scarcity are the sufficient and necessary conditions for anything to have exchange value.

Land, however, is fundamentally different from air and water. Air and water does not have exchange value, not because they don't include labor, but because they are not scarce so that they cannot be traded and exchanged. On the contrary, land, whether it has been cultivated and thus contains the congealed labor in it or has not been cultivated and is without congealed labor, obviously has both use value and the trait of scarcity, and thus can be traded and exchanged. The use value and scarcity of land together have exchange value (and value). This is an indisputable fact. Only an idiot would deny it. Given that humans have long depended on the trade and exchange of land for cultivation, how could it possibly not have exchange value? How can there be things traded or exchanged without exchange value! Land can be traded and exchanged, which means that it has exchange value. Therefore, isn't it

66 *Categories of meta-ethics*

self-contradictory to assert that a thing that can be traded and exchanged has no exchange value?

In conclusion, the mistaken consideration of the "paradox of value" led Smith, Ricardo, and Marx to deny the truth of the utility theory of value, which holds that "a commodity's value is the utility of the commodity," thus falling into the fallacy of the labor theory of value, which holds that "labor is the only source of the creation of value" and that "the value of commodities is the congealed labor in commodities." The theory of marginal utility, through its great discovery that "use value is the marginal utility of commodity," scientifically proves that "the use value is proportional to the exchange value," and hence proves that the "paradox of value" is untenable. It consequently ends the domination of the labor theory of value, and brings us back to the utility theory of value inherited from Aristotle: that commodity value is the utility of a commodity for satisfying human needs and desires.

It is only that the use value of commodities is the marginal utility of the factual property of commodity to consumption needs, while the exchange value of commodity is the utility of the use value of commodity on exchange needs. In the final analysis, it is the utility of the marginal utility of a commodity to *exchange needs*: The use value of commodity—namely the marginal utility of commodity—is the source and substance of the exchange value of commodity. Therefore, the amount of the exchange value is the same as that of the use value, both depending on the amount of the marginal utility. Put simply, the amount of the exchange value of the commodity is equal to the amount of marginal utility. As Schumpeter says: "The theory of marginal utility proved what Adam Smith, Ricardo, and Marx thought impossible to prove: explaining the exchange value with the use value."[54]

The replacement of the theory of marginal utility with the labor theory of value was a revolution in the field of economics. Schumpeter even makes the following comparison: "The replacement of 'classical economic theory' with the theory of marginal utility is similar to the replacement of the geocentric theory with the heliocentric theory."[55] Mark Skousen, commenting on the significance of the revolution of theory of marginal utility, also states: "Its discovery resolved the paradox of value that had frustrated the classical economists from Adam Smith to John Stuart Mill. It was also the undoing of Marxian economics."[56]

1.3 Reaction of value: The concept of evaluation

1.3.1 Reflection and reaction: Truth and falsehood and right and wrong

What is evaluation? Perhaps the most appropriate and widely accepted definition so far is that evaluation is the consciousness or the reflection of value. However, when we examine it carefully, this definition is not exact: It misinterprets "reaction" as "reflection," because truly speaking, evaluation is

The starting concept of ethics   67

a reaction to value, not merely a reflection of value. Then, what is the actual difference between reflection and reaction?

The so-called reaction, as it is known, is the product of the interaction of things. There is no doubt that everything interacts with other things, and thus constantly changes. The change of a thing affected by another is the answer to the function and property of the other thing and this kind of change, answer, or expression is called reaction relative to the function and property of other things: reaction is the change of a thing affected by another thing, which is the answer or expression of the function and property of the other thing. For example, there are four kinds of reaction which reveal the property and the expression of the things interacting under certain effects or forces: these are mechanical, physical, chemical, and biological reactions. Let's take the example of the phenomenon of dripping water wearing away a rock. Water is soft but over time its constancy wins out over the hardness of the rock. The change of the rock is a *mechanical* reaction: it is the expression of the properties or effects of water. Another example is hydrothermal evaporation. The change of water under the effect of heat is a *physical* reaction: it is the expression of the properties or effects of heat. Then there is iron rust. The change to iron under the effect of oxygen is a *chemical* reaction: it is the expression of the properties or effects of oxygen. A final example is the petiole of the mimosa, which droops when the plant vibrates. The change that occurs in the mimosa under the vibration is a *biological* reaction: it is the expression of the properties or effects of the vibration. It is obvious that reaction is a property belonging to everything.

But reflection is not the property that all things have—as it is known, it is a special kind of physical phenomenon, i.e. what is in the mirror is the reflection of what is outside the mirror. Epistemology borrows from the physical phenomenon of reflection to define cognition: cognition is the reflection of the outside world held in the mind. This reflection is a special kind of reaction to externality, belonging to the category of reaction. It is the reaction and expression of the mind to the properties or effects of the external world on sensory organs, just as the image held in the mirror is the reflection and expression of external things that appear before it, and changes accordingly. The mind, though, to move beyond the mirror, responds to both the outside world and to the images held within the mind itself independent of externality. As far as the physical world is concerned, reflection is only the reaction of certain special materials (mirrors, water, eyes, television, photography, etc.), and, in terms of the phenomenal world, reflection is only a reaction of a kind of more specific material, namely the mind and its response to the external world and its internal world, which is the highest form of reaction.

However, reflection and reaction are fundamentally different in nature: reflection has traits of being true or false, while reaction has no traits of being true or false, it only has traits of right or wrong. The so-called "truth or falsehood" of something depends on its consistency, that is, the consistency of the reflection with its object: if the reflection is consistent with the

68 *Categories of meta-ethics*

object, it is true; if the reflection is not consistent with the object, it is false. The so-called "right or wrong" is the utility, that is, the utility of the object to the needs of the subject, referring to whether the object is conducive to satisfying the needs, desires and purposes of the subject: if the utility of the object is conducive to satisfying the needs, desires, and purpose of the subject it is called "right," "good," "ought," and "correct"; if the utility of the object is an impediment to satisfying the needs, desires and purpose of the subject it is called "wrong," "bad," "ought not," and "incorrect." The concepts of right or wrong, good or bad, ought or ought not, correct or incorrect are generally the same. Then, why does reflection have the trait of being true and false but reaction has only the trait of being right and wrong?

This is because the basic nature of reflection, as the theorists of reflection point out, is the reproduction and recurrence of the object. Conforth says: "The reaction process itself consists of such a correlation between two particular material processes, in which the characteristics of the first process are reproduced as the corresponding characteristics of the second process."[57] Ukraintseff also says:

> Reflection is a special aspect and product of the interaction of the objects (or the subject and the object); this product is the reproduction that is more or less consistent with the characteristics of the process of the reflected external object in the variation of the process of the reflected object (or subject).[58]

The Chinese scholar Xia Zhentao writes: "The simplest and most universal nature of the reflection is the reproduction and recurrence of the corresponding characteristics of the prototype."[59] Since reflection is the reproduction and recurrence of the object, there exists the question of whether it conforms to the object: it is true if it conforms to the object, and it is false if it does not. If the reflection is the reflection of the subject on the object, then this reflection is not only true or false, but also right or wrong: true reflection is conducive to satisfying the needs of the subject, and is thus right, good, ought, and correct, while false reflection is detrimental to satisfying the needs of the subject, and is thus wrong, bad, ought not, and incorrect.

On the contrary, although reaction is the same as reflection in the sense that it is also an expression of the effect and the property of the object, and the certain form of expression of the effect and property of the object, it is not the reproduction or recurrence of the effect and property of the object, so it has no issue of whether it conforms to the object and of being true or false. The reaction only has the problem of adapting to the object, hence the problem of conforming to the needs of the subject; therefore, reaction has only the issue of being right or wrong: if adapting to the object to satisfy the needs of the subject then it is correct, good, and ought; if not adapting to the object to satisfy the needs of the subject then it is wrong, bad, ought-not, and incorrect. For example:

The starting concept of ethics 69

Darwin once came across a tiger in the wild. He knew that if he turned his back to the tiger and ran, the tiger would catch up with him and eat him. So, the only way to possibly save his life was to keep facing the tiger and slowly walk backwards. Darwin's perception of the tiger reflected the nature of the tiger in his mind, which is a reproduction and recurrence of the nature of tigers, thus this was a question of whether his reaction conformed with the nature of the tiger and a question of whether his reaction was true or false: it was true because it conformed to the real nature of tigers in the wild. And it was also right, as it ought to be, and correct because it enabled Darwin to avoid being eaten by the tiger, which satisfied his need for survival. Darwin's slow walk backwards facing the tiger was his reaction to the nature of tigers, which was obviously a reaction and expression to the nature of tigers, but not the reproduction or recurrence of the nature of tigers, so his reaction neither had the problem of being true or false, nor the so-called truth, but only the so-called right or wrong and the so-called utility: It was right, as it ought to be, and correct because it enabled Darwin to avoid being eaten by the tiger, which satisfied his need for survival.

1.3.2 Definition of evaluation: Reaction of value

The analysis of reflection and reaction shows that the mainstream view that "consciousness or psychology is the reflection of the mind" is untenable, for "psychology or consciousness," as is well known, is divided into "cognition" (knowledge), "emotion" (feeling, sentiment) and "volition" (will). Among them, only knowledge and cognition are the mind's reflection of external things, while feelings and will are not reflections of the mind of things but only the reaction of the mind to things. Knowledge and cognition are reflection in the mind of external things in the sense that they are the reproduction and recurrence of objects. Consequently, there is the question of whether the objects reflected in the mind conform to the objects themselves, thus have the issue of being true or false: when knowledge and cognition conform to the objects, they are a true reflection; when they do not conform to the objects, they are a false reflection.

As only a reaction to and an expression of an object or objects: emotion is the inner experience of the subject as to whether its needs are satisfied by the object or objects, and volition is the psychological process from the determination to the execution of the subject's behavior. Therefore, although emotion and volition belong to the categories of psychology and consciousness, like actions, they are not the reflection of objective objects but the reaction to objective objects. More precisely, they are not the transcription, reproduction, disclosure, and explanation of objective objects, but the requirements, design, planning, and arrangement of objective objects; they are not intended to provide knowledge about objective objects, but solutions for how to use and transform objective objects; they are not seeking to be consistent with objective objects, but to satisfy the needs of the subject. Therefore, emotion

70   *Categories of meta-ethics*

and volition do not have the issue of whether they are consistent with the object, hence do not have the issue of being true or false. Instead, the issue is only whether the needs of the subject are satisfied, which is a matter of utility, namely right or wrong: if something is conducive to satisfying the needs of the subject it is right, good, correct, and ought to be, and if something is an impediment to the needs of the subject it is wrong, bad, incorrect, and ought not to be.

For example, on the one hand, "Kong Ming (a great strategist in ancient China) thought that Ma Su had the talent of a general." This was his initial impression of Ma Su, which belonged to the category of cognition, but the "reflection" (in Kong Ming's mind) of Ma Su as a general, in terms of the reproduction and recurrence of Ma Su' ability, was an issue of whether the reflection conformed to Ma Su's actual ability, hence was a question of being true or false. It turned out that the reflection was false because it was not consistent with Ma Su's ability, such that under Ma Su's command the city of Jieting fell to the enemy which was historically a significant loss for the State of Shu. On the other hand, "Kong Ming was fond of Ma Su," so this was a sentiment that belonged to the category of emotion, and "Kong Ming intended to make good use of Ma Su," so this was a resolve that belonged to the category of volition. Both in a sense were a "reaction" (in Kong Ming's mind) to the prospect of Ma Su in the role of general. As his emotion and volition were not a reproduction and recurrence of Ma Su's ability, these had no issue of being true or false, they were only a question of being right or wrong. Clearly, the historic defeat meant that his emotional evaluation concerning Ma Su's military appointment to secure the State of Shu was wrong, for it ultimately did not conform to the needs, desires, and purposes of the State or to that of Kong Ming himself.

Defining evaluation as a reflection of value mistakes the part for the whole. This is because evaluation is not only cognitive evaluation: it at least includes evaluations of emotion and volition. Cognitive evaluation is the same concept as value judgment since both are the knowledge and cognition of value belonging to the category of cognition, and hence are reflections of value. But emotional evaluation is the psychological experience of value belonging to the category of emotion, and volitional evaluation is a psychological process of the behavioral choice of value and the process go through from the determination to the execution, which belongs to the category of volition. Therefore, emotional evaluation and volitional evaluation, like emotion and volition or feelings and will, do not belong to the category of reflection but to the category of reaction: they are not reflections of value but reactions to value.

For example, when John sees peony flowers "he thinks that peony is beautiful," "he feels that peony is lovely," and "he decides to buy two peony flowers." The first of the above evaluations, "he thinks that peony is beautiful," is a cognitive evaluation, which reflects the value of peony flowers. As a reproduction and recurrence of the value of the peony flower, it belongs to the category of cognition, and is thus true or false. Indeed, it is true because it is

The starting concept of ethics 71

consistent with the value of the peony flower, namely its beauty. On the contrary, the second evaluation above, "he feels that peony is lovely," is an emotional evaluation, which is the psychological experience of the value of peony, belonging to the category of emotion, and the third evaluation, "he decides to buy two peony flowers," is a volitional evaluation, which is the psychological process of the behavioral choice of value, which in this instance is the decision to purchase two peony flowers, belonging to the category of volition: both evaluations are merely reactions to, not reproductions and recurrences of, the value of peony flowers, and since neither reflects the value of peony flowers, there is no issue of being true or false. Both reactions are only a question of being right or wrong. Indeed, they are right because they conform to the needs, desires, and purposes of the subject (John).

In sum, it can be seen that cognitive evaluation is the reflection of value, and that emotional evaluation and volitional evaluation are the reactions to value. Therefore, defining evaluation as the reflection of value makes the mistake of taking the part for the whole: evaluation is the reaction to value, not merely the reflection of value. However, on closer examination, this definition of evaluation still has its drawbacks: ultimately, for evaluation, who or what does the reaction to value?

Of course, this question is not difficult to answer now because we have already understood that, on the one hand, value is the utility of the object to the needs, desires and purposes of the subject. In short, value is the utility of the object to the subject; on the other hand, reaction is the change of a thing under the effect of other things. The thing that reacts to value is nothing else but the so-called subject. Therefore, where value is the utility of the object to the subject, evaluation is the subject's reaction to value: it is the subject's response or answer to the object. Therefore, Makiguchi writes: "When the subject is aware of the influence of the object to a certain extent it moves accordingly. This activity is called evaluation."[60] To be precise, evaluation is the reaction of the subject to value, and is the reaction of the subject to the value of the object. In short, evaluation is the reaction to value, and the expression and manifestation of value.

1.3.3 Types of evaluation: Cognitive, emotional, volitional, and behavioral evaluations

Evaluation is the subject's reaction to the value of the object, which is undoubtedly only the definition of evaluation, so it is only the definition of the extension of evaluation. To truly grasp the concept of evaluation, it is obviously necessary to divide the things covered by this boundary: that is, the classification of evaluation. Roughly speaking, evaluation is divided into three categories: cognitive evaluation, emotional evaluation, and volitional evaluation. This is what the popular definition that "evaluation is the consciousness of value" implies, for consciousness itself is divided into three categories: cognition, emotion, and volition.

72   *Categories of meta-ethics*

However, this definition and classification of evaluation is wrong because it mistakes the part for the whole. People do not have only conscious reactions to value, they also have behavioral reactions to it. Both are expressions and manifestations of value, hence are evaluations of value. Therefore, there are not only conscious evaluations (including cognitive evaluations, emotional evaluations, and volitional evaluations, which are the consciousness of value, the conscious reaction to value, and the conscious expression of value), but also behavioral evaluations: the action caused by value, the behavioral reaction to value, and the behavioral expression and manifestation of value. For example:

When we see peony, we not only will have a variety of conscious reactions such as that "we think that peony is beautiful" (cognitive evaluation), "we feel that peony is lovely" (emotional evaluation), and "we decide to buy two peony flowers" (volitional evaluation), but will possibly have a behavioral reaction as well such as that, at this point, "we buy two peony flowers" (behavioral evaluation). If "we decide to buy two peony flowers" is the evaluation of the value of peony flowers, then "we buy two peony flowers" is the culmination of the evaluation of the value of peony flowers. The only difference in terms of these reactions to the value of peony is that "we decide to buy two peony flowers" is a volitional evaluation and expression, while "we buy two peony flowers" is a behavioral evaluation and expression. The nature of behavioral evaluation is obviously the same as both volitional evaluation and emotional evaluation. Not one of them has the question of being true or false. Who would say "we decide to buy two peony flowers" or "we buy two peony flowers" is true or false? Isn't it the case that the decision or the action itself is right or wrong?

Notes

1 Louis P. Pojman: *Ethical Theory: Classical and Contemporary Readings,* Wadsworth Publishing Company, U.S.A., 1995, p. 145.
2 Bryan Wilson: *Values Humanities,* Press International, Inc., Atlantic Highlands, 1988, p. 1.
3 Aristotle, in: *Philosophy of Ancient Greece and Rome.* SXD Joint Publishing House, 1957, p. 309.
4 K. Marx and F. Engels, *Complete Works of Marx and Engels*, Volume 2, People's Publishing House, 1956, p. 164.
5 Aristotle: *Complete Works of Aristotle.* Vol. 1. Renmin University of China Press, p. 4.
6 Li Deshun: *Theory of Value.* Renmin University Press, 1987, p. 12.
7 Li Lianke: *Philosophical Theory of Value.* Renmin University Press, 1991, p. 88.
8 Ralph Barton Perry: *General Theory of Value: Its Meaning and Basic Principles Construed in Terms of Interest*, Longmans, Green, New York, 1926, p. 122.
9 Ralph Barton Perry: *General Theory of Value: Its Meaning and Basic Principles Construed in Terms of Interest*, Longmans, Green, New York, 1926, p. 52.
10 Ralph Barton Perry: *General Theory of Value: Its Meaning and Basic Principles Construed in Terms of Interest*, Longmans, Green, New York, 1926, p. 40.

The starting concept of ethics 73

11 Ralph Barton Perry and others: *Value and Evaluation*. Renmin University Press, 1989, p. 45.

12 Ralph Barton Perry: *General Theory of Value: Its Meaning and Basic Principles Construed in Terms of Interest*, Longmans, Green, New York, 1926, p. 27.

13 Ralph Barton Perry and others: *Value and Evaluation*. Renmin University Press, 1989, p. 51.

14 Ralph Barton Perry: *General Theory of Value: Its Meaning and Basic Principles Construed in Terms of Interest,* Longmans, Green, New York, 1926, p. 81.

15 Tsunesaburo Makiguchi: *Philosophy of Value*, Seikyo Press, Tokyo, 1964, p. 75.

16 K. Marx and F. Engels, *Complete Works of Marx and Engels*. Volume 26, People's Publishing House, 1974, p. 326.

17 Edited by Wang Yuliang: *A New Theory of Value Philosophy in China and Japan*. Shanxi People's Education Publishing House, 1994, p. 47.

18 Li Lianke. *Theory of Philosophical Value*. Renmin University of China Press, 1991, p. 62.

19 Edited by Wang Yuliang: *Values and the Views on Values*. Shanxi Normal University Press, 1988, p. 31.

20 Yuan Guiren: "Value and Cognition," *Journal of Beijing Normal University*, 1995, No. 3.

21 Yuan Guiren: *Introduction to the Theory of Value.* Beijing Normal University Press, 1991, p. 49.

22 Wang Yuliang (ed.)*: Values and the Views on Values.* Shanxi Normal University Press, 1988, p. 163.

23 Wang Yuliang (ed.): *A New Theory of Value Philosophy in China and Japan.* Shanxi People's Education Publishing House, 1994, p.47.

24 Wang Yuliang (ed.): *A New Theory of Value Philosophy in China and Japan*. Shanxi People's Education Publishing House, 1994, p. 47.

25 Also see: Sheng Qinglai: *A New Theory of Utilitarianism*, Shanghai Jiaotong University Press, 1996, p. 137.

26 Wang Yuliang (ed.): *Values and the Views on Values*. Shanxi Normal University Press, 1988, p. 185.

27 Tsunesaburo Makiguchi: *Philosophy of Value*, Seikyo Press Tokyo, 1964, p. 20.

28 Knut Wicksell: *Lectures on National Economics*, Shanghai Translation Publishing House, 1983, p. 21.

29 David Ricardo: *Principles of Political Economy and Taxation*. Commercial Press, Beijing, 1972, p. 9.

30 Yan Zhijie. *Restudy of the Theory of Economic Value*, Peking University Press, 2005, p. 9.

31 Yan Zhijie: *A New Probe into the Labor Theory of Value*. Peking University Press, 2001, p. 98, also see Aristotle: *Complete Works of Aristotle*. Vol. 1, Renmin University of China Press, p. 4.

32 Nicholas Barbon: *A Discourse of Trade*. Commercial Press, Beijing, 1982, p. 55.

33 Paul A. Samuelson and William D. Nordhaus, *Microeconomics* (16th Edition), McGraw-Hill, Boston, 1998. p. 81.

34 Paul A. Samuelson: *Economics*, Volume 2, Commercial Press, 1986, p. 77.

35 Paul A. Samuelson and William D. Nordhaus, *Microeconomics* (16th Edition), McGraw-Hill, Boston, 1998, p. 81.

36 David Ricardo, *Principles of Political Economy and Taxation*, George Bell and Sons, London, 1908, p. 6.

74 *Categories of meta-ethics*

37 Eugen V. Böhm-Bawerk, *The Positive Theory of Capital*. New York: G. E. Stechert & Co., 1930, p. 149.

38 Paul A. Samuelson and William D. Nordhaus: *Microeconomics* (16th Edition), McGraw-Hill, Boston, 1998, p. 81.

39 J. S. Mill: *Principles of Political Economy*. Commercial Press, Beijing, 1997, p. 493.

40 Adam Smith: *The Wealth of Nations*, Books I–III, Penguin, Harmonsdworth, 1970, pp.131–132.

41 Karl Marx: *Capital*, Vol. 1, China Social Sciences Press, 1983, p. 27.

42 Friedrich Von Wieser: *Natural Value*. Kelley & Millman, New York, 1956, p. 31.

43 Adam Smith, *The Wealth of Nations*, Books I–III, Penguin, Harmonsdworth, p. 133.

44 Adam Smith, *The Wealth of Nations*, Books I–III, Penguin, Harmonsdworth, p. 140; David Ricardo, *Principles of Political Economy and Taxation,* George Bell and Sons, London, 1908, pp. 5–7, . Karl Marx: *Capital*, Vol. 1, China Social Sciences Press, 1983, pp. 15, 50, 51.

45 Ronald L Meek: *Studies in The Labor Theory of Value,* Second Edition 1973, Monthly Review Press New York, p. 42.

46 This is why Marx said labor is the only source of the creation of commodity value or exchange value, and the latter is the congealed human labor in the commodity. However, the substance of value and value are fundamentally different. Why did Marx say that labor is both value and the substance of value? It turns out that Marx subscribed to commodity realism, believing that the value of a commodity is the intrinsic property of the commodity and is therefore its substance. In this view, value and the substance of value are not different. It is just that the fluid and living labor is the source and substance of value creation, while the congealed labor in the commodity is the value of the commodity (1983).

47 Karl Marx: *Capital*, Vol. 1, China Social Sciences Press, 1983, p. 39.

48 Karl Marx: *Capital*, Vol. 1, China Social Sciences Press, 1983, p. 39.

49 Yan Zhijie: *Marginalism in Economics*, Peking University Press, 1987, p. 49.

50 Yan Zhijie: *Research of the Theory of Value of Economics*. Peking University Press, 1987, p. 9.

51 Karl Marx: *Capital*, Vol. 3, People's Publishing House, 2004, p. 728.

52 Karl Marx: *Capital*, Vol. 3, People's Publishing House, 2004, p. 702.

53 Karl Marx: *Capital*, Vol. 3, People's Publishing House, 2004, p. 729.

54 Joseph A. Schumpeter, *History of Economic Analysis*, George Allen & Unwin Ltd, London, 1955, p. 960.

55 Joseph A. Schumpeter: *History of Economic Analysis*, vol. 3, Commercial Press, Beijing, 1991, p. 251.

56 Mark Skousen, *The Making of Modern Economics: The Lives and Ideas of the Great Thinkers.* Changchun Press, 2009, p. 169.

57 Украинцев,БС Ukraintseff: *Reflections in Non-Biological Circles*, Renmin University of China Press, 1988, p. 6.

58 Украинцев,БС Ukraintseff: *Reflections in Non-Biological Circles*, Renmin University of China Press, 1988, p. 80.

59 Xia Zhentao (ed.): *The Theory of Emergence of Cognition*, The People's Publishing House, 1991, p. 63.

60 Tsunesaburo Makiguchi: *Philosophy of Value*, Renmin University of China Press, 1989, p. 22.

2 Primitive concept of ethics

2.1 Good

2.1.1 The definition of good: The satisfaction of desire is good

The meta-ethical concept of "good," just as Moore said, is "goodness," "good in itself" but not good things such as good actions, good strategies, or good characters. "Good" in meta-ethics is not the good of actions, good of characters, good of moralities, and good of strategies, but the commonality of the goodness of all these concrete things. The "good" as the object and concept of meta-ethics is therefore different from the concept of "good" as the object and concept of normative ethics: the former is "good" and the latter is "moral good." This distinction is so important that the meta-ethicist A. C. Ewing insists in the preface of *The Definition of Good* that "The question *What is the definition of good* must be distinguished from the question *What things are good*; and it is the former, not the latter, question which I discuss in this book."[1] Therefore, what exactly is the definition of good? What is the difference between "good" and "what things are good" or "good things"?

Originally, from the etymological point of view, "good," "positive value," "ought," and "beauty" are synonymous with "goodness." According to *ShuoWenJieZi,* "Good means fortunate, it is affiliated with 'words' and 'lamb,' and is synonymous with ought and beauty." In the *Oxford English Dictionary*, "good" is synonymous with "positive value." It characterizes "good" as "the most general adjective of commendation, implying the existence in a high, or at least satisfactory degree of characteristic qualities which are either admirable in themselves or useful for some purpose."[2] Can we say, then, that the conceptual definition of good and its etymological meaning are the same?

Yes, "good and bad," "positive value and negative value" are all the same concept. In his in-depth analysis of good and evil, Feng Youlan concludes: "The so-called good and bad are also the so-called positive value and negative value."[3] And on the matter of value, Stegmüller writes: "The bearer of an affirmative value is good; if it involves a negative value, then we call it bad."[4] That is to say, the category of "good and bad" originally belong

76 *Categories of meta-ethics*

to the category of "value" as a classification of the concept of value: value is the property of good or bad existing in behaviors, characteristics, and objects.[5]

Therefore, according to our study of the value category, good and bad are the utility of the object to the needs of the subject, as well as to the needs' various forms of transformation in the subject's consciousness, such as the subject's desires and purposes, while the needs, desires, and purposes of the subject are the standard of good and bad: the utility of the object that is conductive to satisfying the needs, desires, and purposes of the subject is positive value, thus is the so-called good, while the utility of the object that is an impediment to satisfying the needs, desires, and purposes of the subject is negative value, thus is the so-called bad. That is why Feng Youlan stated: "good refers to those [objects] that meet this standard, and bad refers to those [objects] that are against this standard."[6]

Mencius fully understood that standards of good and bad are based on the needs, desires, and purposes of the subject, simply stating: "The satisfaction of desires is good."[7] In the same era as Mencius, Aristotle wrote: "The definition of good reveals that the thing of this nature that is desirable by itself is [a] common good."[8] Two thousand years later, Russell, settling the issue from a more rigorous scientific perspective, echoed the definitions of Aristotle and Mencius: "It is obvious that the definition of good must come from desires. I think that when a thing fulfills the desire, it is good, or to be more precise, we can define good as the satisfaction of desires."[9]

Can this definition however be tenable? If one's desire to steal is bad, isn't the satisfaction of this desire bad? Indeed, it is bad, and its satisfaction is even worse. But on what basis do we say that the desire to steal and its satisfaction are bad? Clearly, we base this on the harm it causes to others and society. The desire to steal and its satisfaction is harmful to other people's need of "not to fall victim." thus is bad. However, any satisfaction of a desire to steal is bad *only* because it obstructs and harms the wishes of others and society, not because it satisfies the wishes of the thief; stealing satisfies the wishes of the thief, thus it is good for the thief.

To be more precise, the satisfaction of the desire to steal is both bad and good: good for the thief but bad for others and society. It is good for the thief only because it satisfies the desire of the thief; it is bad for others and society only because it harms and impedes other people's desires of "not to fall victim." Therefore, in the final analysis, the satisfaction of any desire is good, and the harming of any desire is bad.

Although the satisfaction of a certain desire can be bad, we cannot deny the definition that "good is the satisfaction of desires." Similarly, the suppression of a certain desire can be good for oneself as a protection against a harm (e.g., self-preservation), or good for benefiting the needs of others even if this is a harm to oneself (e.g., self-sacrifice), but this doesn't mean that we can deny the definition that "bad is the suppression of desires" either. This is because the suppression or satisfaction of many desires has a dual nature: the suppression of a certain desire or the harm caused by a certain desire can also

Primitive concept of ethics 77

be the satisfaction of other desires, and, at the same time, the satisfaction of a certain desire can be the suppression of other desires or the harm resulting from this or other desires. We often say that self-sacrifice is good, and theft is bad, but when analyzed carefully, we see that the actions are not pure good and pure bad. We say that self-sacrifice is good only because it satisfies and preserves the wishes of others and in a broader sense benefits society at large. But it cannot be all good because it likely suppresses and impairs the desires of the one who makes the self-sacrifice. In terms of one's self-preservation, the self-sacrifice may be bad: Who can say that self-sacrifice is a good thing for the one who self-sacrifices?

Therefore, whether some desires (such as theft) and their satisfaction are bad, or the suppression and harm of some desires (such as self-sacrifice) are good, we cannot deny the definition that good is the satisfaction of desire, and bad is the suppression or harm of desire. It implies that both good and bad are the utility of the object to the desires of the subject: "Good" or "positive value" is the utility of the object that is conductive to the satisfaction of the needs, desires, and purposes of the subject, while "bad" or "negative value" is the utility of the object that is harmful to the satisfaction of the needs, desires, and purposes of the subject. Starting from this definition we can further assert that "Good things" are things that possess "goodness," that is, things with utility that can satisfy subject's needs, realize subject's desires and conform to subject's purposes, which, in the final analysis, are interests or things that can bring pleasure. On the one hand, interests are the things that can satisfy the needs and desires of the subject and thus conform to the purpose of the subject, that is, interests are the "object" of the needs and desires of the subject.

As David Braybrooke puts it: "A person's interest may be defined as at bottom—bedrock—what meets basic or vital NEEDS, adding that it extends upward to include the command of any resources that can be converted into provisions for needs."[10] On the other hand, pleasure, as we know, is the psychological experience of the satisfaction of needs, the satisfaction of desires, and the achievement of purpose, and thus is the psychological experience of the obtaining of interests. As Mozi simply stated "interest is the thing that brings pleasure."[11]

Therefore, all good things and all things that can satisfy a subject's needs, realize a subject's desires and conform to a subject's purposes are interests or things that can bring pleasure, while all interests or things that can satisfy a subject's needs, realize a subject's desires, and conform to a subject's purposes, are also good things: the "good things," the "things that can satisfy a subject's needs, realize a subject's desires and conform to a subject's purposes," and the "interests or the things that can bring pleasure" are all the same concept.

However, "good things" is fundamentally different from "good." "Good" is the utility of "good things" (i.e., "interests or things that can bring pleasure") to the needs of the subject, which exists dependently on the needs and desires of the subject, and thus belong to the category of "value." Conversely, the "good things" (i.e., "interests or things that can bring pleasure") which can

78 *Categories of meta-ethics*

satisfy a subject's needs, realize a subject's desires and conform to a subject's purposes are the object of the needs and desires of the subject, existing independently of the needs and desires of the subject as "things of goodness," and thus belong to the category of "fact" or the "substance of value" or the "substance of good." However, many thinkers such as Spinoza equate "good" with "good things" (i.e. things that can bring pleasure):

> Good or bad is something that is conductive to or hinders the maintenance of our existence. That is to say, it means something that is sufficient to increase or decrease, encourage or hinder our activities. Therefore, whenever we feel anything that makes us happy or [feel pain], we call it good or bad.[12]

2.1.2 *Types of good: Intrinsic good, instrumental good, and ultimate good*

Ross and Ewing have thoroughly enumerated the meanings and types of good, which (and this is a slightly abridged account) fall into the following categories: (1) "pleasant or liked"; (2) "capable of satisfying of desire"; (3) "efficient"; (4) "productive of something intrinsically good"; (5) "good as a means" or "efficiently produced"; (6) "intrinsically good"; (7) "ultimately good"; and (8) "morally good."[13]

However, interests are nothing but things that can satisfy needs, realize desires, and achieve purposes, while pleasure is the psychological experience of the satisfaction of needs, the realization of desires, and the achievement of purposes; success is undoubtedly the realization of the purpose of life, while efficiency is the degree to which human activities achieve their purpose. Therefore, the first four meanings and types of good can be summed up as follows: good is the utility of the object to meet the needs of the subject, to realize the desire of the subject and to achieve the purpose of the subject, which is actually the definition of good. The last meaning of "morally good" is the so-called "right," which is also a kind of utility to purpose, that is, not a utility to someone's purpose but a utility to the purpose of society which is to establish and maintain morality. However, "morally good" is not the object of meta-ethics but the object of normative ethics. What really constitutes the types of "good" that are the object of meta-ethics obviously are the other three meanings and types listed above, namely (5) instrumentally good, (6) the intrinsically good, and (7) the ultimately good. Both Ewing and Ross agree that these three kinds of good are the most important and fundamental to philosophy.[14] This is correct; however, their status belongs not so much to philosophy as it does ethics. Then what are the connotations of these three goods?

The division of "intrinsically good," "instrumentally good" and "ultimately good" originates from Aristotle, as he wrote: "It is manifest then the goods may be so called in two senses, the one class for their own sake, the other because of these"[15] Thus so-called "intrinsically good" also can be

Primitive concept of ethics 79

referred to as "good as an end" or "good-in-itself," which is that the good "itself rather than its result is desirable, and is able to satisfy the needs people pursue." For example, health and longevity can produce many other results that are good, such that one can achieve more things or gain more pleasure from things. However, even without these good results, as an end that people pursue, health and longevity itself is desirable, hence is good. Therefore, longevity and health is an intrinsically good. That is why Ross says: "The intrinsically good is best defined as that which is good apart from any of the results it produces."[16]

So-called "instrumentally good," which can also be called an "extrinsically good" or "good in result," is that good in which the "result is desirable, and able to satisfy the needs, thus is the ends that people pursue"; it is the good that "can produce a certain result that is good," the good in which the "result, but not the itself, is the ends people pursue," and is the good in which "itself is the means by which people pursue it, and its result is the ends that people pursue." For example, the result of winter swimming is a long and healthy life, which is desirable and is a kind of good, and thus is the end people pursue; while winter swimming is the instrument to achieve this good, hence is also a kind of good. However, the good of winter swimming is different from its result—a long and healthy life—swimming itself is not the end people pursue, but the means for achieving this end, it is an "instrumentally good." Therefore, discussing "instrumentally good," Ross wrote:

> "good" in this usage is a complex notion implying both a causal relation between the thing judged good and a certain effect, and the goodness of the effect. Thus this usage points directly to another...that in which the "good" means "intrinsically good."[17]

It is not difficult to see that the distinction between intrinsically good and instrumentally good is often relative, because an intrinsically good can often be an instrumentally good at the same time, and vice versa. Health is intrinsically good, and, at the same time, instrumentally good because it enables people to accomplish certain things, effectively becoming the means for achieving them. Similarly, freedom is instrumentally good in that it enables people to realize their own creative potential and thereby achieve self-fulfillment. But freedom is also intrinsically good since freedom itself is what is desired to begin with. Benevolence is another example, as Ewing said:

> Something may be good by means as well as good by ends, which is a better thing in all things. Benevolence is this kind of thing, because it is not only good in itself, but also produces happiness.[18]

Is there, then, absolute *intrinsic good*? Yes. It is the highest good, or, to use Ross and Ewing's sense of the term, the ultimate good, which is absolutely

80   *Categories of meta-ethics*

good as an end—that is, it has "no instrumental good at all." This kind of good, as Aristotle stated, is happiness, because happiness can only be the end people pursue, and it can't be a means to achieve any other ends:

> We choose always for its own sake, and never with a view to anything further…happiness is manifestly something final and self-sufficient, being the end of all things which are and may be done.[19]

As kinds of good, "ultimate good," "good as an end," and "instrumental good" are the same as the other "good"'s listed by Ross and Ewing, in the sense that all the types of good refer to the utility that can satisfy the needs, desires, and purposes of the subject. It is only that "good as an end" and "ultimate good" are themselves desirable and can satisfy certain needs, thus are ends people pursue, while that which is "instrumentally good" is the means by which people pursue a desirable result that can satisfy certain other needs. Therefore, any good is the utility of the object that can satisfy the needs, realize the desires and achieve the purposes of the subject. In sum, it is what people praise, choose, desire, and pursue:

> We might adopt a technical term and define "good" as what ought to be the object of a pro attitude (to use Ross's word). "Pro attitude" is intended to cover any favorable attitude to something. It covers, for instance, choice, desire, liking, pursuit, approval, admiration.[20]

2.1.3 Types of bad: Pure bad and necessary bad

The opposite of good, as Ewing says, is bad: "the former may be called pro attitudes, the latter anti attitudes."[21] Thus, in his view, bad has opposite meanings to the meanings of good, the types of which correspond to the different types of good: (1) "unpleasant"; (2) "contrary to what we desire"; (3) "inefficient in fulfilling certain purpose"; (4) "productive of something intrinsically evil"; (5) "inefficiently made"; (6) "intrinsically bad"; (7) "ultimately bad"; (8) "morally bad."[22]

Obviously, the first four kinds of meanings can be summed up in one sentence: bad is the utility that hinders the satisfaction of needs and desires of the subject and, therefore, prevents the achievement of purpose. The last kind of meaning, "morally bad," is also the so-called "wrong," which is also a negative utility to "purpose," namely the negative utility to the purpose for which a society establishes morality. However, "morally bad" is not the object of meta-ethics but the object of normative ethics. The types of "bad" that truly constitute the object of meta-ethics are namely three kinds of bad that respectively correspond to (5) "instrumentally good," (6) "intrinsically good," and (7) "ultimately good," namely, the things that cause "intrinsical bad," are "intrinsically bad," and "ultimately bad."

Primitive concept of ethics 81

If what is "ultimately good" is happiness, that which is "ultimately bad" must be misfortune. If "intrinsic good" is "good-in-itself," "intrinsic bad" is "bad-in-itself." If "instrumental good" is "good-in-result," "the thing that causes an intrinsic bad," is "bad-in-result." However, because good-in-result is an end that people pursue, the thing that facilitates the achievement of the good-in-result can be called an "instrumental good." On the contrary, something that is "bad-in-result" cannot be an end that people pursue, so the thing that causes the bad-in-result cannot be an "instrumental bad," it can only be "bad-in-result." "Ultimately bad" is misfortune, which is self-evident, but the meanings of "bad-in-itself" and "bad-in-result" are very complicated: What exactly do they mean?

The thing with a "bad result" may hinder the satisfaction of needs, the realization of desires, and the achievement of purposes; hence, while it is bad, the result may also be conducive to satisfying needs, realizing desires, and achieving purpose, which is good. The thing that is bad in itself with a bad result, such as incurable cancer, can be called a "pure bad." Generally speaking, a thing with a "result that is bad but itself is good," of which the good is small, and the bad is great, producing the greatest net balance of bad over good, also belongs to the category of "pure bad." For example, most "bad" things, such as excess, laziness, and lust, in themselves involve all kinds of satisfactions of needs, realizations of desires, or the achievement of some purpose, hence are also "good." But as far as "bad-in-result" is concerned, "bad" things hinder the fulfillment or realization of more important needs, desires, and purposes, thus produce the greater net balance of bad over good, falling under the category of "pure bad."

On the contrary, the result of a thing that is bad in itself can be both bad and good. As mentioned, certain types of cancer are bad, and fall into the category of "pure bad," but something "bad" like undergoing surgery for appendicitis, for example, is also good because the removal of the appendix in most cases is a good result. In this instance, the bad can be called a "necessary bad" but it as such can be designated as a category of good. A "necessary bad" is very complex but extremely important. It can be best defined as "a thing that is bad in itself with a good result, producing a net balance of good over bad consequences." It is still, itself, a kind of bad because it is a complete suppression of, and obstacle to, needs and desires. However, because it is a kind of bad that can prevent greater bad or enable greater good, it has a net balance of "good" over "bad," hence it is not bad but a "necessary bad" which is good. For example:

The surgery, itself, for appendicitis, is a total kind of bad since it involves a large amount of blood loss which makes the patient weak. However, because it prevents greater bad, i.e. more severe complications from appendicitis and even death, the net balance of good over bad makes surgery a kind of necessary bad. Winter swimming, itself, is also a total kind of bad since one endures the physical effects of cold water and could be at risk of hypothermia.

82 *Categories of meta-ethics*

However, because it can bring the greater good of health and longevity, the net balance of good over bad makes winter swimming a kind of necessary bad. Taking the example of pain, Bernard Gert offers a profound insight into the essential nature of necessary bad:

> To say that pain is an evil is not to say that pain never serves a useful purpose. Pain sometimes provides a warning that we need medical attention. If we did not feel pain, then we might not seek the necessary medical attention, and as a result might even die. This fact about the function of pain is sometimes used in an attempt to solve the problem of evil. It is sometimes claimed that this is the best of all possible worlds, and all the evil in it is a necessary evil.[23]

The above examples make it clear that the net balance of a necessary bad is good, and therefore it belongs to the category of good. However, since the good exists only in the result, it belongs to the category of instrumental good or extrinsical good or good-in-result. To put it another way, a necessary bad cannot be an intrinsically good because it is completely bad-in-itself. If, as we say, the ultimate good or absolute intrinsical good can only be "happiness," then there are many things that are an absolute instrumental good or a necessary bad to prevent greater bad: things like surgery or pain, discussed above, or, more broadly, things in the social or moral sphere to prevent greater bad, such as politics, law, prison, and penalties. Because these things, in terms of themselves, are all sorts of restrictions, suppressions, infringements, or harms to certain desires and freedoms, they are bad; but this kind of bad can prevent greater bad (i.e., the collapse of society) and enable greater good for individuals or for society as a whole (i.e., the preservation and development of society), thus because the net balance of its results are good over bad, it is a necessary bad and is also an absolute instrumental good.

As far as what they reference, the terms "necessary bad," "pure bad," and "ultimately bad" are different, but it is obvious in the sense of being bad they are the same. All refer to the utility of objects to suppress the realization of the needs, desires, and purposes of subjects: the necessary bad suppresses wants of a smaller value to achieve wants of greater value, while pure bad completely suppresses the realization of wants or suppresses wants of a greater value to fulfill wants of smaller value. However, in terms of the academic value of these concepts, the "necessary bad" is far more important than "pure bad" and "ultimately bad." It is in fact one of the most important concepts of meta-ethics, for it is the key to unlock the puzzle of "the origin and goal of morality," namely, whether morality originates from morality itself, that is, for the perfection of everyone's moral character, or if it originates beyond this sense of morality for the promotion of everyone's interests and happiness.

Having understood what is "good," we can then further study "ought" and "right," because, in the final analysis, "ought" and "right" are nothing more

Primitive concept of ethics 83

than a special kind of "good": ought is the good of actions and right is the moral good of actions.

2.2 Ought and right

2.2.1 *Ought: The good of action*

Good is the utility of the object that is conductive to satisfying the needs, realizing the desires and conforming to the purpose of the subject. It implies that good is the aim pursued by all activities or actions of humans or the subject, because the purpose of all activities or actions of humans or the subject is undoubtedly to satisfy needs and desires. Aristotle wrote at the beginning of the *Nicomachean Ethics*: "Every art and every *inquiry*, and similarly, every *action* and every intention is thought to aim at some good. "[24] Ewing simply regards the pursuit of good as the definition of good: it is "the sense of 'good' in which it means [a] 'fitting object of choice or pursuit.'"[25]

However, no matter who one is, the pursuit of good may or may not achieve the desired aim. The actions of a person to achieve their aims, thus satisfying their needs and desires, is like the good they pursue, and undoubtedly belongs to the category of good because it is consistent with the definition of good, and hence is called the action of good. Conversely, the action that hinders the realization of aims and the satisfaction of desires conforms to the definition of bad, and belongs to the category of bad, and so can be called an "action of bad." For example:

If I want to be healthy and enjoy a long life, then a moderate diet and a balanced lifestyle are actions of good because they help me realize my desires and aim; conversely, if I have an excessive diet and an unbalanced lifestyle, it is then they are actions of bad for they obstruct the realization of the desires for a healthy and long life.

However, as Moore and Ross state, the "good action" is different from the "good" in the "good action." The good or goodness in the "good action" is the utility of the action for achieving purpose, satisfying needs, and realizing desires. In short, it is the utility of the action for achieving its purpose. This kind of good or goodness of action is the so-called "ought." Conversely, the bad or badness of a bad action is the utility of an action that cannot achieve purpose, satisfy needs, and realize desires. It is the utility of action that cannot achieve its purpose. This kind of bad or badness of action is called "ought-not."

One ought to have a moderate diet for a long and healthy life, but what does "ought to" mean? Obviously, it means that a moderate diet has utility for achieving the purpose of a healthy and long life. Conversely, what does "ought-not" mean in the statement that one ought not to have an immoderate diet? Doesn't this mean that an immoderate diet has no utility for achieving the purpose of a healthy and long life? Therefore, "ought" and "ought-not" do not necessarily have moral implications. They are only the utility of the

84 *Categories of meta-ethics*

actions to purpose. No matter how evil, for instance, one's purpose is, if the action can achieve one's purpose, then this kind of action is what one ought to do; if the action fails to achieve one's purpose, then the action is what one ought not to do. That is why Ewing says:

> "Ought" is sometimes used merely to indicate the best means of achieving a certain goal, regardless of whether the purpose is good or bad. For example, "the killer ought not leave his fingerprint on the weapon".[26]

Therefore, as the good of action, *ought* is the utility of action to purpose. But is "ought" merely the good of action? The field of good undoubtedly can be divided into two categories: "good in the field of consciousness and purpose," and "good in the field of unconsciousness and purposelessness." The good in the field of unconsciousness and purposelessness is only good without the question of ought or ought-not. We can say, for instance, that "water at zero degrees is good or harmful for people" but can't say that "water ought to or ought not be at zero degrees." And we can say that a "diamond is hard and useful, which is a kind of good" but can't say "a diamond ought to be hard." That is why Kant said: "to ask what nature 'ought' to be is as absurd as to ask what nature a circle 'ought' to have."[27]

Therefore, the good of "ought" must exist only in the field of consciousness and purpose, that is, only as a "good" in the field of consciousness and purpose. However, what exactly is the good in consciousness and purpose? Is it the flesh and blood of people or subjects? No, because we can't say "one ought to be born beautiful, and ought not to be born ugly." Why can we not say "one ought or ought not to be born beautiful or ugly"? This is because such qualities can't be freely chosen. Ought and ought not only apply to things that can be freely chosen. In the field of consciousness and purpose what exactly are then the things that can be freely chosen?

Obviously, they can only be actions and the traits of character expressed and formed by actions. In general, the category of action can also contain the traits of character expressed and formed by action. This is why Ewing says that "ought" is different from "good" mainly in that it is related to behavior.[28] Only the good of action is called "ought." Or, in other words, "ought" can only be the good of action, that is, the utility of action to a purpose, the utility of action that can realize a purpose, and the utility that can achieve a purpose, thus satisfying certain needs and realizing certain desires. In the end, in the field of action, "ought," and "good" or "positive value" are just different names for the same utility of the object to the needs of the subject, and therefore are different terms for the same concept. This is probably the reason that every judgment with the concept of "ought" is called a "value judgment."

2.2.2 *Right: Moral good of action*

Right or wrong is also called a moral good or a moral bad. Meta-ethicists, such as Ross, Ewing, Hare, Schlick, and Russell all take "moral good" as

Primitive concept of ethics 85

an important and specific type of good as the object for detailed analysis. This is probably because, on the one hand, people tend to equate "good" with "moral good," and if we do not have a comparative analysis of them we cannot truly understand "good" or "moral good." On the other hand, the analysis of "good" is just a method and means, its purpose is to analyze "moral good" and establish moral principles that can guide actions. But what exactly is "moral good"?

What exactly can be said to be a moral good or a moral bad, right, or wrong? This is undoubtedly the first question we must settle to define moral good or moral bad (i.e., right or wrong). Almost everything can be said to be good or bad. For example, a brisk morning wind, a lovely sunset, a full moon, green trees, beautiful flowers, liberty, democracy, science, and art are beneficial to our well-being, thus are good; an earthquake, a flood, absolutism, ignorance, and superstition are harmful to our well-being, thus are bad. However, the things we can say to be a moral good or moral bad, right or wrong are extremely limited. Just as Frankena says: "The sort of things that may be morally good or bad are persons, groups of persons, traits of character, dispositions, emotions, motives, and intentions—in short, persons, groups of persons, and elements of personality."[29]

In fact, not all of these things can be said to be a moral good or a moral bad, i.e., the human body, a congenital temperament, genetic type, characteristics, and so on. The things that can be said to be a moral good or a moral bad no doubt are the things belonging to consciousness and freedom of choice, which, in the final analysis, can only be actions and the moral character that actions express. So, what kind of action and moral character is a moral good or a moral bad?

Since the moral good of action and virtue is a kind of "good," then, just as J. L. Mackie says, they are bound to have the general properties of "good," that is, the utility of the object that can satisfy the needs, realize the desires and conform to the purpose of the subject: "in moral contexts 'good' still has its general meaning, that it still characterizes something as being such as to satisfy the requirements or interests or wants of the kind in question."[30] The question is, whose needs, desires, and purposes the good of action and virtue, or the moral good satisfy? "It is still unsolved whether such requirements (etc.) are fed in point of view of the speaker, or of (some or all?) other people, whether the reference is somehow to all the interests of everyone."[31]

Richard Taylor also contends that if a person lives alone and isolates himself from society, he would only have good or bad rather than right or wrong, just as he says, "To whom could he own any obligation to do anything? And by what standard, other than good and evil themselves, over which he is the sole judge, could any action of his be deemed right or wrong?"[32] Why does right and wrong exist only in society, and only good or bad for individuals who are separated from society?

Obviously, this is because, first of all, good is to satisfy the needs, desires, and purposes of any subject, while what is right satisfies only the needs, desires and purposes of a special subject—society—that is to say it is the needs,

86   *Categories of meta-ethics*

desires and purposes of the society to establish morality. Secondly, good is a property of all things that can satisfy the needs, desires, and purposes of any subject, while right is a property of the action that can satisfy the needs, desires, and purpose of the society to establish morality. Furthermore, "good" and "bad" belong to the category of value as classifications of value (and as synonyms of positive value and negative value), while "right" and "wrong" belong to the category of moral value as classifications of moral value (and as synonyms of positive moral value and negative moral value).

Finally, good and bad are the utility of the object (of all things) to the needs, desires, and purposes of the subject, which, in the final analysis, is the utility of all things to the purpose of the subject: the utility that conforms to the purpose is good, and the utility that does not conform to the purpose is bad. Right and wrong are the utility of the object of morality (the actions) to the needs, desires, and purposes of the subject of morality (the society) to establish morality, which, in the final analysis, is the utility of the action to the goal of morality: those actions that conform to the goal of morality are the so-called right or moral good actions, and those actions that violate the goal of morality are the so-called wrong or moral bad actions.

It can be seen that right or wrong, or moral good or moral bad, as Schlick says, are subjected to good or bad, that is, move from particular to the general: "Moral good is only a special case of a more general good." The difference between the two is expressed in the following aspects: On the one hand, the objects of both good and bad, which are fundamentally different, pertain to the general because good and bad are all objects and all things, while the objects of moral good and moral bad are only special kinds of objects, which are an individual's actions and moral character.

On the other hand, the subjects of good and bad are also fundamentally different. The subject of good or bad can be the needs, desires, and purposes of any subject, which in the final analysis, is any purpose. On the contrary, the subject of moral good or moral bad is a special subject: "society," and its needs, desires, and purposes for establishing morality, which, in the final analysis, is the goal of morality. Schlick also writes: "Only when the word good (1) refers to a person's decision, and (2) expresses some kind of social approval of this decision, does it have moral significance."[33]

Based on the differences between these two aspects, we can then, as Frankena points out, separate "moral good and moral bad" from "good and bad," so that good and bad can be divided into two types of morally good and morally bad, and non-morally good and non-morally bad.[34] The so-called moral good or moral bad is right or wrong, and refers to the utility of action to the needs, desires, and purposes of society to establish morality: that which conforms to the goal of morality is the moral good or "right," that which does not conform to the goal of morality is the moral bad or "wrong." On the contrary, non-moral good or bad is the utility of all things to other needs, desires, and purposes (excluding those needs, desires, and purposes of society to establish morality), which mainly the utility to

Primitive concept of ethics 87

personal purpose: it is a non-moral good when it conforms to personal purpose, and a non-moral bad when it does not conform to personal purpose. Therefore, moral good and bad and non-moral good and bad may be consistent or inconsistent. For example:

"Benefiting others for one's self-interest" can satisfy my desires and achieve my purpose, hence it is a kind of good for me, namely a "non-moral good"; in the meantime "benefiting others for one's self-interest" is beneficial to the existence and development of society, which is consistent with the goal of morality, and hence is right and also a kind of "moral good." For instance, a successful act of theft is in line with the purpose of thieves, so it is a kind of non-moral good; at the same time, it is harmful to the existence and development of society, violating the goal of morality, hence is a moral bad and is wrong. If one makes some sort of self-sacrifice it is beneficial to the existence and development of society conforming to the goal of morality, hence is a moral good and is right, but, at the same time, it can be harmful to the person who makes the self-sacrifice because he or she may sacrifice certain desires that are of some importance to their well-being, thus is a kind of non-moral bad.

It is wrong to deny the definition that "good is the satisfaction of desire" according to the judgment that the satisfaction of certain desires (such as theft) is bad. The reason for this mistake, in the final analysis, is that "good" is seen as the same as "moral good." If good and the moral good are the same concept, it follows that a lot of desires and their satisfaction (theft, envy, slander, and so on) would be completely bad (or by no means good) because they are harmful to others and society, violating the goal of morality. Indeed, in this sense, the definition of "good" as the "satisfaction of desire" would undoubtedly make the mistake of being too broad.

If, however, we distinguish "moral good" from "good," then theft would be just a moral bad rather than a non-moral bad: it is clearly a good thing for the thief to satisfy the desire to steal, which is a kind of good or non-moral good. Thus, though the satisfaction of a certain desire, such as theft, is of course bad, it is not a complete bad, but rather a moral bad or non-moral good. Therefore, only "defining moral good as the satisfaction of desires" is wrong, while, alternatively, defining "good as the satisfaction of desires," is a truth that is universally applicable.

The analysis of right or moral good shows that the question of what action and moral character are right is a very complex one: it is directly dependent on the utility of the action and moral character to the goal of morality, ultimately, on both the nature of the action and the goal of morality. Throughout history people have been arguing over "what action or moral character is right," which, in the final analysis, is a controversy surrounding "the goal of morality," "the nature of action" and "the utility of action to the goal of morality."

Why do some people today still think that right and moral good are different, just as Ross does?[35] Why do they believe that "benefiting others for one's self-interest" is right but not a moral good, and that only "selflessly

88 *Categories of meta-ethics*

benefiting others" is a moral good? In answer to that the advocators of the heteronomous theory of the goal of morality often mistake the goal of morality for morality itself—that it is to perfect everyone's moral character. In this way, on the one hand, only "selflessly benefiting others" is morally good because it's a perfect moral realm that conforms to the goal of morality, thus is morally good; on the other hand, "benefiting others for one's self-interest" is not seen as the perfect realm of moral character, thus does not conform to the goal of morality but only to a legal or "selfish" purpose, which thus means it is right and lawful but not morally good.

This view is wrong. The study of normative ethics will tell us that the goal of morality is not autonomy but heteronomy; that it is not to perfect everyone's moral character, but rather to safeguard the existence and/or development of society and promote everyone's interests. In view of this, regardless of whether one benefits others or is self-interested, as long as it does not harm others, it is not only right, but also a moral good because it conforms to the goal of morality: right and moral good are the same concepts. Therefore, to determine whether an action is right or a moral good, and what kind of action conforms to a moral good that guides the particular actions, we must start from the definition of meta-ethics that "moral good and moral bad is the utilities of actions to the goal of morality" to study "the goal of morality," "the nature of action" and "the utility of action to the goal of morality." However, these problems have unfortunately gone beyond the field of meta-ethics enquiry and entered the field of normative ethics.

2.2.3 *Right and ought: The universalizability of moral ought*

Scholars often equate "ought" with "right." For example, Burton F. Porter said that "whatever is right ought to be done and, conversely, that an act that ought to be done because it is right."[36] Ewing even stated that " 'The right action' is synonymous with the action which ought to be done."[37] Following this, one could argue that "a killer ought not to leave fingerprints at the crime scene" is equal to "it is right that a killer leaves no fingerprints at the crime scene." Would this ever be a plausible argument?

It is not difficult to see that the extension of "ought" is much broader than that of "right." Mackie classifies "ought" into two categories of "moral ought" and "knowledge ought":

> We must take account not only of moral and prudential and, hypothetically imperative "ought," but also of such statements as "This ought to do trick," "they ought to be across the border by now," and "it ought to have dissolved; I wonder why it didn't," which we can perhaps call epistemic.[38]

However, according to the logical rules of classification, it is better to call it a "non-moral ought" than a "knowledge ought." In this way, "ought" is divided into two large types of "moral ought" and "non-moral ought." The

Primitive concept of ethics 89

so-called moral ought and moral ought-not, that is, right or wrong, or moral good or moral bad, is the utility of action to the needs, desires, and purposes of society to establish morality. In the final analysis, it is the utility of action to the goal of morality: when it is consistent with the goal of morality it is a moral "ought," a moral "good" or right, and when it is not consistent it is a moral "ought not," moral "bad," or wrong. For example:

Regardless of how the crime fits the killer's purpose, the crime is harmful to the existence and development of society and violates the goal of morality, and thus is a moral "ought not," moral "bad," or wrong. On the contrary, no matter how harmful self-sacrifice is for the purpose of self-preservation, it may be beneficial to the existence and development of society, conforming to the goal of morality, thus is a moral "ought," a moral "good" or right.

However, "non-moral ought and non-moral ought not" are different from "non-moral good and non-moral bad." Good and bad are the utilities of all things, so "non-moral good and non-moral bad" are the utilities of all things to the purpose of the things other than the goal of morality (i.e., are beyond morality), and are the utilities of everything to the purpose of non-moral purpose such as personal purpose. Conversely, ought is only the utility of action. Therefore, "non-moral ought" is only the utility of action to a purpose other than the goal of morality, that is, a personal purpose: if it is consistent with personal purpose it is a "non-moral ought," and if not consistent, a "non-moral ought-not."

For example, not to leave fingerprints at the crime scene conforms with the purpose of the killer to avoid being caught, so for the killer it is an "ought." On the contrary, to leave fingerprints at the crime scene does not conform with the purpose of the killer, which is to avoid being caught, so it is an "ought not" for the killer. Because these oughts conform or do not conform to the killer's purpose, they are a "non-moral ought" and "non-moral ought not" because they hold to personal purpose not to the goal of morality.

It can be seen that "moral ought" and "non-moral ought" are the utilities of actions. The difference between the two lies in that "moral ought" is the utility of action to the goal of morality, while "non-moral ought" is the utility to the non-moral purpose. Therefore, on the one hand, "moral ought" and "non-moral ought" can be consistent or inconsistent. For example, "benefiting others for one's self-interest" conforms to my purpose of self-interest, thus it is a "non-moral ought," but it is also beneficial to the existence and development of society, conforming to the goal of morality, thus it is a "moral ought." Conversely, where it is inconsistent with my purpose, it is a "self-sacrifice," which violates my own purpose of self-preservation, and thus is a "non-moral ought not," but, at the same time, it is beneficial to others and society, conforming to the goal of morality, and thus is a "moral ought." In the same way, not to leave fingerprints at the crime scene conforms with the purpose of the killer to avoid being caught, so it is a "non-moral ought." At the same time, it is harmful to the existence and development of society and violates the goal of morality, thus is "moral ought not."

90 *Categories of meta-ethics*

On the other hand, "moral ought" has "universalizability," while "non-moral ought" has no "universalizability." The concept of universalizability of "moral ought," as is well known, originates from Kant and was established by Hare, who believed that "moral ought" has two features:

> The second feature of the word "ought" that I shall be relying on is usually called *universalizability*. When I say that I ought, I commit myself to more than that *I* ought. Prescriptivity demands that the man who says "I ought" should himself act accordingly, if the judgment applies to him and if he can so act.[39]

Why does "moral ought" have universalizability? Obviously, it is only because the ultimate goal of morality is universal, general, and the same in all societies: it safeguards the existence and development of society and promotes everyone's interests. On the contrary, personal purposes are significantly different because the utility of "non-moral ought" actions—that is, of so many people with so many different purposes—clearly means it lacks the feature of universalizability. John's "ought" is not Jim's "ought." In this way, "moral ought" has universalizability because it is the utility of action to the ultimate goal of morality, which is the same goal for all societies: an ought that is applicable to everyone.

To sum up, we can see that "ought" is broader than "right" and hence becomes an intermediary between "good" and "right": "Good" is the utility of the object (of all things) to the purpose of the subject; "ought" and "right" are the utility of action to the purpose of the subject; "ought" is the good of action and the utility of the action to every purpose; right is the moral good of action and the utility of action to the goal of morality. Therefore right, ought, and good are all certain utilities of the object to the needs of the subject, belonging to the category of value. However, we might ask: Where do right, ought, and good come from? What are their sources? In the final analysis, how to answer is-ought problem? The analysis of the categories of value, good, ought, and right will inevitably lead to the study of "is" or "fact": They are the end category of the system of meta-ethics.

2.3 Fact and is

2.3.1 Fact: The concept of fact in a broad sense

All things, according to their nature of existence, undoubtedly can be divided into two categories: "fact" and "non-fact." Fact is "a thing that actually exists outside of thought," and "the thing that exists independent of thought." Non-fact is "the thing that merely exists in thought." If a person is diagnosed with cancer, for instance, regardless of whether he believes it, of whether he admits it to others, or of whether he is physically suffering from the cancer, the fact is that he has cancer. Any denial of it to the contrary is a non-fact. In defining the concept of fact Russell wrote: "I mean by a 'fact' something which is there, whether anybody thinks so or not."[40] "The fact itself is objective and independent of our thoughts or opinions about it."[41]

In view of this, value undoubtedly belongs to the category of fact, because a thing that has value is obviously "a thing that actually exists independently of thought." The nutritional value of egg, for instance, "exists independently of how we think of it." Whether you think the egg has nutritional value or not it still has it. The nutritional value of an egg "exists independently of human thought," so it is a fact, and can be called a "value fact."

This extension of the concept of "fact," which includes "value," is a concept of "fact in a broad sense": it applies only to non-value sciences such as epistemology, and is not applicable to value sciences, such as ethics, because the fundamental problems of all value sciences are undoubtedly about the sources and basis of "ought" or "value," and, more specifically, in regards to ethics, is the relationship between "ought," "value," and "is" or "fact," which is the nub of Hume's guillotine.

The very existence and persistence of the guillotine, especially the attempts to prove "that value can be derived from fact," obviously already implies that value is not fact, or that fact does not include value: That fact and value are two opposite concepts with no overlapping extensions. Otherwise, if fact is "a thing that actually exists independently of thought," hence containing value, then "to derive value from fact" would be the same as "to derive fact from fact," consequently there would be no problem of "whether value can be derived from fact."

Since the birth of Hume's guillotine, there has almost been a consensus that value and fact belong to opposing fields. In *Human Knowledge: Its Scope and Limits* and *Our Knowledge of the External World as a Field for Scientific Method in Philosophy*, Russell defined "fact" as "something which is there, whether anybody thinks so or not," and claimed that "value" belongs to the category of fact, but, in *Religion and Science*, he seemingly denied that value is fact: "When we assert that this or that have 'value,' we are giving our expression of our own emotions, not for the fact which is still true, if our personal feelings were different."[42]

Russell, however, does not contradict himself. His statement that fact is "something which is there, whether anybody thinks so or not," which includes value, refers to the concept of fact in non-value sciences, such as epistemology which holds to the concept of "fact in a broad sense," while his statement that value is not fact—that fact does not include value—refers to the concept of fact in value sciences, namely the concept of "fact in a narrow sense."

The value sciences instituted the concept of "fact in a narrow sense" because the is–ought problem is a fundamental concern. The difference then between the broad and narrow senses of the concept of fact boils down to the extent the respective definitions include or exclude value. Given that

92 *Categories of meta-ethics*

the concept of fact "in a broad sense" in epistemology and other non-value sciences is that "a thing actually exists independently of thought" what is, then, "the concept of fact in a narrow sense" since it excludes value?

2.3.2 Is: The concept of fact in a narrow sense

It turns out that the fact in a broad sense—the thing that actually exists independently of thought—can be divided into the fact of subjectivity and the fact of objectivity: The fact of subjectivity is "the autonomous agent" that actually exist independently of the thought; the fact of objectivity is "the object of action" that actually exists independently of the thought. For example, when a sculptor is sculpturing an eagle, the sculptor is an autonomous agent, and consequently the sculptor and his needs, desires and purposes, etc. are the facts of subjectivity, while the eagle he is sculpturing and its size, material, and color and so on are the facts of objectivity.

What is crucial is that the fact of objectivity can be further divided into "value fact" and "non-value fact" based on the nature of whether each depend on the needs, desires and purposes of the subject. "Value fact" is also "value," which is the property of the utility of the object to the needs, desires, and purposes of the subject, thus is the thing of the object that exists depending on the needs, desires, and purposes of the subject. Why, however, can "value" be called "value fact"? It is because value, which exists depending on the needs, desires, and purposes of the subject, also exists independently of the subject's thought: Value is a kind of fact, belonging to the category of fact in a broad sense (things that actually exist independently of thought), which is also applicable in non-value sciences such as epistemology.

On the contrary, "non-value fact" actually exists not only independently of thought, but also independently of the needs, desires, and purposes of the subject. It is the thing of the object that actually exists independently of the needs, desires, and purposes of the subject, and is the property of non-value that actually exists in the object—that is, as an objective fact beyond value, which is the "fact" of the object exclusive of "value" and opposed to value. This is the concept of "fact" in ethics and other value sciences, which is also "the concept of fact in a narrow sense": Fact is the thing of the object that actually exists independently of the needs, desires, and purposes of the subject. The fundamental problem of ethics and of other value sciences is that the question of whether "value" can be derived from "fact" implies that value is not fact and fact does not include value: that fact and value are opposite concepts with no overlapping extensions.

Based on the concept of "fact in a broad sense," and because of the fundamental problem of the value sciences (whether "value" can be derived from "fact"), we have formed the concept of "fact in a narrow sense" to discern it from "value": we define fact in a broad sense as "the thing that actually exists independently of thought," which includes value and is applicable to non-value science; and we define fact in a narrow sense as "the thing that actually

Primitive concept of ethics 93

exists independently of the needs, desires and purposes of the subject," which is exclusive of value and applicable to every value science. For instance:

Is it or is it not a fact that pork is nutritious? It is a fact because the nutrition of pork "exist independently of how we think." It is only that the "nutrition of pork" is a kind of value which can be called a "value fact." Although its nutrition exist independently of thought, they also exist depending on human needs and so are the utility of pork to human needs. Hence the nutrition of pork belongs to the concept of "fact in a broad sense" (which is applicable to epistemology and all other non-value sciences). Conversely, it is also a fact that pork has weight, but the weight itself is not the utility of pork to human needs, hence is neither a value nor a value fact but a non-value fact instead. The weight of pork is a fact beyond value which exists not only independently of our thought, but also independently of the needs of a subject. Hence the weight of pork belongs to the concept of "fact in a narrow sense" (which is also applicable to ethics and all other value sciences).

Therefore, the fundamental problem of the value sciences, namely whether "value" can be derived from "fact," determines that the concept of "fact" is the fact in the narrow sense, that is, that it is not just exclusive of "value" but also the opposite of value, which, in the final analysis, is the thing of the object that exists independently of the needs, desires, and purposes of the subject; on the contrary, "value" is the utility of the object to the needs, desires, and purposes of the subject, and is the property of object that exists depending on the needs, desires, and purposes of the subject, which varies with the changes of the needs, desires, and purposes of the subject, so value is not a fact.

The concept of fact in the narrow sense, which is exclusive of "value," and is opposite to value, is not only the concept of fact in value sciences, but also the same concept of fact in the natural sciences such as physics. Einstein repeatedly pointed out that natural science only studies "fact" and not "ought": "Science can assert only 'what is,' and not 'what is ought'; however, besides its range, all kinds of value judgments are still necessary."[43] He further writes:

> There is another feature of the scientific way of thinking. It does not express any sentiments for the use of the concepts used in the establishment of its consistent system. For scientists, there is only "existence" but not wishes, value, good, bad and purpose. As long as we stay in the field of science we would never encounter sentences such as "you should not lie"....Although scientific statements about facts and relationships cannot produce ethical rules, logical thinking and empirical knowledge can enable ethical rules to conform to rationality and to be consistent.[44]

Obviously, from Einstein's point of view, natural science only studies "fact" and "what is," but not "value" and "what is ought." Does this not imply that the concept of "fact" in the natural sciences is the concept of fact in a narrow sense—that it is exclusive of and opposite to "value"? Therefore, Hume's

94 *Categories of meta-ethics*

guillotine (whether "value" can be derived from "fact") takes "fact" as a concept that is exclusive of and opposite to value. It is not only based on the fundamental difference between "fact" and "value" (where the former does not depend on the desire of the subject, while the latter depends on the desire of the subject), but is also based on the concept of fact in the natural sciences, which it inherited.

In this way, not only the narrow sense of the concept of fact in Hume's guillotine conforms to the concept of fact in the natural sciences, but also the answer to the guillotine problem can determine whether a value science such as ethics can be a true science, that is, a science like that of the natural sciences. This is because the objects of study of the natural sciences are facts in a narrow sense exclusive of "value" and opposite to "value," while the objects of study of ethics are ought and value. Therefore, whether "value" can be derived from "fact" is key to determining if value sciences can be true sciences. If value can be derived from fact, then the object of ethics, in the final analysis, is "fact." It follows, then, that ethics, like the natural sciences, is also a true science. Indeed, if we were not able to derive value from fact, ethics would only be the study of ought and value, not facts, thus not a true science.

Hume's guillotine is certainly the most important, fundamental and decisive problem of all value sciences, as many ethicists, such as W. D. Hudson, also acknowledge: "The central problem in moral philosophy is that commonly known as the is-ought question."[45] Where, however, this guillotine makes the concept of "fact" in all value sciences the same as the concept of "fact" in the natural sciences, which is exclusive of value and opposite to value, it follows that the concept of "value fact" in all value sciences may be seen to be the equivalent of arguing the "square of a circle," which is an absurd, contradictory, and untenable concept.

However, "value fact," we know, is a scientific concept in epistemology and other non-value sciences because, in these fields, "fact" is used in a broad sense to refer to a thing that actually exists independently of thought, and also because the existence of value no doubt only depends on the needs, desires, and purposes of the subject, not on the thought of the subject (i.e., the nutritional value of eggs merely depends on human needs, not on human thought). Since in some non-value sciences value belongs to the category of fact, we likewise assert that the concept of "value fact" is scientific, and further claim that value fact and non-value fact are the two major types of the concept of fact. In the field of value sciences, however, some Chinese scholars, for instance, when discussing things in relation to "value fact," quite often confuse the different meanings of the concept of "fact" in the value sciences and non-value sciences.

In all value sciences, including ethics, just as Hume discovered, this narrow sense of fact, which is exclusive of value and opposite to value, is often expressed through the uses of "is" or "is not" as the judgment of copulatives ("what is" and "not what"), whereas, those with "ought" or "ought not" as the judgment of copulatives, are often the expressions of value.[46] Therefore,

Primitive concept of ethics 95

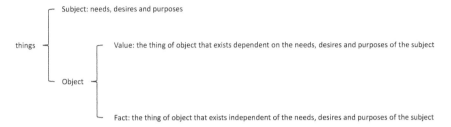

Figure 2.1 The categories of things in value sciences.

in a value science like ethics, "fact" and "is" are treated as the same concept, so that "is" also is the "fact" exclusive of value and opposite to value, which is the thing that exists independently of the needs, desires, and purposes of the subject. Furthermore, the "fact" that is relative to "ought" is called "is," and the "fact" that is relative to "value" is mostly called "fact," consequently in ethics there exist two pairs of terms: "fact-value" and "is-ought."

Therefore, in all value sciences, all things fall into two categories: object and subject. And object is further divided into two categories: value and fact. Thus, everything is actually divided into three categories: value, fact, and subject. Value is the utility of the object to the needs, desires, and purposes of the subject, which is the thing of the object that exists dependent on the needs, desires, and purposes of the subject. "Fact" is also "is," which is the opposite of value and is the thing of the object that exists independently of the needs, desires and purposes of the subject. The subject with its needs, desires, and purposes is the opposite of the object—the subject and object are two opposites that constitute all things—hence is neither value nor fact, but is the basis to divide "object" into "value" and "fact," and the intermediary connecting value and fact, which can be illustrated as in Figure 2.1.

2.3.3 Conclusion: Two concepts of fact

To sum up, all things can be divided into two categories based on their nature of existence: fact and non-fact. However, there are two kinds of facts: fact in a broad sense and fact in a narrow sense. The concept of fact in a broad sense applies to some non-value sciences such as epistemology, which is everything that actually exists beyond thought and independent of thought, hence include "value": value actually exists independently of thought, and can be called "value fact." The concept of fact in a narrow sense can also be called "is," which is exclusive of value and is the concept opposite to value with no overlapping extension: "is" or "fact in the narrow sense" is the thing of the object that exists independently of the needs, desires, and purposes of the subject, while value is the utility of the object to the needs, desires, and purposes of the subject, which is the thing of the object that exists depending on the

96 Categories of meta-ethics

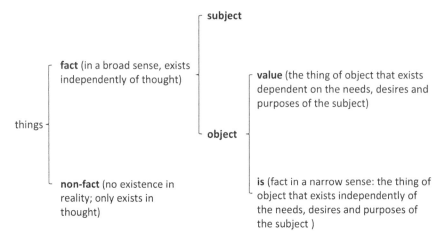

Figure 2.2 The categories of things in non-value sciences.

needs, desires and purposes of the subject. The birth of the concept of fact in the narrow sense is mainly due to the fundamental problem of value sciences—whether "value" can be derived from "fact"—which, in the final analysis, is due to the concept of fact in natural sciences, a concept that is applicable to all value sciences and natural sciences. This can be illustrated as in Figure 2.2.

Now we have completed the analysis of the categories of meta-ethics or the primitive concepts of ethics—"value," "good," "ought," "right" and "is" or "fact." When we relate these concepts and further explore their general nature—especially the relationship between "ought" and "fact," it is not difficult to discover the primitive propositions and primitive inference rules, which can be summed up in two major series of axioms and postulates, namely "the existential axioms and postulates of ethics" and "the deductive axioms and postulates of ethics," which are the objects of study in the following two chapters.

Notes

1 A. C. Ewing: *The Definition of Good,* Hyperion Press, Westport, CN, 1979, Preface.
2 *The Oxford English Dictionary*, Second Edition, p. 668.
3 Feng Youlan: *Complete Works of Sansong Tang*, Vol. 4, Henan People's Publishing House, 1986, p. 91.
4 Wolfgang Stegmüller: *The Mainstream of Contemporary Philosophy*. Translated by Wang Bingwen and others, Commercial Press, 1989, p. 329.
5 Lawrence C. Becker: *Encyclopedia of Ethics*, Volume II, Garland Publishing, Inc., New York, 1992, p. 897.
6 Feng Youlan: *Complete Works of Sansong Tang*. Vol. 4, Henan People's Publishing House, 1986, p. 98.

Primitive concept of ethics 97

7 Mencius: *Jinxin*.
8 Aristotle: *Complete Works of Aristotle*, Vol. 1, Renmin University of China Press, p. 244.
9 Bertrand Russell, *Human Society in Ethics and Politics*, China Social Sciences Press, 1992, p. 66.
10 Lawrence C. Becker. *Encyclopedia of Ethics*, Volume II, Garland Publishing, New York, 1992, p. 189.
11 Mozi: *Universal Love*.
12 Baruch Spinoza: *Ethics*, Commercial Press, Beijing, 1962, p. 165.
13 C. E. M. Joad: *Classics In Philosophy and Ethics,* Kennikat Press, London, 1960 pp. 194–199; A. C. Ewing: *The Definition of Good*, Hyperion Press, Westport, CN, 1979, pp. 112–117.
14 Also see: *Classics in Philosophy and Ethics*, p. 198, *The Definition of Good*, p. 117.
15 *The Nicomachean Ethics of Aristotle*. Translated by D.P. Chase, China Social Sciences Publishing House, Chengcheng Books, Ltd, 1990, p. 8.
16 W. D. Ross: *The Right and Good,* Clarendon Press, Oxford, 1930, p. 68.
17 W. D. Ross: *The Right and Good,* Clarendon Press, Oxford, 1930, p. 68.
18 A. C. Ewing: *Ethics,* The Free Press, New York, 1953, p. 13.
19 Aristotle: *The Nicomachean Ethics of Aristotle*. Translated by D.P. Chase, China Social Sciences Publishing House, Chengcheng Books, Ltd, 1990, pp. 10–11.
20 A. C. Ewing: *The Definition of Good*, Hyperion Press Inc, Westport, CN, 1979, pp. 148–149.
21 A. C. Ewing: *The Definition of Good*, Hyperion Press Inc, Westport, CN, 1979, p. 150.
22 A. C. Ewing: *The Definition of Good*, Hyperion Press Inc, Westport, CN, 1979, p. 117.
23 Bernard Gert: *Morality: A New proof of the Moral Rules*, Oxford University Press, New York, Oxford, 1988, p. 48.
24 Aristotle: *Aristotle's Nicomachean Ethics,* Translated by Hippocrates G. Apostle, The Peripatetic Press, Grinnell, 1984, p. 1.
25 A. C. Ewing: *The Definition of Good*, Hyperion Press Inc, Westport, CN, 1979, p. 190.
26 A. C. Ewing: *The Definition of Good*, Hyperion Press Inc, Westport, CN, 1979, p. 15.
27 Immanuel Kant: *Selected Works of Kant's Philosophy*. Commercial Press, Beijing, 1963 Edition, p. 161.
28 A. C. Ewing: *The Definition of Good*, Hyperion Press Inc, Westport, CN, 1979, p. 15.
29 William K. Frankena: *Ethics*, Prentice-Hall, Inc., Englewood Cliffs, N.J., 1973, p. 62.
30 J. L.Mackie: *Ethics: Inventing Right and Wrong*, Richard Clay Ptd Ltd, 1977, p. 59.
31 J. L.Mackie: *Ethics: Inventing Right and Wrong*, Richard Clay Ptd Ltd, Singapore, 1977, p. 59.
32 Louis P. Pojman: *Ethical Theory: Classical and Contemporary Readings*, Wadsworth Publishing Company, 1995, p. 136.
33 Moritz Schlick: *Ethical Problems*, translated by Zhang Guozhen and others, Commercial Press, Beijing, 1997, p. 29.
34 William K. Frankena: *Ethics*, Prentice-Hall, Inc., Englewood Cliffs, N.J., 1973, p. 62.

98   *Categories of meta-ethics*

35 C. E. M. Joad: *Classics in Philosophy and Ethics*, Kennikat Press, London, 1960, p. 200.
36 Burton F. Porter: *The Good Life: Alternatives in Ethics*, Macmillan, New York, 1980, p. 33.
37 A. C. Ewing: *The Definition of Good*, Hyperion Press, Inc., Westport, CN, p. 123.
38 J. L.Mackie: *Ethics: Inventing Right and Wrong*, Richard Clay Ptd Ltd, Singapore, 1977, p. 73.
39 R. M. Hare: *Essays in Ethical Theory*, Clarendon Press, Oxford, 1989, p. 179.
40 Bertrand Russell: *Human Knowledge: Its Scope and Limits*, Routledge, 2009.
41 Bertrand Russell: *Our Knowledge of the External World as a Field for Scientific Method in Philosophy.* Shanghai Translation Publishing House, 1990, p. 40.
42 Bertrand Russell: *Religion and Science*, Oxford University Press, 1974, pp. 230–231.
43 Albert Einstein, *Works of Einstein*, vol. 3, Commercial Press, 1976, p. 182.
44 Albert Einstein, *Works of Einstein*, vol. 3, Commercial Press, 1976, p. 280.
45 W. D. Hudson: *The Is–Ought Question: A Collection of Papers on the Central Problem in Moral Philosophy,* St. Martin's Press, New York, 1969, p. 11.
46 David Hume: *A Treatise of Human Nature.* The Commercial Press, 1983, p. 509.

Part II
The meta-ethical proof

3 The axiom of the existence of value and the postulate of the existence of moral value in ethics

3.1 The axiom of the essence of the existence of value and the postulate of the essence of the existence of moral value in ethics

A question pertaining to the most fundamental concepts of meta-ethics—right, ought, good, and value—in terms of the things they are said to connote, is whether they actually exist. At first glance, the question seems quite absurd: do such concepts only refer to things in our imagination? On the matter of things having value Rickert writes, "we cannot say whether [things] actually exist or not, but can only say whether [things] are meaningful or meaningless." Is what Rickert says true? Or can we assert otherwise that "right, ought, good, and value" do exist? These question concerns the essence of the existence of right, ought, good, and value, that is, the essence of the existence of value and moral value.

3.1.1 The essence of the existence of value: The property of object

Right, ought, and good belong to the category of value, and because each are utilities of the factual properties of the object to the needs, desires, and purposes of the subject, they also belong to the category of "property." Typically, however, value, right, ought and good are thought of as a kind of relationship between subject and object, hence as belonging to the category of "relationship," not "property." This view is absurd, because as we know, since Aristotle, everything has been divided into two categories: substance and property. What is a substance? Substance, according to Aristotle, in its strictest sense "can neither be described as a subject nor exists in a subject." A substance, for instance, could be an "individual man" or "horse." Yet we do often refer to the first substance of a thing in its most generic sense as a secondary substance. An individual man, for instance, belongs to the "human" species and to the genus "animal," both which are secondary substances.[1]

This means that substances are things that can exist independently, thus are the things that are unique, singular, individual, and perceptible, and are also the sum of these things, that is, as the "genus" or "species" of a single thing. The single thing is the first substance, and the genus or species of the

102   *The meta-ethical proof*

single thing is the second substance. On the contrary, properties are things that cannot exist independently but are subordinate to, and depend on, the substance, that is, as things outside of the substance (colors, emotions, psychology, etc.). Although property and substance are extremely broad concepts, as Zhu Guangqian pointed out, everything is either a substance or a property without exception: "If a concept does not belong to the category of 'noumenon,' it must belong to the category of 'property'."[2] Therefore, the view that holds that value does not belong to the category of "property" but to the category of "relationship" is absurd. Even if value is a kind of "relationship" between the subject and the object, because each thing in a "relationship" obviously cannot exist independently and must belong to certain substances, each thing thus belongs to the category of "property." If value is not the property, then it can only be the substance, but isn't it just as erroneous to regard value as belonging to substance as it is to assign value to a "relationship" between subject and object?

If right, ought, good, and value all belong to the category of property, are they the property of the object or the subject? Doesn't the definition that "right, ought, good and value are the utilities of factual properties of the object to the needs of the subject" clearly indicate that they are all the properties of the utility of the object? Indeed, the object does have value, but the subject does not. Value is the property of the object, but not the property of the subject. Take, for example, a subject–object relationship in which a person (the subject) eats bread (the object). Is it the bread or the person that has nutritional value? Obviously, it is the bread. Nutritional value is the property of the bread rather than the person. I am afraid that only a mad person would say that the person has nutritional value. By reason of this sort of subject–object relationship, R. M. Anderson says: "value does not exist in the subject, but in the object."[3] Or, as E. J. Bond puts it: "Value is in the object itself, rather than in its affecting me agreeably."[4]

But some Chinese scholars, such as Lai Jinliang, believe that not only does the object have value, the subject has value as well. He says, "If mankind has no value as a subject of value, how can he measure and judge whether the thing as the object of value has value?"[5] Indeed, everything has value. Therefore, the existent as a subject also have certain values. Let's consider the case of two individuals called John and Mary. Both have certain values, however, when we refer to these people as subjects with value, they are no longer subjects but objects. For example, when John tries to court Mary, John is the subject and Mary is the object (i.e., the object of his affection). So, for John, Mary has great value: Value is the property of the object. But, does the subject, John, also have value?

Of course he has. However, when we say that John, as the subject, also has value, it is obviously relative to Mary or to other certain needs of John. If John has value that is relative to Mary, then John, as the subject, is no longer the subject but the object of Mary: John is the object that Mary pursues. If John, however, has value out of certain other needs for himself—such as writing

The axiom of the existence of value 103

and reciting poems—John is then both the subject and the object: John, who has these needs, is the subject, while John, who can satisfy these needs, and thus himself has value, is the object. Therefore, value can only be the property of the object. It is impossible for value to be the property of the subject: once we state that existents as subjects have value, these existents are no longer the subject but the object.

If value is the property of the object, then, according to the deductive axiom of logic, all lower concepts that subordinate to the category of value, such as ought, right, and good, are undoubtedly only the properties of the object. However, from the correct premise that "ought is just a property of action, which is only the property of activity with consciousness and purpose," some scholars have drawn the wrong conclusion that "ought" is the property of the subject rather than the object; that only the subject, not the object, has the so-called ought. According to Chen Huaxing, "Ought is a pure activity of the subject activity,"[6] and Yuan Guiren writes:

> "Ought" is the ought of the subject rather than that of the object. Strictly speaking, the object itself does not have the problem of ought or ought not, it always moves, changes and develops according to the objective laws, and there is only the question of "is" or "will be."[7]

According to this view, "ought" does not belong to the categories of good and value, but is contrary to them where ought is said to be the property of the subject, and value and good are said to be the properties of the object. Thence, it follows, an "ought" judgment cannot be a value judgment. Clearly, this exposes what is wrong with this argument. Although conscious and purposeful activities can only be the actions or activities of the subject, all activities or actions of the subject do entail some object and so are a duality of subject and object: while the activity of a subject is the property of the subject, and hence belongs to the category of the subject, the activity is also the object of the subject so it is also the property of the object, and hence belongs to the category of object. The argument is also flawed because it is possible for a subject to understand and evaluate an action before and after it acts: if the action can achieve a purpose, and thus as it ought to be, the subject will engage it. Thence the action has a dual relationship with the subject: on the one hand, since it is the subject doing the action, the action belongs to the category of subject; on the other hand, since the action is the object of the understanding and evaluation of the subject, that is, whether the action ought or ought not to be done, the action belongs to the category of object.

For example, I am an autonomous agent, and so am a subject who does winter swimming. This is undoubtedly an activity I do as a subject, hence, as my activity, winter swimming is a property of a subject. However, before and after my swim I may consider and evaluate my activity of winter swimming: Should or should I not swim in winter? Thus, the activity in question becomes the object of my understanding and evaluation, and is the object belonging to the

104   *The meta-ethical proof*

category of object. When I am sure that winter swimming meets my purpose of being healthy and living a long life, and is what I ought to do, I persist with it. Therefore, the statement "I swim in the winter" is fundamentally different from "I ought to swim in the winter." "I swim in the winter" is the activity and property of the subject, belonging to the category of subject; while "I ought to swim in the winter" is the object of the understanding and evaluation of the subject, belonging to the category of object.

Obviously, the mistake in holding that "ought" is the "activity and property of the subject" lies in equating "action" ("I swim in the winter") with "the property of the action that ought or ought not to be" ("I ought to swim in the winter"), thus asserting that "the action that ought or ought not to be" is the activity and property of the subject from the premise that "action is the activity and property of the subject." However, despite that action is the activity of the subject belonging to the property of the subject, the action of the subject also can be the object of the evaluation of the subject and becomes object: the utility of an action which is consistent with the purpose of the subject is *ought*, while the utility of an action which is not consistent with the purpose of the subject is *ought not*. Therefore, the property of action that is *ought* or *ought not* is the utility of action as object to the purpose of the subject. Consequently, although "action" is the activity of the subject, and thus belongs to the category of the subject, "the property of the action that ought or ought not to be" is the utility of action as the object, no matter whether it conforms to the purpose of the subject, and hence belongs to the category of object.

3.1.2 The essence of the existence of value: The relational property and tertiary qualities of the object

Ought, good, and value are all properties of the object, but do they belong to the "primary qualities" of the object, such as the size and mass of a substance, or do they belong to the "secondary qualities" of the object, such as weight and color? Or are they "intrinsic properties" that exist independently of the subject, or the "relational properties" that exist dependent on the subject? The key to any further confirmation of the essence of the existence of ought, good, and value is the study of the types of "property." First published in 1950, Stephen Edelston Toulmin begins his metaphysics classic, *The Place of Reason in Ethics*, with three types of property; however, for the verification of the nature of existence of ought, good, and value, he divides properties, in the tradition of Moore, into pure nature and compound nature, which is unscientific.[8] The nature of the existence of ought, good and value has nothing to do with pure or compound nature. As C. D. Broad states, it concerns "relational properties or pure properties" or, to be more exact, "relational" or "intrinsic" properties of the object.[9]

The so-called intrinsic property is the property that a thing uniquely possesses. A thing has its own intrinsic property regardless of whether it is by

The axiom of the existence of value   105

itself or in relation to other things. As Marx put it, this property "is not caused by the relationship between this thing and other things, but only manifested in this relationship."[10] The so-called relational property is the property that emerges when the intrinsic property of the object is related to other things. Therefore, a thing itself does not have a relational property; only when it has a relationship with other things does it have a relational property. For example, while the mass of an object is unrelated to gravity, and thus is an intrinsic property of the object, weight is a property that emerges with the force or acceleration of gravity on the object. The object itself does not have weight, so weight is the relational property of an object.

Take, as another example, electromagnetic waves and color. An object has a certain length of electromagnetic waves in terms of both the object itself and in relation to the light our eyes can detect. Thus, the length of the electromagnetic wave is the intrinsic property of the object. Conversely, color is a property that emerges when an object's electromagnetic wave reaches our eyes. The object itself does not have color. In general, electromagnetic waves with a wavelength of 760 to 400 nm are detected by cones in the eye which send a signal to the brain converting light to color. For example, an electromagnetic wave with the wavelength of 590 to 560 nm generates yellow, and an electromagnetic wave with the wavelength of 560 to 500 nm generates green. The object itself does not have color. Thus, color is the relational property of an object.

Like yellow, green, and other colors, ought, good, and value are the relational properties of the object. However, ought, good, and value, as mentioned above, are the utilities of the object to the needs of the subject, and thus are properties of an object that exist independently. Then what is the difference between colors and values, or yellow and good? Understanding this difference is key to revealing the essence of the existence of values, which has been much debated among meta-ethicists from Moore to Toulmin. The best way to settle this problem is probably to compare the relationships of three types of properties, namely intrinsic properties, relational properties, and factual properties.

Let's first consider factual and intrinsic properties. The factual property and intrinsic property of an object are not the same concept. Like the intrinsic property, the so-called factual property of an object exists independently of the needs of the subject, but it can also be dependent on other things of the subject, and thereby intersects with the so-called relational property instead of the intrinsic property. Color, taste, and sound are such properties that are independent of the needs of the subject, but still exist dependent on the subject: color depends on the eyes of the subject, taste depends on the tongue of the subject, and sound depends on the ears of the subject. Therefore, color, taste, and sound are the factual properties and the relational properties of an object. On the contrary, the intrinsic property of an object certainly is the factual property of the object. The intrinsic property is the property that a thing has alone. This is to say, the intrinsic properties of an object, such as

106 *The meta-ethical proof*

mass, and the length of the electromagnetic wave, are properties that exist independently of anything of the subject, and hence are properties that exist independently of the needs of the subject. These are therefore also the factual properties of an object.

Therefore, the intrinsic property of an object and the factual property of an object are subordinate relations of genus and species: all intrinsic properties of an object are factual properties of the object; but the factual properties of an object can either be intrinsic properties or relational properties of the object. More precisely, the factual properties of an object are mainly the intrinsic properties of the object, such as mass, and the length of the electromagnetic wave, which exist independently of a subject, but also include the relational properties of the object such as color, taste, and sound that exist dependent on the subject. Are then all the relational properties of an object also the factual property of the object? The answer is no. This is because value is the property of an object that exists dependent on a subject. Hence, it is a relational property not factual property. The relational property and the factual property of the object can best be described as a cross-relationship: On the one hand, some of the factual properties of the object such as color are the relational properties of the object, while some factual properties such as electromagnetic wavelengths are not relational properties; on the other hand, some of the relational properties of the object such as color are the factual properties of the object, while some of the relational properties such as value, are not factual properties.

Therefore, red, yellow, and other colors, as well as ought, good, and value are all relational properties rather than intrinsic properties of the object. However, red, yellow, and other colors are the relational properties that exist independently of the needs of the subject and are factual properties of the object. On the contrary, ought, good, and value are the relational properties that exist dependent on the subject's needs and hence are the value properties of the object. Value, therefore, as Perry articulates well, can be defined "as a particular relationship between any interest and its object; or, rather, it is such a property of an object that renders the interest to it satisfied."[11]

Thus, all properties can be divided into three categories after two divisions. The first division is based on whether the property of a thing depends on the relationship between the thing and other things whereby it is divided into intrinsic properties and relational properties. The second division is based on whether the property depends on the needs of the subject whereby the relational property is further divided into two categories: value (property of value relation) and fact (property of factual relation). Therefore, all properties are divided into three categories: (1) intrinsic properties or intrinsic factual properties, e.g., mass and electromagnetic wavelengths; (2) the factual property of relation or the property of factual relation, e.g., red and yellow; and (3) the property of value relation, e.g., right, ought, and good, which can be shown as in Figure 3.1.

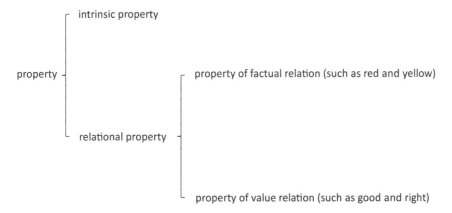

Figure 3.1 The categories of property.

It is not difficult to see that the objectivity and fundamentality of these three properties are different and diminishing in order. Intrinsic factual properties (mass, electromagnetic wavelengths, etc.) are things that exist completely independent of other things, and are therefore completely objective, so we can call them "primary qualities" as Locke had also termed them. Factual relational properties (red, yellow, etc.) are the products of the relationship between the intrinsic properties or the primary qualities of the object and a certain objective organ of the subject, such as the eyes. In other words, these are produced by primary properties but exist dependently on a certain organ of the subject; they are neither independent nor completely objective, so, to use Locke's term, we can call them "secondary qualities." Value relational properties (ought, good, etc.) are the products of the interactions between the factual properties of an object—the primary and secondary qualities—and some subjective things of the subject, such as desires, wishes, and purposes. These are produced by primary and secondary qualities but exist dependently on certain subjective things of the subject; therefore, they are the less independent and less objective things. We can call them "tertiary qualities" just as Samuel Alexander and George Santayana termed them.

The distinction between "good" and "yellow" lies in the difference of the substances to which they belong, namely the primary qualities or secondary qualities which are the basis in which they emerge: The substance of good is the broader factual property of the object and thus may be either a "primary quality" or a "secondary quality," while the substance of yellow is the narrower intrinsic property of the object, and thus is only a "primary quality." To reiterate, colors are the result of the relationship between the property of the object which is independent of the subject (the electromagnetic wave length) and the subject, and thus are the intrinsic properties of an object

108   *The meta-ethical proof*

and the result of the relationship between "primary qualities" and the subject. Conversely, good or ought are value properties that emerge from the interactions between "the property of an object that exist independently of the needs, desires and purposes of the subject" and "the needs, desires and purposes of the subject," which is the utility of the factual relation of the object (that is, its "primary qualities" and "secondary qualities") to the needs, desires, and purposes of the subject.

On the other hand, the distinction between good and yellow also lies in the different properties of the subjects that they depend on. Yellow is the result of the relationship between an object and a certain "objective thing" of the subject (i.e., the physiological organ of the eye); on the contrary, good is the result of the relationship between an object and some "subjective things" of the subject (i.e., the subject's psychological needs, desires, and purposes). In short, without the subject, both good and colors cannot exist. However, colors can exist without the needs, desires, and purposes of the subject. Hence, it belongs to the category of "facts" as a secondary quality of an object. On the contrary, the existence of good depends on the needs, desires and purposes of the subject, belonging to the category of "value" as a tertiary quality of the object.

3.1.3 Conclusion: The axiom of the essence of the existence of value and the postulate of the essence of the existence of moral value

Based on the comparison between the essence of the existence of color and value, we can see that the essence of the value of "ought" or "good," like the essence of the color of "red" or "yellow," is the same in the sense that they are relational properties of the object existing in the object. However, colors are properties of an object that exists independently of the needs of the subject, that is, colors are properties that an object has regardless of the interaction between the subject's needs and the object, and thus are the factual properties of the object, as well as the properties of the factual relations of the object, otherwise known as its "secondary qualities." Conversely, ought, good, and value are the properties of the object that cannot exist without the needs of the subject, that is, they only emerge when the subject' needs interacts with factual properties of the object. In this respect, they are the utilities of the factual properties of the object to the needs, desires, and purposes of the subject, as well as the properties of the value relations of the object, otherwise known as the "tertiary qualities" of the object. In short, good and ought belong to the category of value and red and yellow belong to the category of fact. Though colors and electromagnetic waves differ from each other as "primary qualities" and "secondary qualities," both belong to the category of fact which is opposite to value, and constitute two parts of fact: color is the property of the factual relation of the object, while the electromagnetic wave is the property of the intrinsic fact of the object. Consequently, we can draw a number of conclusions.

Ought, good and *value* and *is* or *fact* are properties of an object that exist in the object. *Is* or *fact* is the property of an object that is independent of the needs of the subject: it is the property of an object irrespective of whether it is related to the needs of the subject, as well as the intrinsic property or the property of the factual relation of an object, and the "primary quality" or "secondary quality" of an object. Conversely, *Ought, good*, and *value* are the property of an object that depends on the needs of the subject: They are the property that emerge when the *fact* of the object is related to the needs, desires, and purposes of the subject, as well as the utility of the *fact* to the needs, desires, and purposes of the subject, and the relational property of the object, namely the property of the value relation of the object, which, in the final analysis, is the "tertiary quality" of the object. This is the essence of the existence of *ought, good*, and *value*. In short, it is the essence of the existence of value, which is "the axiom of the essence of the existence of value in ethics" applicable to all fields of ought, good, and value.

For example, the shape and color of peony and the beauty of peony are all properties of peony. However, its shape and color is the "is (fact)" of peony: as the properties of peony its shape and its color are independent of human needs—that is, exist regardless of whether its shape and color appeals to human's needs—as intrinsic properties and properties of factual relations, which can also be respectively called "primary qualities" and "secondary qualities" of peony. Conversely, the beauty of peony is the "value" of peony, and is a property of the peony that depends on the needs of people—that is, it emerges when the shape and color of peony appeals to human needs—which is the utility of the shape and color of peony to human needs, desires and purposes, and the property of the value relation of peony, belonging to "tertiary qualities" of peony.

The axiom of the essence of the existence of value in ethics reflects the "universal essence of the existence of all ought, good and value" which is applicable to all value sciences, such as stateology (the value science concerning the goodness and badness of state institutions) and Chinaology (the value science concerning goodness and badness of the Chinese state institutions). Therefore, the axiom of the essence of the existence of value in ethics is also the axiom of the essence of existence of value in all value sciences. If we deduce the axiom to the fields of moral value, moral good, and moral ought, we would then discover the essence of the existence of moral ought, moral good, and moral value, namely "the postulate of the essence of the existence of moral value in ethics." The postulate, however, is only applicable to ethics, since, according to Aristotle and Euclid, "Axioms are the common truths of all sciences, and postulates are only the first principles accepted by a science."[12]

What exactly is the postulate of the essence of the existence of moral value? In the field of moral value, it is that society is the agent that makes moral norms, and hence is a subject; the purpose for which it makes moral norms (namely the goal of morality) is the purpose of activities of society as a subject. The object therefore is all the actions in society that can be morally

110 *The meta-ethical proof*

evaluated and regulated by morality. Thence, if we deduce the axiom of the essence of the existence in ethics to the fields of moral ought, moral good, and moral value, there are several conclusions that can be drawn. The moral ought, moral good, and moral value of behavior that "ought to be" and "behavioral fact" are both properties that exist in behavior, however, there are fundamental differences. The "behavioral fact" is the property of the behavior that is independent of the goal of morality: It is the property behavior that exists irrespective of whether it is related to the goal of morality, as well as the intrinsic property or the property of the factual relation of the behavior, and are "primary qualities" or "secondary qualities" of behavior. Conversely, the moral good, moral ought, and moral value of behavior that "ought to be" are the properties of behavior that depend on the goal of morality: they are the properties that emerge when the behavioral facts are related to the goal of morality, as well as are the utilities of the "behavioral facts" to the goal of morality, and are the relational property of the behavior, namely the property of the value relation of the behavior, which, in the final analysis, are the "tertiary qualities" of the behavior. This is the essence of the existence of moral ought, moral good, and moral value, and the "postulate of the essence of the existence of the moral value in ethics."

For example, both "ought to be honest" and "honesty" are properties of honest behaviors. But "honesty" is the property of honest behavior alone, which is independent of the goal of morality, that is to say, it exists whether or not it is related to the goal of morality. Thus, it is the intrinsic property or the property of the factual relation of honest behavior, as either one of the "primary qualities" or "secondary qualities" of honest behavior. Conversely, "ought to be honest" is not the property of the honest behavior alone, but the property of honest behavior that exists dependently on the goal of morality. It is the property that emerges when the honest behavior relates to the goal of morality, and is also the utility of honest behavior conforming to the goal of morality (the safeguarding of the existence and development of society and the promotion of everyone's interests), and is the property of the value relation of the honest behavior and the "tertiary qualities" of the honest behavior.

3.2 The axiom of the structure of the existence of value in ethics and the postulate of the structure of the existence of moral value in ethics

3.2.1 Substance and standard: The structure of the existence of value

The essence of the existence of value (i.e., *ought, good,* and *value* are the property of an object that depends on the needs of the subject, and the property that emerge when the *fact* of the object is related to the needs, desires and purposes of the subject, as well as the utility of the *fact* of the object to the needs, desires and purposes of the subject, and the relational property of the object) shows that without the needs, desires, and purpose of the subject,

The axiom of the existence of value 111

the object itself has no ought, good, and value; only when the factual properties of the object are related to the needs, desires, and purposes of the subject can the object have ought, good and value. Therefore, the existence of "ought," "good," and "value" consists of two aspects: The factual properties of the object and the needs, desires, and purposes of the subject. The factual property of the object is the source from which "ought," "good," or "value" emerge and is the substance for their existence (simply called the substance of ought, good, or value); the needs, desires and purposes of the subject are the conditions of the emergence of "ought," "good," and "value," and are the value standard for the measurement of the factual property of the object (simply termed the standard of ought, good, or value). This is the structure of the existence of value, good, ought, and other such ethical concepts such as "right." In short, it is the "structure of the existence of value" which is of extreme importance in the value sciences and is the key to unlocking Hume's guillotine. Let's take some examples.

(1) The beauty of the peony is the utility of the peony to people's aesthetic needs; without this need peonies themselves do not have beauty as we usually understand it. It is only when the peony's factual properties such as its shape and colors are related to people's aesthetic needs that it is deemed beautiful. Therefore, the peony's "beauty" consists of the peony's factual properties such as its colors and people's aesthetic needs: the factual properties are the source from which the beauty of the peony emerges, and are the substance of the existence of its beauty, which can be called the "substance of the peony's beauty." People's aesthetic needs are then the condition for the emergence and existence of the beauty of the peony, and are also the value standard for measurement of the factual property of the beauty of the shapes and colors of the peony, which can be called the "standard of the peony's beauty."

(2) The nutritional value of eggs is the utility of eggs to people's dietary needs. Without people's dietary needs eggs themselves do not have nutritional value; it is only when the factual properties of eggs, such as protein and yolk, are related to people's dietary needs that we can say that eggs have nutritional value. Thus, the nutritional value of eggs consists of factual properties and people's dietary needs: the factual properties of eggs, such as protein and yolk are the source and substance of the nutritional value of eggs, while people's dietary needs are the condition and standard of the existence of the nutritional value of eggs.

(3) The recommendation that we "ought" to have a moderate diet is the utility of the behavior of following a moderate diet to people's need for a healthy and long life. Without people's needs for a healthy and long life, the behavior of following a moderate diet itself does not have the property of "ought"; it is only when the behavioral fact of a moderate diet relates to people's needs for health and longevity that it can have the property of "ought." Thus, the existence of the property of "ought" in this instance

112 *The meta-ethical proof*

is composed of the factual property of the behavior of following a moderate diet and people's need for a healthy and long life: The factual property of a moderate diet is the source and substance of the property of the "ought" of following a moderate diet, while people's need for a healthy and long life is the condition and standard of the existence of the property of the "ought" of following a moderate diet.

It can be seen that any value is nothing but the utility of the object to the needs, desires, and purpose of the subject, consisting of two aspects: The factual property of the object and the needs, desires, and purposes of the subject. The factual property of the object is the source from which value emerges and the substance for its existence, which can be called the "substance of value"; the needs, desires, and purpose of the subject are the condition that value emerge from the factual properties of the object, which are the standards for the measurement of the factual properties of the object, and hence can be called the "standard of value." As Protagora pointed out, in the field of value, "mankind is the measurement of everything." To be more exact, however, it is the needs, desires, and purposes of the subject that are the measurement of everything.

3.2.2 Reality and potentiality: The duality of the structure of the existence of value

When we further examine the structure of the existence of ought, good, and value, we can see that some of the factual properties of the object are known to the subject and some are not. The factual properties of the object that are known to the subject, can be called the "real substance" of value, good, or ought, for the utility to the subject's needs is realistic. The factual properties of the object that are not yet known to the subject, can be called the "potential substance" of value, good, or ought, for the utility to the subject's needs is potential. For example, iron ores and oil fields, before being discovered, have potential utility for humans, so are a potential substance of value and good. Once discovered, iron ores and oil fields are a real substance of value and good, for their utility to humans is realistic.

Similarly, the standard of ought, good, and value also have the distinctions of being real and potential. This is because all the purposes of a subject emerge from its needs and desires: All the purposes of a subject are to satisfy its needs and desires; conversely, all the needs and desires of a subject to be satisfied are also its purposes. Thus "purposes" and "needs and desires to be satisfied" actually mean the same thing, so it logically follows that not all the needs and desires of a subject lead to actions and purposes. The needs and desires that trigger actions and purposes are the "needs and desires to be satisfied," and hence are the purpose, which can be called "real needs and desires," or rather "effective needs," while the needs and desires that do not trigger actions and purposes are not the "needs and desires to be satisfied,"

The axiom of the existence of value   113

and not the purpose, which can be called "potential needs and desires," or rather "ineffective needs."

For example, a young man focused on studies to be admitted into a doctoral program thinks that having a girlfriend would be a distraction from this purpose. While he does have a need and desire for a girlfriend it does not trigger the actions and purpose of finding a girlfriend. Thus, it is not a need and desire to be satisfied, nor the young man's purpose, but a potential need and desire or simply an ineffective need. However, when he is finally admitted into the doctoral program the need and desire for a girlfriend triggers the actions and purpose of finding a girlfriend, which is a need and desire to be satisfied, i.e., the purpose, and hence a real need and desire or effective need.

The purpose is the real need and desire, so it is a real and substantial standard that measures the value and ought of the factual properties of an object. It is the real standard of ought, good, and value. What we may call "unpurposed" needs and desires are potential needs and desires, and therefore are the potential standards of measuring the value and ought of the factual properties of an object, and are the potential standards of measuring ought, good, and value.

> The young man we mentioned above had a need and desire for a girlfriend and a need and desire to get into a doctoral program. However, in the years preparing for the Ph.D. entrance examination, his need and desire for a girlfriend was suppressed and consequently remained in a state of potential. The time spent finding a girlfriend and developing a relationship would have gone against his purpose of getting admitted to a doctoral program, so it was something he ought not to realize; nevertheless the potential of a girlfriend conformed to his unpurposed need for a girlfriend, so potentially finding a girlfriend was something he ought to realize. Therefore, his purpose to pass the examination for a doctoral program, namely the real need and desire, was the real standard for measuring the ought or ought-not of his actions; the unpurposed need for a girlfriend, namely a potential need and desire, was only a potential value standard for the ought or ought-not of his actions.

3.2.3 Conclusion: The axiom of the structure of the existence of value and the postulate of the structure of the existence of moral value

To sum up:

> ought, good, and value are the utilities of the fact of the object to the needs, desires and purpose of the subject, hence consist of two aspects: The factual properties of the object and the needs, desires, and purposes of the subject. The factual properties of the object are the source from which ought, good, and value emerge and are the carrier, noumenon, and substance for their existence, simply referred to as the substance of ought,

114   *The meta-ethical proof*

good, or value, while the needs, desires, and purposes of the subject are the conditions for the emergence of ought, good, and value, which are the measurements of the existence of the value or good of the factual properties, and are called the standard of ought, good, and of value—the purpose is the "real standard of value," while unpurposed needs and desires are the "potential standard of value."

This is the structure of the existence of ought, good, and value, in short, the structure of the existence of value, namely "the axiom of the structure of the existence of value in ethics," which is universally applicable to every field of ought, good, and value, and, in the final analysis, is "the axiom of the structure of the existence of value in the value sciences" which is universally applicable, for instance, to ethics, stateology, and Chinaology, all of which are concerned with the goodness and badness of state institutions.

For example, the use value of a commodity is the marginal utility of the factual properties of the commodity to people's consumption needs, desires, and purposes, hence is composed of the factual properties of the commodity and the needs, desires and purposes of people's consumption: The factual property of a commodity is the source from which the use value emerges and is the carrier, noumenon, and substance of its existence, and is called the "substance of use value," while people's needs and desires regarding consumption are the conditions for the emergence and existence of the use value of a commodity from the factual property of the commodity, which is the standard for the measurement of the existence of the use value of the factual property of the commodity, and is called the "standard of the use value of a commodity."

Although the commodity owner has the needs and desires to consume the commodity he owns, and the commodity is also able to satisfy his consumption needs and desires, the purpose of producing the commodity is nevertheless for exchange rather than for one's own consumption. Therefore, in reality, for him, the commodity has no use value, it has only exchange value; the use value is only a potential. As Marx stated: "The commodity of the commodity owner has no direct use value to him. All commodities are non-use value for their owners."[13] To be more comprehensive, the purpose (exchange) of a commodity for the owner is the real standard of the commodity's value, so, in real terms, for him, the commodity has no use value, it only has exchange value; the commodity owner's unpurposed needs and desires (consumption) are the potential standard of the commodity value, so, potentially, the commodity also has use value: The use value is merely a potential for the owner.

In the field of moral value, society is the agent that makes moral norms, and hence is a subject; the purpose for which it makes moral norms (namely the goal of morality) is the purpose of society's activities as a subject. The object therefore is all the actions in society that can be morally evaluated and regulated by morality. So, if the "axiom of the nature of the existence of value in ethics," which is universally applicable to all fields of the ought, good, and

The axiom of the existence of value 115

value, is deduced to the field of the moral ought, moral good and moral value, we can draw the following conclusion:

The moral ought, moral good, and moral value of the behavior that ought to be are the utilities of the behavioral facts to the goal of morality, hence consist of two aspects: The "behavioral fact" and the "goal of morality." The behavioral facts are the source from which the behavior that ought to be emerges and are the carrier, noumenon, and substance of its existence, which can be termed the "substance of moral ought" or the "substance of moral good," and, in the final analysis, is the "substance of moral value"; the goal of morality is the condition for the emergence and existence of the behavior that ought to be from the behavioral fact, and is the standard of the measurement of the existence of moral value of the behavioral fact, which can be termed "the standard of moral value" or "the standard of moral good," and, in the final analysis, is "the standard of morality." This is the structure of the existence of moral ought, moral good, and moral value, in short, is the structure of the existence of moral value, namely the postulate of the structure of the existence of the moral value of ethics, which is only applicable to ethics.

For example, "ought to be honest" is the utility of the fact of honest behavior to the goal of morality—to safeguard the existence and development of society and promote everyone's interests—and, hence, consists of the fact of honest behavior and the goal of morality: the fact of honest behavior is the source of the emergence of "ought to be honest" and the carrier, noumenon, and substance for its existence, which, in the final analysis, is the substance of the moral value of "ought to be honest," while the goal of morality is the condition for the emergence and existence of "ought to be honest," which is the standard for the measurement of the existence of the moral value of the fact of honest behavior, which, in the final analysis, is the standard of the moral value of "ought to be honest."

In other words, the fact of honest behavior is the substance of the moral value of "ought to be honest," while the goal of morality is the standard of the moral value of "ought to be honest," which implies that not all honesty is an ought: honesty is an ought only under the condition that it conforms to the goal of morality; if it violates the goal of morality it is an "ought not." Take the example Kant gave us: if a murderer asks me whether his intended victim is in my house, I certainly ought not to be honest but ought to lie that he is not.[14]

Clearly, when the murderer makes the inquiry, the good of "honesty" conflicts with the good of "saving a life." If I am honest, he will be murdered, so I lie and he survives. In this situation, honesty is a small good, while saving a life is a great good; lying is a small evil, while killing is a great evil. If being honest causes the death of the victim, its net balance is to harm him and violates the ultimate goal of morality, hence one ought not be honest. Conversely, if merely lying can save his life, its net balance benefits him because it conforms to the goal of morality, and hence he ought to lie. Mencius was right when said: "The virtuous man does not have to keep his word, his every

116 *The meta-ethical proof*

action merely ought to comply with rightness."[15] Otherwise, to avoid a small evil (lying) and commit a greater evil (killing), or to attain a small good (being honest) and lose a greater good (saving a life), the net balance harms the victim, which violates the goal of morality and is an immoral act: "to keep every word so as to be honest, obviously is the actions of a virtueless man."[16]

3.3 The axiom of the nature of the existence of value and the postulate of the nature of the existence of moral value in ethics

3.3.1 *The nature of the existence of value: Particularity and universality*

It was said Spinoza was under a tree one day when he discovered that there are no two pieces of leaves that are completely the same, and from this he realized that everything had its particularity. However, he neglected the other side of the issue, namely there are also no two completely different pieces of leaves. All things have their commonality and universality. Universality is the property that all things of a kind have, and it is the commonality of one kind of thing. Conversely, particularity is the property that some things of a kind have; it is what makes some things of a kind different from one another. For example, the human "species" has a love of delicious food and a love of games. These are "properties" belonging to all humans, and thus are universal human traits. On the contrary, the preference for eating carrots over cabbage, or the preference for playing cards rather than playing tennis, is the "property" of some and not others, and hence is a particular human trait.

Accordingly, the particular ought, good or value is that which exists for some individuals or subjects of a kind but not for others. Thus, there is great variation as to what ought to be, is good, or has value, such that for some subjects a thing has value but for other subjects it is valueless, or even bad in that it has negative value. Conversely, a universal ought, good, or value exists for all the subjects of a kind. Thus, there is no variation as to what ought to be, is good, or has value, such that a thing has value to every subject.

For example, chrysanthemums have value for many people, especially for the famous ancient Chinese poet Tao Yuanming who wrote a lot of poetry in praise of the flower; however, they do not have value for everyone, especially for those who are allergic to them. Therefore, the value of chrysanthemums is particular. Conversely, *beauty* has value for all people regardless of whether they are allergic to chrysanthemums, so it can be said that the value of beauty is universal.

It is not difficult to see that the distinction of the universality and particularity of ought, good, and value first emerges from the distinction of the universality and particularity of the needs of the subject (and the various forms of transformation of the needs in the subject's consciousness, such as desires and purposes). The particular needs of the subject refer to the different needs of the subjects of a kind, that is, the needs that only some subjects of a kind have; the so-called universal needs of the subject are also

The axiom of the existence of value 117

the common needs of a kind of subject, which are the same needs for all subjects within that kind.

Take our food preferences for example. Some like to eat cabbage and some like to eat carrot. The preference of either food source simply belongs to a different type of human need and is therefore a particular need of the subject. However, no matter the different needs of the human species regarding taste or nutrition, everyone has the same need of delicious food, which is the common need of the human species, and hence is the universal need of the subject.

The particular ought, good, and value are the utilities of the factual properties of the object for satisfying particular needs of the subject. Since what they satisfy are the particular needs of the subject, ought, good, and value are different for different subjects. The universal ought, good, and value are the utilities of the factual properties of the object to the universal needs of the subject. Since what they satisfy are the universal needs of the subject, ought, good, and value are the same for any subject, thus never vary for the different subjects of that kind.

Why is the value of a chrysanthemum particular? Why is it of value for some people, but not for others? Isn't it because its factual properties, its shape, colors, and scent, satisfy the particular needs of some subjects? The pleasures of the shape, color, and scent of chrysanthemums are the needs of only certain people. On the contrary, why is the value of beauty universal? Why does beauty have value to any subject? Because the factual properties of a beautiful object, such that it has "proportional harmony," satisfies the universal needs of all human subjects: all people have a love of beautiful things.

Then, what kinds of objects have particular value which can satisfy the particular needs of some subjects? Obviously, it can only be the universal objects and the universal facts of the objects. And what kinds of objects have universal value which can satisfy the universal needs of the subject? Similarly, it can only be the particular facts of the object and particular objects. However, all universalities exist in particularity and all particularities contain universality. "Food," as a universal object, certainly exists in the "cabbage" or "carrot" and the "cabbage" or "carrot," as particular objects, certainly also contain the universal object "food."

Therefore, the factual properties of a particular object, such as the cabbage or carrot, have a particular good and a particular value for they have particular tastes that can satisfy the particular needs of the subjects. They also contain the universal object of "food," which, on being digested and absorbed by the subject, has the function of metabolism (along with other universal factual properties) that satisfies the universal needs of nutrition and survival. Thus, cabbages and carrots have universal value and universal good. However, the universal factual properties of food are certainly contained in particular objects, such as the particular color and taste of a carrot which can satisfy the particular needs of the subject's love of carrot, and thus food has a particular value or good.

118 *The meta-ethical proof*

Generally speaking, it can be concluded that *ought*, *good*, and *value* are particular and universal since both the "standard of value" (the needs, desires, and purposes of the subject) and the "substance of value" (the factual properties of the object) are particular and universal. The utility of the particular fact of an object to satisfy the particular needs of a subject is a particular *ought*, *good*, or *value* for they are good or valuable or an ought only for a subject with this kind of particular need. Conversely, the utility of universal fact of an object to satisfy the universal needs of a subject is universal *ought*, *good*, or *value* for they are good or valuable or an ought for all subjects.

Put another way, "ought," "good," and "value" have both particularity and universality, because "ought," "good" and "value" are the utilities of the object to the needs, desires and purposes of the subject, consisting of two aspects: the "factual property of the object (the substance of value)" and the "needs, desire and purposes of the subject (the standard of value)." On the one hand, ought, good, and value are determined by the particular needs, desires, and purposes of the subject and the particular fact of the object: They have particularity only for subjects with certain needs. On the other hand, they are also determined by the universal needs, desires, and purposes of the subject and the universal fact of the object: They have universality for every subject. This is the principle of universality and particularity of the existence of "ought," "good," and "value." In short, it is the principle of universality and particularity of the existence of value.

3.3.2 *The nature of the existence of value: Relativity and absoluteness*

The particularity and universality of ought, good, and value are closely related to their relativity and absoluteness: all particularity are relativity and all absoluteness are universality. This is because absoluteness, i.e., unconditionality, is something that does not vary with conditions, it remains the same for any object all the time; on the contrary, relativity is conditional, it is something that varies under different conditions. For example, as matter/substance, Cao Xueqin is absolute for he is matter/substance under any conditions. Although Cao Xueqin was the author of the famous novel Dream of the Red Chamber, he was also a father, husband, and someone's son in the years lived 1715–1763. So, his actual life or existence was relative in that he lived and died at a certain time in history and under certain conditions. In short, he was of his time. Hence, while as matter/substance, Cao Xueqin is absolute, it is also relative to his lived experience such that to his parents he was only ever a son.

The so-called absolute ought, good, and value are the unconditional ought, good, and value which exist at any time for any individual subject of a kind; on the contrary, relative ought, good and value are conditional ought, good, and value which exist only for some individuals of a kind, or for any individual for a certain period of time. For example, the value of food is absolute because it has value to anyone all the time. Conversely, a food source, such as beef, is relative (as are cabbages and carrots) because it only has value for some

The axiom of the existence of value   119

people (e.g. taste, certain dietary needs). Relativity applies to human subject–object relations as well. The desire for a lover, for instance, which is somewhat different from the relativity of the food source beef, is not only conditional, it also only has relative value for humans once they are of a sexual age.

It is not difficult to see that all particular ought, good, and value are relative because they exist only for some individuals of a kind but not for others; for other subjects they can be valueless, an ought-not, even bad in that they have negative value. For example, pork has both particular and relative value for those who need pork, but for those who have no need for pork, or for those who deem that eating pork is bad, such as Muslim people, it has no value.

Does this mean then that all universal ought, good, and value are absolute? The answer is negative. Let's consider the value of the so-called object to human beings. Universal value undoubtedly is the value that has value for all people, so it exists without conditions for its object, while absolute value also exists without conditions for its object it also has no conditions of time, so it is the value that exists for all people at all times. Therefore, all absolute values are universal values, while not all universal values are absolute values: Objects that have absolute value exists for all people through all times. So, as not to confuse the terms, we might say they have "absolute universal value," which is conceptually no different from what is meant by "absolute value."

For example, ancient philosophers used to say that "both the desire for food and sexual desire are human nature," but their values are actually not the same. Food has not only value for everyone, thus has universal value, it also has value for everyone at any time, thus has absolute value. In regard to the matter of sexual desire, while we can say that having a lover, generally speaking, has value for everyone, thus is a universal value, it does not, however, have absolute value. Clearly, it is a relative value with conditions, for although it has value for everyone, it does not have value for everyone at any time. Since children do not have sexual needs, it only has relative value for humans who have reached sexual maturity. Doesn't the saying "life is dear, love is dearer" sound ridiculous to a child?

The distinction between relative and absolute ought, good and value first emerges from the relative and absolute needs, desires, and purposes of the subject. The so-called absolute needs of the subject are the universal needs of any individual of a kind. These needs occur at any time, such as the human need for games, food, art, or leisure. The so-called relative needs of a subject (e.g., the need for beef) are only the needs of some individuals of a kind, or are the needs of humans (e.g., sexual needs) only at certain times or under certain conditions.

The ought, good, or value that satisfy the absolute needs of the subject are the same ought, good, and value for all subjects every time, thus are absolute. On the contrary, the ought, good, and value that satisfy the relative needs of the subject are different because of different subjects or different needs of the subject at different times, so they are only an ought, a good, or value for the subjects who have these needs, hence are relative.

120　*The meta-ethical proof*

Why is the value or good of food absolute? Obviously because the satisfaction of food meets people's absolute needs and because anyone at any time has the need for food. Why is the value or good of beef relative, or the value or good of a sexual relationship relative? It is undoubtedly because they satisfy people's relative needs: Only some people have a need to eat beef, and only those of sexual age have sexual desires.

Then what kind of objects that satisfy the relative and particular needs of the subject are relative value, good and ought? What kind of objects that satisfy the absolute needs of the subject are absolute value, good and ought? Undoubtedly, only the object with absoluteness can satisfy the absolute need of the subject; and only the object with relativity can satisfy the relative need of the subject. However, both absoluteness and universality exist in relativity and particularity, and both relativity and particularity contain absoluteness and universality. For example, as an object of appreciation, "beauty" is absolute and universal and can exist in relative and particular objects, such that we refer to the beauty of chrysanthemums or to the beauty of Lu Mountain; conversely, relative and particular objects, such as chrysanthemums and Lu Mountain, can contain absolute and universal beauty.

As an object with both relativity and particularity, the chrysanthemum, its special shape, its unique seasonal blooming and tolerance of the cold, was esteemed by the ancient poet Tao Yuanming whose love of the flower was a source of fascination for the Chinese philosopher Zhou Dunyi who named the chrysanthemum "the hermit of flowers," after the reclusive poet. And so, this very same feature or property of the chrysanthemum, along with its "beauty," is what satisfied the relative and particular needs of the poet, serving as the inspiration for his poems. At the same time, its beauty (i.e., its "harmonious proportion"), which is its absolute and universal factual property, satisfied the absolute need of Tao Yuanmin's love of beauty, as it has for others throughout the ages, and thus has absolute value and good.

On the contrary, a universal object of the absoluteness, such as the object of "beauty," is contained in other objects of particularity and relativity which comprise the absolute and universal factual property of "harmonious proportion." It satisfies the absolute and universal needs of Zhou Dunyi's love of beauty, thus has relative value and relative good. The particular and relative factual property of the lotus is expressed by his admiration for how it "grows out of mud yet is clean." This unique feature of the lotus, along with other factual properties of its beauty, satisfies the particular and relative needs of Zhou Dunyi's love of the flower, so he refers to the lotus as the "gentlemen of flowers." Thus, the lotus has relative value and relative good.

To sum up, "ought," "good," and "value" are relative and absolute. This is because both the "standard of value" (needs, desires, and purposes of the subject) and "the substance of value" (factual properties of the object) are relative and absolute, and particular and universal; that is, on the one hand, as the object's utilities for satisfying the particular and relative needs of the subject and, on the other hand, as the object's utilities for satisfying the absolute and universal needs of the subject. The former have relativity because they have value, are good or ought to be for subjects with certain kinds of needs but not for other subjects, while the latter have absoluteness because they have value, are good or ought to be for any subject at any time.

In other words, the existence of ought, good, and value is both relative and absolute because these are the utilities of an object to the needs, desires, and purposes of the subject consisting of two aspects: the "factual properties of the object (the substance of value)" and the "needs, desires and purposes (the standard of value)." Therefore, on the one hand, ought, good, and value are determined by "particular and relative needs, desires and purposes of the subject" and by "particular and relative facts of the object," and thus have relativity. On the other hand, ought, good, and value are also determined by "absolute and universal needs, desires and purposes of the subject" and "absolute and universal facts of the object," and thus have absoluteness. This is the principle of absoluteness and relativity of the existence of "ought," "good," and "value," and, in short, is the principle of absoluteness and relativity of the existence of value.

3.3.3 *The nature of the existence of value: Subjectivity and objectivity*

After clarifying the universality, particularity, absoluteness, and relativity of the existence of ought, good, and value, we are then able to analyze the more complicated problem of objectivity and subjectivity which are based on the above principles. The objectivity and subjectivity of ought, good, and value, first of all, emerge from the objectivity and subjectivity of the needs of the subject—and the various forms of the transformation of these needs in the subject's consciousness. However, as we all know, subjectivity and objectivity have two meanings. One is that subjectivity refers to consciousness or mind and objectivity refers to the material world outside of the consciousness or mind. If we subscribe to this meaning, desires belong only to the category of consciousness or mind, so all desires are only subjective. The meaning is that subjectivity refers to the properties of things that can change at will and objectivity refers to the properties of things that cannot change at will. The "subjectivity and objectivity" of the needs, desires, and purposes of the subject refer to this meaning: That is, whether things can change at will. Accordingly, desires that can change at will, such as the desire to steal, we can classify as subjective desires, and the desires that cannot change at will, such as sexual desire or appetite, we can classify as objective desires.

Therefore, the so-called subjective needs of the subject are the needs that can change at will, while the objective needs of the subject are the needs that cannot change at will. Then, what are the needs of the subject that can change at will? Undoubtedly, they are the particular needs of the subject: All the subjective needs of the subject are particular needs of the subject because everyone's particular needs, desires, and purposes are mostly accidental, variable, and freely chosen, and thus have the subjectivity that can change at will.

122 *The meta-ethical proof*

For example, John is addicted to poker and Jim is obsessed with playing chess. They are both highly competitive individuals with different means of satisfying the strong urge to outsmart their opponents. When John and Jim realize, however, that sitting for hours on end playing poker and chess is detrimental to their health, they take up the healthier activity of ping-pong instead. The strong urge to satisfy their competitive streak through the particular needs of playing poker and chess is transferred to the particular need to compete in ping-pong. Since all three activities or hobbies are by choice, they are subjective and arbitrary. Particular needs such as these therefore are mostly subjective because they can change at will.

The subjective arbitrariness of the particular needs of the subject determines the subjective arbitrariness of ought, good and value, for the needs of the subject are the *standard* of ought, good, and value: if the standard for the measurement of the good or value of the object are subjective and arbitrary, then how can the good or value of the object not be subjective and arbitrary? If the constant need or urge to play poker or chess is subjective and arbitrary, then the good or value of playing poker or chess is also subjective and arbitrary. The need to play poker or chess means that playing poker or chess has value and thus is a kind of good. But once they quit these hobbies, that is, no longer need them, playing poker or chess is no longer a kind of good, and thus is of no value to them.

Therefore, questions regarding worthwhile pursuits, such as whether one should play poker, chess, or ping-pong, are really no different from questions concerning other life choices or vocations, such as whether it is better to be an official, to be rich, or to be a professor, in the sense that they can change at will and are subjective, arbitrary. This is to say that the ought, good, and value that satisfy the particular needs of subjects vary in different times and situations since they can change at will and are subjective, arbitrary, and accidental.

However, ought, good, and value are not completely subjective. To claim otherwise would mean that, as long as something in our desires and thoughts has value, its value is beyond any doubt. Can such a claim be feasible? No, in reality it is *quite the opposite*. Frogs and spiders, for instance, are beneficial to humans because they eat mosquitoes and flies that spread harmful diseases. They have value to us as a matter of fact not because we wish it so. Conversely, then, to reprise the previous point, our wishing, desiring, or hoping that something has value certainly does not mean that it has value. As E. J. Bond put it: "valuing something cannot make it valuable."[17] "Ought," "good," and "value" obviously have a certain kind of objectivity that cannot change at human will.

When we say ought, good, and value have objectivity, however, it is first because of the objectivity of the standard of the needs, desires, and purposes of the subject. The objective needs of the subject, as mentioned above, are the needs that cannot change at will. Then what are the needs of the subject that cannot change at will? Undoubtedly, they are the universal needs of the subject because everyone's universal needs, desires, and purposes are necessary,

The axiom of the existence of value   123

unchangeable, and cannot be freely chosen. For example, everyone has dietary needs, sexual needs, the needs of leisure, aesthetic needs, and needs for self-realization; and every society has its moral needs such as continence, honesty, self-respect, the doctrine of the mean, courage, and justice—all of which are universal needs as well. The reason that every subject has these universal needs is because they are inevitable, unchangeable, and cannot be freely chosen, and hence have the objectivity that cannot change at will.

It is not the case, for instance, that one wishes to have sexual desire and then has it, or, vice versa, one wishes one did not have sexual desire, and so does not have it. It occurs regardless. Marx once declared that for a person who pursues a great cause, falling in love and getting married is the most stupid thing to do. So, why did Marx fall in love and get married against his so-called better judgment? No doubt sexual desire played a role: sexual desire has the objectivity that cannot change at will. Marx remarks that sensuality, which is man's "own *natural* destination...reveals the extent to which man's *natural* behaviour has become *human*, or the extent to which the human essence in him has become a *natural* essence." As Freud said, people are not the masters of their own physical desires and actions: "The ego ... is not even master in its own house."[18] "Man becomes an animal with weak intelligence and is subject to instinctive desires."[19]

So, aside from the kinds of subjectivity that we attribute to say marriage, love, etc., Marx and Freud express in different ways the instinctual drive of sexual desire, which is also to say that the value or good of a sexual partner is something that exists independently of human will as a universal need of the subject (as do the good or value of food, love, leisure, beauty, self-realization, honesty, courage, etc.). In short, objective ought, good, and value are the ought, good, and value that exist independent of human will.

"Ought," "good," and "value" have objectivity where they are the standard of value—the universal needs, desires, and purposes—and, more importantly, the utility of the factual property of the object to the needs, desires, and purposes of the subject: The factual properties are the source of the emergence of ought, good, and value and the substance of their existence; thus their existence has the nature of being independent of human will. The reason that facts are facts is because they are things existing independently of the needs, desires, and purposes of the subject. For example, the fact that cabbage has value not only depends on people's dietary needs, but, more importantly, on its factual properties such that it contains protein, fat, carbohydrates, calcium, carotene, riboflavin, etc., which exist independently of human will.

If cabbages didn't have these properties but some other factual properties, such as hepatitis B virus and HIV, would we still say that they have value? No. So we say cabbages have value not just because of our desires, but, more importantly, because they have certain factual properties that exist independently of human will. Conversely, even if a person does not like to eat cabbage, it is still of nutritional value to him. The nutritional value of cabbage is independent of the taste, food habits and desires of a subject because it contains

124   *The meta-ethical proof*

protein, fat, carbohydrates and other factual properties so it is objective and has objective value: Objective value is the value independent of the desires, wishes and will of the subject.

To sum up, ought, good, and value have both subjectivity and objectivity. On the one hand, ought, good, and value are subjective because their standards (the needs, desires, and purposes of the subject) are particular, thus subjective, accidental, variable, and can change at will. On the other hand, ought, good, and value are also objective, not only because their substance (the factual property of the object) is objective and independent of human will, but also because their standard (the needs, desires, and purposes of the subject), have universality and hence are also objective, inevitable, unchangeable, and independent of human will.

In other words, ought, good, and value have both subjectivity and objectivity because ought, good, and value are utilities of the object to the needs, desires, and purpose of the subject, consisting of two aspects: The factual properties of object (the substance of value) and needs, desires, and purposes of the subject (the standard of value). Therefore, on the one hand, ought, good, and value are determined by the subject's needs, desires, and purposes which are particular, subjective, and can change at will: They are subjective ought, good, and value. On the other hand, ought, good, and value are also determined by the factual property or properties of the object and the subject's needs, desires, and purposes which are universal, objective, and cannot change at will: They are also objective ought, good, and value. This is the principle of the objectivity and subjectivity of the existence of "ought," "good," and "value," which, in short, is the principle of objectivity and subjectivity of the existence of value.

3.3.4 The axiom of the nature of the existence of value and the postulate of the nature of the existence of moral value in ethics

From the analysis of the nature of the existence of *ought, good*, and *value*, it can be concluded that ***ought, good,*** *and* ***value*** *have not only particularity, relativity and subjectivity, but also universality, absoluteness and objectivity. This is because* ***ought, good,*** *and* ***value*** *are the utilities of the object to the needs, desires, and purposes of the subject, consisting of two aspects: The factual properties of the object (the substance of value) and the needs, desires, and purposes of the subject (the standard of value). Therefore, on the one hand, ought, good, and value are determined by "the needs of particularity and relativity of the subject" and "the facts of particularity and relativity of the object," and thus vary with different needs of subject, and are particular, relative and subjective and can change at will; on the other hand,* ***ought, good,*** *and* ***value*** *are determined by "the needs of universality and absoluteness of the subject" and "the facts of universality and absoluteness of the object," thus are the same for every subject, and are universal, absolute, objective, and independent of human will.*

The axiom of the existence of value 125

This is the nature of the existence of *ought, good*, and *value*, in short, the nature of the existence of value, namely the axiom of the nature of the existence of the value in ethics, which is universally applicable to every field of *ought, good*, and *value*, and, in the final analysis, is the axiom of the nature of the existence of value in the value sciences.

In the field of moral value, society is the agent that makes moral norms, and hence is a subject; the purpose for which it makes moral norms (namely the goal of morality) is the purpose of society's activities as a subject. The object therefore is all the actions in society that can be morally evaluated and regulated by morality. So, if the "axiom of the nature of the existence in ethics," which is universally applicable to all fields of *ought, good*, and *value*, is deduced to the field of *moral ought, moral good*, and *moral value*, we can draw the following conclusion:

> The moral ought, moral good, and moral value of the behavior that ought to be not only have particularity, relativity, and subjectivity, but also have universality, absoluteness, and objectivity. This is because the moral value of the behavior that ought to be is the utility of the behavioral fact to the goal of morality, consisting of two aspects: The "behavioral fact" (the substance of moral value) and the "goal of morality" (the standard of moral value). Therefore, on the one hand, the moral value of the behavior that ought to be is determined by "the particular and relative purpose for which a certain society establishes morality" and "the particular and relative behavioral facts," which varies from society to society; thus it is particular, relative, and subjective. On the other hand, the moral value of the behavior that ought to be is also determined by the "the universal and absolute purpose for which each society establishes morality" and "the universal and absolute behavioral facts," which are the same for any society, so it is universal, absolute, and objective and does not change according to human will.

This is the nature of the existence of moral ought, moral good, and moral value, and "the postulate of the nature of the existence of the moral value in ethics" which is only applicable to ethics.

For example, many primitive societies were at the same stage of social development with extremely low productivity, and couldn't provide enough food for all people. However, the moral rules made and practiced in these societies were different. The Eskimos' rule was to freeze some baby girls and aging parents in the snow. The rule of Yanomamos in Brazil was to kill or starve the baby girls and let the men engage in bloody fighting among themselves. The rule for certain people in New Guinea was that men could only establish gay relationships in the early years of puberty. The different rules fully show the particularity, relativity, and subjectivity of moral values and moral norms, which, undoubtedly depended on the particular and relative goal of morality for the primitive societies to "avoid starving everyone to death."

126　*The meta-ethical proof*

However, every society in every era in history advocated moral norms such as honesty, self-respect, love, loyalty, diligence, generosity, courage, justice, integrity, probity, happiness, modesty, wisdom, continence, courage, etc., fully demonstrating the universality, objectivity, and absoluteness of moral values and norms, which, unquestionably depend on the universal, ultimate and absolute goal of morality that all societies establish: To safeguard the existence and development of society, and to promote everyone's interests.

3.4　Theories about the axiom of the existence of value and the postulate of the existence of moral value in ethics

3.4.1　Conclusion: Three axioms of the existence of value and three postulates of the existence of moral value in ethics

The axiom of the existence of value and the postulate of the existence of moral value in ethics can be summed up as six "sets of primitive propositions" or "axioms and postulates":

3.4.1.1　The axiom of the essence of the existence of value in ethics

Good, value and *ought* are the properties of the object that exist dependently on the needs of the subject, and which emerge when the *fact* of the object are related to the needs, desires, and purposes of the subject. They are the utilities of the *fact* of the object to the needs, desires, and purposes of the subject, and so are relational properties of the object and the "tertiary qualities" of the object.

3.4.1.2　The axiom of the structure of the existence of value in ethics

Ought, good, and *value* are the utilities of the fact of the object to the needs, desires, and purpose of the subject, consisting of two aspects: The factual properties of the object and the needs, desires, and purposes of the subject. The factual properties of the object are the source from which ought, good, and value emerge and are the carrier, noumenon, and substance for their existence, simply referred to as *the substance of value*, while the needs, desires, and purposes of the subject are the conditions for their emergence and existence from the factual properties of object, which are the standard of the measurements of the value or good of the factual properties of object, and are called *the standard of value*—the purpose is the "real standard of value," while unpurposed needs and desires are the "potential standard of value."

3.4.1.3　The axiom of the nature of the existence of value in ethics

The existence of ought, good, and value has not only particularity, relativity, and subjectivity, but also universality, absoluteness, and objectivity. This is

The axiom of the existence of value 127

because *ought, good,* and *value* are the utilities of the object to the needs, desires, and purposes of the subject, consisting of two aspects: The factual properties of the object (the substance of value) and the needs, desires, and purposes of the subject (the standard of value). Therefore, on the one hand, ought, good, and value are determined by "the particular needs of the subject" and "the particular facts of the object," which are different because of the different needs for subjects, and thus are particular, relative, and subjective; on the other hand, ought, good, and value are determined by "the universal needs of the subject" and "the universal facts of the object," thus are the same for every subject, and are universal, absolute, objective, and independent of human will.

3.4.1.4 *The postulate of the essence of the existence of moral value in ethics*

The moral good, moral ought, and moral value of the behavioral ought are the properties of behavior that depend on the goal of morality: They are the properties that emerge when the behavioral facts are related to the goal of morality, and are the utilities of the "behavioral facts" to the goal of morality, and are the relational property of the behavior, namely the property of the value relation of the behavior, which, in the final analysis, are the "tertiary qualities" of the behavior.

3.4.1.5 *The postulate of the structure of the existence of moral value in ethics*

The moral good, moral ought, and moral value of the behavioral ought are the utility of the behavioral facts to the goal of morality, consisting of two aspects: The "behavioral facts" and "goal of morality." The behavioral facts are the source from which the behavioral ought emerges and are the carrier, noumenon, and substance for the existence of behavioral ought, which can be termed the "substance of moral value"; the goal of morality is the condition for the emergence and existence of the behavioral ought from the behavioral fact, and is the standard of the measurement of moral value of the behavioral fact, which can be termed "the standard of moral value."

3.4.1.6 *The postulate of the nature of the existence of moral value in ethics*

The moral good, moral ought, and moral value of the behavior that ought to be not only have particularity, relativity, and subjectivity, but also have universality, absoluteness, and objectivity. This is because the moral value of the behavior that ought to be is the utilities of the behavioral facts to the goal of morality, consisting of two aspects: The behavioral facts (the substance of moral value) and the goal of morality (the standard of moral value). Therefore, on the one hand, the moral value of the behavior that ought to be is determined by "the particular and relative purpose for which a certain society establishes morality" and "the particular and relative behavioral facts," which

128   *The meta-ethical proof*

varies from society to society; thus it is particular, relative, and subjective. On the other hand, the moral value of the behavior that ought to be is also determined by the "the universal and absolute purpose for which every society establishes morality" and "the universal and absolute behavioral facts," which is the same for any society, so it is universal, absolute, and objective and does not change according to human will.

The reason that the combination of these six sets of primitive propositions is termed the axiom of the existence of value and the postulates of existence of moral value in ethics is that it is the theoretical premise for solving whether "ought" can be derived from "fact," further deduce the deductive axiom of value and deductive postulate of moral value in ethics, and finally deduce all objects and propositions of ethics. This will be the contents of the next chapter "The proof of meta-ethics: The deductive axiom of value and deductive postulate of moral value in ethics." These six axioms and postulates are so important that four meta-ethical theories, namely "objectivism," "realism," "subjectivism," and "the theory of relation," were established as fields of research.

3.4.2 Objectivism and realism

Meta-ethical objectivism is the proof theory of meta-ethics that contends *ought*, *good*, and *value* exist in the object, which is a theory concerned with the proof of the axiom of the existence of value and the postulate of the existence of the moral value in ethics. There are many thinkers such as Plato, Aristotle, Thomas Aquinas, Anthony Ashley-Cooper, 3rd Earl of Shaftesbury, Francis Hutcheson, Edmund Burke, Kant, Goethe, Hegel, Moore, E. J. Bond, David O. Brink, C. E. M. Joad, Holmes Rolston III, etc., who advocate this view of objectivism. Objectivism can be divided into two schools, the first of which is moderate objectivism holding that ought, good, and value cannot exist in the object independently of the subject. The other school is extreme objectivism believing that ought, good, and value can exist in the object independently of the subject.

In the view of moderate objectivism, *ought*, *good*, and *value* exist in the object, but they cannot exist in the object independently of the subject: The object is the source for their existence while the subject is the condition for their existence, which is well-expressed by Rolston:

> The value of a flower is constructed through appreciation; it is not something long existing in flowers themselves has nothing to do with people's appreciation. But it is such value that although it appears to be a product of human subjective consciousness, it is still objectively attached to the flowers blooming on the grass.[20]

The Chinese scholar Zhu Di also draws a similar conclusion after examining objectivism:

The axiom of the existence of value 129

In general, objectivists also recognize that one not only needs an object but also a subject to produce the entire aesthetic process... .Objectivists only admit that the attainment of the aesthetic pleasure needs an object, but do not believe that the source of beauty needs both the existence of the object and the subject.[21]

This view of objectivism, as Zhu Di points out, is "general" objectivism, namely the moderate objectivism held by most objectivists.

On the contrary, extreme objectivism holds that *ought, good*, and *value* are the facts of the object that can exist independently of the subject, hence is also called "realism" or "meta-ethical realism," which is the theory of meta-ethical proof holding that *ought, good*, and *value* are the facts of the object that can exist independently of the subject. E. J. Bond, David O. Brink, David Wiggins, John Mcdowell, Richard N. Boyd, Nicholas L. Sturgeon, Geoffrey Sayre-McCord, Mark Platts, C. E. M. Joad, and the Chinese esthetician Cai Yi all are advocators of this meta-moral realism. They see that *ought, good* and *value* exist in the object, but they deny that the needs of the subject are the conditions for the existence of ought, good, and value. They believe that ought, good, and value can exist independently of the needs, desires, and purposes of the subject and exist in the object alone, so ought, good, and value are a kind of facts of the object that can exist independently of the subject, and are the intrinsic or factual properties of the object, which is well-expressed by Bond:

It is neither a necessary nor a sufficient condition of the end's being worthwhile that it is in fact desired, even when the relevant factual beliefs are true.[22]

All values were objective, in the same sense, namely, that all values were "external", i.e. their existence was independent of desire and will...Values have and independent existence, even if there were no persons, even if there were no conscious appetitive agents in the world.[23]

It is obvious that the common view of both moderate objectivism and realism is that *ought, good, beauty*, and *value* completely exist in the object, and thus both belong to objectivism. However, moderate objectivism believes that *ought, good, beauty*, and *value* are the properties that emerge when the object is related to the subject; that, although the properties exist in the object, they depend on the subject, so they the relational properties of the object; on the contrary, realism believes that *ought, good, beauty*, and *value* exist only in the object—as facts of the object—completely independent of the needs of the subject, so are the kind of exclusive reality intrinsic to the object. Therefore, realism is an extreme objectivism.

It is easy to see that moderate objectivism is the truth, and that realism is fallacy. This is because, as discussed earlier, *ought, good, value*, and *beauty* are the relational properties of the object, emerging only when the factual

130 *The meta-ethical proof*

properties of the object are related to the needs, desires, and purpose of the subject: The factual property of the object is the source for the emergence of *ought, good, beauty*, and *value*, and the substance for their existence; the needs, desires, and purposes of the subject are the condition and the standard for their emergence from the factual properties of the object. The mistake of realism, firstly, lies in that it only sees that the object is the source and the substance of the existence of *ought, good, value*, and *beauty*, but fails to see that the subject is the condition and the standard of the existence of *ought, good, value*, and *beauty*; secondly, it only sees that *ought, good, beauty*, and *value* emerge from and exist in the object, but fails to see that they can emerge from and exist in the object only when the object is related to the subject. Thus, realism mistakenly believes that whether there exists the subject, the object has *ought, good, beauty*, and *value*, so they are not relational properties of the object but the intrinsic or factual properties of the object. Therefore, the mistake of meta-moral realism is to regard the relational properties of the object as the intrinsic properties of the object, and the property of value relation of the object as the property of factual relation of the object, taking the source and substance of ought, good, beauty, and value as ought, good, beauty, and value themselves.

3.4.3 Types of theory of realism

Meta-ethical realism is widespread in the field of value sciences, such as ethics, aesthetics, and economics. Its expression in the field of morality is the so-called "moral realism," the basic feature of which is the acknowledgement of the existence of "moral facts." As Pojman states: "A moral realist is one who holds an analogous thesis about ethics: [that] there are moral facts and that they exist independently of whether we believe them."[24] David O. Brink also writes that "Moral realism claims that there are objective moral facts."[25] However, what exactly is "the existence of moral facts"?

In explaining this point, Hare writes:

> On the face of it, it means the view that moral qualities such as wrongness, and likewise moral facts such as the fact that an act was wrong, exist in rerum natura, so that, if one says that a certain act was wrong, one is saying that there, existed, somehow, somewhere, this quality of wrongness, and that it had to exist there if that act were to be wrong. And one is saying that there also existed, somewhere, somehow, the fact that the act was wrong, which was brought into being by the person who did the wrong act.[26]

Obviously, the so-called "existence of moral facts" means that right, moral good, and moral value are a kind of facts, even are the intrinsic properties of things, belonging to the category of facts, hence are properties that exist independently of the needs of the subject. As they do not depend on the subject,

The axiom of the existence of value 131

are they separate substances that have nothing to do with physical properties, as A. J. Mackie states? David O. Brink's answer is negative, since moral realism holds that moral properties are produced from the base of physical properties.[27] Then, what kind of properties are produced from the physical properties of behavior? Hare elaborates on Brink's statement: "So far we have been talking about the property of wrongness, and the fact that an act was wrong, in just the same terms as the property of redness, and the fact that a thing is red."[28]

The mistake of moral realism lies first of all in the equivalence of the property factual relation of the object and the property of value relation of the object. Most of moral realists correctly see that moral good, like red, is a relational property of the object dependent on the subject, but not an intrinsic property of the object, but fail to see that, on the one hand, red is a property of the object independently of the needs, desires and purpose of the subject, hence is the factual property of the object, and is also the property of factual relation of the object, and the "secondary qualities" of the object; on the other hand, moral good is the property of the object that cannot exist without the needs, desires, and purpose of the subject, which is the utility of the factual property of the object to the needs, desires, and purpose of the subject (the utility that behavioral facts conform to the goal of morality)—hence is the property of value relation of the object and the "tertiary qualities" of the object. The mistake of moral realism lies in that it equates the nature of the existence of value with that of color, and hence draws the wrong conclusion that moral good is also a fact and that there exist "moral facts," from the correct view that color is a fact.

The mistake of moral realism also lies in its confusion of the concepts of fact in the broad and narrow senses. Because, as mentioned earlier, on the one hand, facts in the broad sense are things that exist independently of thought, including values, which, undoubtedly, is the thing that exist independently of thought: This concept is applicable to epistemology and other non-value sciences; on the other hand, facts in the narrow sense are things that exist dependently on the needs of the subject, which do not include value (value is the thing that exists dependent on the needs of the subject), the relationship between facts and value is the opposite conceptual relationship. This concept of fact in the narrow sense is applicable to all value sciences, such as ethics, because the fundamental problem of value science, namely whether "value" can be deduced from "facts," implies that value is not a fact and fact does not include value: fact and value are opposite concepts.

The key problem is that "moral good" is an ethical concept belonging to the category of "value," which is opposite to the "fact" with no overlapping extensions, thus cannot belong to the category of "fact" and cannot be "fact." In the final analysis, there exists no "moral fact." The so-called "moral fact" is at variance with the fundamental problem in value science, namely *whether "value" can be deduced from "fact,"* hence is as absurd as "a round square," and is an absurd, contradictory, and untenable concept.

132   *The meta-ethical proof*

However, in epistemology and other non-value sciences "moral fact" is a scientific concept, because in non-value sciences, "fact" is the broad sense referring to things that actually exist independently of thought, while the existence of "moral good" merely depends on the needs, desires, and purpose of the subject, and on the purpose for which society establishes morality, but not on thought, and hence belongs to the category of fact: "moral fact" is a scientific concept in epistemology and other non-value sciences.

Thus it is wrong for moral realists to talk about "moral facts" in the field of ethics: they confuse the different meanings of the concept of "facts" in non-value sciences and value sciences, and confuse the concept of facts in the broad and narrow senses. Indeed, the concept of "moral fact" is a scientific concept in non-value sciences, such as epistemology, but it is a ridiculous concept in ethics and other value sciences.

The manifestation of meta-ethical realism in the aesthetic field, namely "aesthetic realism," defines beauty as the "proportional harmony" of the object, which implies that if beauty is the proportional harmony of object then the beauty is the property possessed by the object alone, and that existence of beauty is independent of human's aesthetic needs, desires, and purpose, thus is the fact of object that can exist independently of humans, that is, the intrinsic property of the object. Thus, the aesthetic realist Joad writes:

> Beauty is an independent, self-sufficient object. It is a real and unique element in the universe... When we say a picture or a piece of music is the beauty... [it] refers to the particular qualities and properties of the picture and the music itself.

In a word, as China's aesthetic realist Cai Yi concludes: "Beauty exists independently of those who appreciate it."[29]

Therefore, if there were no human beings in the world the beauty of Raphael's painting *St. Sebastian* would remain the same, as one might ask: "Would there be any changes in this painting? Would there be any change in the experience of it?"

> The only possible change is that it is no longer appreciated, but does it automatically make it no longer beautiful? The unquestionable truth is that all of us would think that *St. Sebastian* without viewer would be better than the stinking puddle without viewer.[30]

The mistake of this view is obviously to equate the value of beauty with the value substance of beauty: proportional harmony is the substance of beauty but not beauty itself; beauty is the utility of the proportional harmony of the object to the aesthetic needs of human beings.

The manifestation of meta-ethical realism in the field of economics is "the theory of realism of commodity value," mainly Marx's "labor theory of value," which defines commodity value as the general human labor congealed

The axiom of the existence of value   133

in commodities: "All commodity as value are only crystallized human labor."[31] However, the congealment of human labor in commodities clearly depends neither on human needs nor even on human beings in terms of their existence. The human labor that a gold jewelry congeals is still there in the gold jewelry even when human beings cease to exist. Therefore, if commodity value is the general human labor congealed in the commodity, the commodity value then is independent of human needs and contained in the commodity alone, hence an intrinsic property of the commodity. Marx indeed contends that value is an intrinsic property of commodity: "The labor taken for the production of the good manifests as the intrinsic nature of the good, that is, its value."[32]

The error of the theory of realism of commodity value obviously is that it equates commodity value to the substance of commodity value. This is because "labor and products" are the source and substance of the commodity value instead of commodity value itself; commodity value is the utility of "labor and products" to human needs: the use value of commodity is the marginal utility of "labor and products" to the consumption needs, while the exchange value of commodity is the marginal utility of commodity to the exchange needs.

3.4.4 Subjectivism

Subjectivism in meta-ethics, namely meta-ethical subjectivism, is a proof theory of meta-ethics holding that good and value exist in the subject, which, in the final analysis, is a proof theory about the axiom of value existence and postulate of existence of moral value of ethics. Its representatives include R. B. Perry, W. James, J. L. Mackie, Lord Kames, and Gao Ertai. Subjectivism is further away from the truth than realism. Even though it correctly sees that in the object itself there exist no ought, good, beauty, and value: ought, good, beauty, and value exist only with the existence of the needs, desires, and purpose of the subject. However, from that it wrongly concludes that the needs, desires, and purpose of the subject are the sources of emergence and existence of ought, good, beauty, and value; that ought, good, beauty, and value exist in the needs, desires, and purpose of the subject and are the functions and properties of the needs, desires, and purpose of the subject, and, consequently, that ought, good beauty, and value are not objective but totally subjective.

Gao Ertai writes "Is there objective beauty? My answer is negative"[33] because "beauty exists as long as people perceive it and does not exist as long as it is not experienced."[34] Therefore the "human mind is the source of natural beauty as well as artistic beauty."[35] Lord Cames also says: "beauty does not exist in the beloved but in the eyes of the lover."[36] And Perry writes that value must be seen as the function of will or love in its most fundamental sense.[37] In the primary and general sense, when a thing (anything) is an object of interest (any interest), it has value or is valuable.[38] James also says: "The values, interests, or meanings that the world around us seem to have are purely gifts of the viewer's mind to the world."[39]

134 *The meta-ethical proof*

It is true that ought, good, beauty, and value do not exist in the object itself: They emerge when the object is related to the needs, desires, and purpose of the subject. They cannot exist without the needs, desires, and purposes of the subject. Although we cannot say that they exist in the needs, desires, and purposes of the subject, we can say, however, that they exist in the object. This is because they are properties that emerge from the factual properties of the object—not from the needs, desires and purpose of the subject—when the factual properties of the object are related to the needs, desires, and purposes of the subject. The needs, desires, and purposes of the subject can only be the conditions for their emergence and existence from the factual properties of the object: the factual properties of the object are the source of their emergence and existence. The error of subjectivism lies in that it takes the conditions for the emergence and existence of *ought, good, beauty*, and *value* as the source of the emergence and existence of ought, good, beauty, and value.

On the other hand, meta-ethical subjectivism correctly sees that the existence of ought, good, and value is determined by the particular needs, desires, and purpose of the subject, hence possess particularity, relativity, and subjectivity: they vary with the different desires, wishes, and wills of the subject, and are different with the difference of the needs of the subject. However, it wrongly concludes that ought, good, beauty, and value are completely subjective, and that there is no objective ought, good, beauty, or value. For instance, Mackie has repeatedly pointed out that "There are no objective values…values are not objective, are not part of the fabric of the world."[40]

> The argument from relativism has as its premise the well-known variation in moral code from one society to another and from one period to one another, and also the differences in moral beliefs between different groups and classes within a complex community. Some people think that something is good or right while others consider it is bad or wrong.[41]

Dukas also writes that beauty is purely subjective because

> one of the most well-known facts of beauty is its mutability: one regards as beauty another does not; one can regard something monotonous today which he judged as beautiful yesterday, or what he judges as beautiful today may be judged to be monotonous or even ugly tomorrow.[42]

The error of meta-ethical subjectivism obviously lies in its one-sidedness. It only perceives that, on the one hand, the existence of ought, good, or value is determined by the particular needs, desires, and purpose of the subject, which can change according to the will of the subject, hence have particularity, subjectivity, and relativity: They can change according to the needs, desires, and purpose of the subject, and are different with the difference of the needs of the subject. But it fails to see that, on the other hand, the existence of ought,

The axiom of the existence of value   135

good, or value is also determined by the factual property of the object (e.g., a cabbage's value is determined by its factual properties which exist independently of human will, such as protein, fat, carbohydrates, calcium, carotene, riboflavin), as well as by the universal needs, desires, and purpose of the subject which are independent of the will of the subject, hence possess objectivity, universality, and absoluteness: They are independent of the desires, wishes, and will of the subject, and are the same for each subject.

3.4.5 Theory of relationship

In meta-ethics, the theory of relationship, namely the theory of the subject–object relationship, is a proof theory of meta-ethics holding that ought, good, and value exist in the relationship between the subject and the object, which, in the final analysis, is a kind of proof theory concerned with the axiom of the existence of value and the postulate of existence of moral value. Its representatives include Wilhelm Windelband, H. S. Langfeld, Zhu Guangqian, and Li Deshun, etc. The theory of relationship looks like the truth because it correctly sees that "there is value neither in subject nor object alone."[43] Consequently, it concludes that ought, good, and value certainly emerge and exist in the relationship between the object and the subject. Windelband writes: "Value is never discovered as a feature of the object itself, but exists in a relationship with someone who appreciates it."[44] Langfeld says that beauty

> is neither completely dependent on human experience nor completely on the material being experienced. It is neither subjective nor objective, neither the outcome of a purely intellectual activity nor an intrinsic value of the objective object, but rather a changing relationship between the two, that is, the relationship between the human body and the objective object.[45]

Zhu Guangqian also writes: "Beauty is the unification of the objectivity and subjectivity."[46] "[It] is in the relationship between the mind and the object...the so-called 'values' are all due to the relationship between things and people."[47] Li Deshun concludes that:

> Value is neither outside the real world and things, nor the existing real things and their properties themselves, nor the subjective phenomenon of human minds and hearts. Then where is it? The answer is: value exists in the relationship between the subject and the object. It is the state and content of this relationship itself. This view can be called [the] "theory of relationship."[48]

Although the theory of relationship has been accepted by many scholars in China, it is not the truth. This is because value is the property of the object

136 *The meta-ethical proof*

which emerges when the object is related to the needs, desires, and purpose of the subject, rather than abstractly "the property which emerges in the subject–object relationship." The former means that value emerges and exists in the object, and is a relational property of the object, while the latter means that value emerges and exists in the relationship between subject and object, and is a subject–object relationship.

The mistake of the theory of relationship lies in that it regards "value is the relational property of the object" *as* "value is the relationship between object and subject," and "value emerges from the object when the object is related to the subject" *as* "value emerges in the relationship between the object and the subject," so it consequently believes that value emerges and exists in the relationship between object and subject, and is a subject–object relationship. According to this logic, the nutritional value of bread does not exist in bread but in the relationship between bread and people; that it is not the bread that is nutritious but the relationship between bread and people is nutritious, or that what I value or enjoy is not the nutrition of bread but the relationship between bread and me: Isn't it absurd?

Upon the discussion of the four proof theories of the axioms and postulates of existence in ethics, we can see that only the moderate objectivism is the truth: "ought," "good," and "value" exist in the object, but not in the object itself without the subject—the object is the source of their existence while the subject is the condition of their existence. The mistake of realism, subjectivism, and the theory of relationship lies in that they exaggerate some aspects of this truth. Realism exaggerates the source and substance of ought, good, and value, neglecting that the subject is the condition and standard of their existence, hence only sees that the object is the source and substance of their existence, and consequently misunderstands that good and value are objective facts that can exist independently of the subject. Subjectivism exaggerates the condition of the emergence and existence of ought, good, and value, thus regards the condition of their emergence and existence as the source of their emergence and existence, and further mistakenly believes that ought, good, and value exist in the subject. The theory of relationship exaggerates "value is the relational property of the object" as "value is the relationship between the object and subject" (and "value emerges from the object when the object is related to the subject" as "value emerges in the relationship between the object and the subject"), thus mistakenly believes that ought, good, and value emerge and exist in the relationship between object and subject, and is the subject–object relationship.

Notes

1 Aristotle: *The Complete Works of Aristotle*, Volume I, Renmin University of China Press, 1990, p. 6.
2 Zhu Guangqian: *Works of Zhu Guangqian*, Shanghai Literature and Art Press, 1983, p. 67.

The axiom of the existence of value 137

3 Ralph Barton Perry: *General Theory of Value: Its Meaning and Basic Principles Construed in Terms of Interest*, Longmans, Green, New York, 1926 p. 70.

4 E. J. Bond: *Reason and Value*, Cambridge University Press, 1983, p. 63.

5 Wang Yuliang (eds.): *A New Theory of Sino-Japanese Value Philosophy*, Shanxi People's Education Press, 1994, p. 47.

6 Chen Huaxing: "Ought: The Unity of Truth and Purpose," *Philosophical Studies*, No. 8, 1993.

7 Yuan Guiren: *An Introduction to Axiology*. Beijing Normal University Press, 1991, p. 395.

8 Stephen Edelston Toulmin: *The Place of Reason in Ethics,* The University of Chicago Press, 1986, pp. 10–18.

9 C. D. Broad: *Ethics of the Five Modern Schools*, Commercial Press, Beijing, 21 Edition, p. 215.

10 Karl Marx: *Capital*, Volume 1, People's Publishing House, 1975, p. 103.

11 Ralph Barton Perry: *General Theory of Value: Its Meaning and Basic Principles Construed in Terms of Interest*, Longmans, Green, New York, 1926, p. 124.

12 Also see Felix Christian Klein: *The Thought of Mathematics: Ancient and Modern*. Vol. 1, Shanghai Science and Technology Press, 1979. (Aristotle: *Complete Works of Aristotle*, Vol. 1, Renmin University of China Press, 1990, p. 266.)

13 Karl Marx: *Capital*, Volume 1, People's Publishing House, 1975, p. 103.

14 Sissela Bok: *Lying: Moral Choice in Public and Private Life*, New York: Vintage Books, 1989, p. 269.

15 Mencius: *Lilou.*

16 *The Analects of Confucius.*

17 E. J. Bond: *Reason and Value*, Cambridge University Press, 1983, p. 100.

18 Sigmund Freud: *Introductory Lectures on Psycho-Analysis,* Translated by James Strachey, W. W. Norton & Company, New York, 1966, p. 353.

19 Luther J. Binkley: *Conflict of Ideals*. Commercial Press, 1983, p. 131.

20 Holmes Rolston: *Environmental Ethics*. China Social Sciences Press, 2000, p. 153.

21 Ju Di: *Contemporary Western Aesthetics*. The People's Publishing House, 1984, p. 176.

22 E. J. Bond: *Reason and Value*, Cambridge University Press, 1983, p. 58.

23 E. J. Bond: *Reason and Value*, Cambridge University Press, 1983, pp. 84–85.

24 Louis P. Pojman: *Ethical Theory: Classical and Contemporary Readings*, Wadsworth Publishing Company, 1995, p. 456.

25 Louis P. Pojman: *Ethical Theory: Classical and Contemporary Readings,* Wadsworth Publishing Company, 1995, p. 469.

26 Ted Honderich: *Morality and Objectivity*, Routledge & Kegan Paul, London, 1985, p. 40.

27 Louis P. Pojman: *Ethical Theory: Classical and Contemporary Readings,* Wadsworth Publishing Company, 1995, p. 533.

28 Ted Honderich: *Morality and Objectivity*, Routledge & Kegan Paul, London, 1985, p. 45.

29 Ju Di: *Contemporary Western Aesthetics*. The People's Publishing House, 1984, p. 172.

30 Ju Di: *Contemporary Western Aesthetics*. The People's Publishing House, 1984, p. 173.

31 Karl Marx: *Capital*, Volume 1, People's Publishing House, 1975, p. 27.

32 Karl Marx: *Capital*, Volume 1, People's Publishing House, 1975, p. 39.

138   *The meta-ethical proof*

33 Gao Ertai: *On Beauty*, Gansu People's Publishing House, 1982, p. 1.
34 Gao Ertai: *On Beauty*, Gansu People's Publishing House, 1982, p. 4.
35 Gao Ertai: *On Beauty*, Gansu People's Publishing House, 1982, p. 4.
36 Ju Di: *Contemporary Western Aesthetics*. The People's Publishing House, 1984, p. 172.
37 Ralph Barton Perry: *General Theory of Value: Its Meaning and Basic Principles Construed in Terms of Interest*, Longmans, Green, New York, 1926, p. 54.
38 R. B. Perry: *Realms of Value*, Cambridge, MA, 1954, p. 2.
39 Cited from Holmes Rolston, *Environmental Ethics*, Chinese Social Sciences Press, 2000, p. 15.
40 J. L. Mackie: *Ethics: Inventing Right and Wrong*, Richard Clay Ptd Ltd, Singapore, 1977, p. 15.
41 J. L. Mackie: *Ethics: Inventing Right and Wrong*, Richard Clay Ptd Ltd, Singapore, 1977, pp. 36–37.
42 Ju Di: *Contemporary Western Aesthetics*. The People's Publishing House, 1984, p. 205.
43 Li Deshun: *Theory of Value*. Renmin University Press, 1987, p. 124.
44 Cited from Holmes Rolston, *Environmental Ethics*, Chinese Social Sciences Press, 2000, p. 151.
45 Ju Di: *Contemporary Western Aesthetics*. The People's Publishing House, 1984, p. 215.
46 Zhu Guangqian: *A Collection of Aesthetic Works of Zhu Guangqian*. Volume 3, Shanghai Literature and Art Publishing House, 1982, p. 43.
47 Zhu Guangqian: *A Collection of Aesthetic Works of Zhu Guangqian*. Volume 3, Shanghai Literature and Art Publishing House, 1982, p. 153.
48 Li Deshun: *A New Theory of Value*. China Youth Press, 1993, p. 68.

4 The deductive axioms and deductive postulates in ethics

By analyzing the axiom of the existence of value and the postulate of moral value in ethics, we know what the "source and condition" and the "substance and standard" of "value," "good," and "ought" are. From this, we can then analyze the process of their production and deduction, which is also the so-called "logic of deduction" of "value," "good," "ought," and "right," and, in the final analysis, is the response to the so-called Hume's guillotine: Whether "ought" can be derived from "is."

The analysis of the guillotine leads us to the discovery of the deductive axioms and deductive postulates in ethics. However, the process of the production and deduction of "ought" from "is" is not a simple and single process but a complicated and compound one, which is actually a four-stage process starting from "value" to "evaluation" then from "evaluation" to "the truth or falsehood and rightness or wrongness of evaluation," ending at "excellent moral norms." Therefore, the deductive axioms and deductive postulates in ethics are divided into the following categories accordingly: (1) the deductive axiom of value and deductive postulate of moral value; (2) the deductive axiom of evaluation and deductive postulate of moral evaluation; (3) the deductive axiom of the truth and falsehood and right and wrong of evaluation and deductive postulate of the truth or falsehood and right or wrong of moral evaluation; (4) the deductive axiom of excellent norms and deductive postulate of excellent moral norms.

4.1 The deductive axiom of value and deductive postulate of moral value in ethics

4.1.1 The answer to is-ought problem

In the 1730s, 24-year-old Hume made the greatest discovery in value sciences, which he articulated in his *A Treatise of Human Nature*:

> In every system of morality, which I have hitherto met with, I have always remarked, that the author proceeds for some time in the ordinary way of reasoning, and establishes the being of a God, or makes observations

140   *The meta-ethical proof*

concerning human affairs; when of a sudden I am surprised to find, that instead of the usual copulations of propositions, *is*, and *is not*, I meet with no proposition that is not connected with an *ought*, or *an ought not*. This change is imperceptible; but is, however, of the last consequence. For as this *ought*, or *ought not*, expresses some new relation or affirmation, 'tis necessary that it should be observed and explained; and at the same time that a reason should be given, for what seems altogether inconceivable, how this new relation can be a deduction from others, which are entirely different from it. But as authors do not commonly use this precaution, I shall presume to recommend it to the readers; and am persuaded, that this small attention would subvert all the vulgar systems of morality.[1]

The challenge put forward in this passage, often referred to as "Hume's guillotine" or "Hume's Law," as W. D. Hudson says, became "The central problem in moral philosophy...commonly known as the is-ought question,"[2] that is, whether "ought" can be derived from "is (fact)." This has relevance not just for moral philosophy or, moreover, meta-ethics, but for all value sciences because it is key to determining whether the respective disciplines can become a science congruent with the hard sciences. However, because of the difficulty of the question, no one from Hume's time to the end of the nineteenth century had systematically discussed it.

It was not until 1903 when G. E. Moore published his epoch-making *Principia Ethica* which marked the birth of meta-ethics, that the question was systematically analyzed. However, at best, Moore only reveals the "naturalistic fallacy" of this problem in ethics past but did not analyze it. Since then, many value scientists in ethics and other fields, have conducted studies of it and a number of them, such as MacIntyre, Foot, Alan Gewirth, J. L. Mackie, and Max Brink, have come close to settling the problem because they have more or less, explicitly or implicitly pointed out how "ought" is derived from the "facts" through "the needs, desires, and purposes" of the subject.[3] However, it is perhaps Brink who has expressed it most clearly as he writes:

To those who claim the existence of an unbridgeable logical gap between "ought" and "is", I offer for consideration the following counter-example:

Fischer wants to mate Botwinnik.

The one and only way to mate Botwinnik is for Fischer to move the Queen.

Therefore, Fischer should move the Queen.[4]

Further illustrating this example, Brink puts forward another reasoning:

You want to achieve E.

Doing M is the one and only way to achieve E.

Therefore, you should do M.[5]

Deductive axioms and deductive postulates   141

By analyzing these inferences, Brink concludes that: "between the factual premises and the practical conclusion there is a sort of gap, bridgeable only by an agent's willingness to engage in the relevant activity or practice,"[6] which quite clearly points out that "ought" is derived from "fact" through the "needs, desires, and purposes of the subject":

> The facts of the object → the needs, desires and purposes of the subject→ the ought of the object.

Brink's view is quite right, because, undoubtedly, the process of the production and deduction of *ought*, *good*, and *value* is a particular case of the process of the production and deduction of the relational property. That is to say, *ought*, *good*, and *value* belong to the general process of the production and deduction of the relational property, hence can be derived from it. It is not difficult to see that the process of the production and deduction of the relational property is obviously different from that of intrinsic property: the intrinsic property directly produces from and exists in a certain substance without an intermediary, while the relational property indirectly produces from and exists in the substance through an intermediary. For example, mass is the intrinsic property of an object, so it produces and exists in that object without any intermediary, while weight is a relational property of an object, so it needs the intermediary of earth's gravity to indirectly produce from and exist in the object. Thus, the processes of the production and deduction of the intrinsic and relational property are different:

> Formula 1: deduction of intrinsic property: object → mass
> Formula 2: deduction of relational property: object → earth's gravity → weight

This difference is evident in all intrinsic and relational properties. It can be seen that the process of the emergence and deduction of the relational property is different from that of the intrinsic property of the object: The intrinsic property directly emerges from and exists in the object without an intermediary, while the relational property indirectly emerges from and exists in the substance through an intermediary. For instance, the electromagnetic wave, as the intrinsic property of an object, directly emerges from and exists in the object without an intermediary (the eyes of the subject). On the contrary, yellow, red, and other colors are relational properties that indirectly emerge from and exist in the object through intermediaries (the eyes of the subject).

Similarly, as the relational properties of an object the production and deduction of value, good, and ought need the intermediary of the subject. But there are clearly differences concerning the cognitive processes. Where colors, such as yellow and red, are the relational property of facts of the object and the secondary qualities, the intermediary is certain objective things of the subject, principally the eyes. However, where value, good, and ought

142 *The meta-ethical proof*

are the relational property of values of the object, these are the tertiary qualities, and hence need the intermediary of certain subjective things of the subject, such as needs, desires, and purposes. Thus, the process of the production and deduction of "colors," such as yellow and red, and that of "values," such as ought and good, can be summed up as follows:

> Formula 3: reasoning of the relational property of facts: object → the eyes of the subject → colors such as yellow and red
>
> Formula 4: reasoning of the relational property of value: object → the needs, desires and purposes of the subject →values such as good and ought

4.1.2 Proof of the answer to is-ought problem: Deductive axiom of value in ethics

Through the analysis we can see that Brink's response to Hume's guillotine—that "ought" emerges and is derived from "fact" through "the needs, desires and purposes of the subject"—is right, because, as discussed above, the axiom of the existence of value shows that:

"Is" or "fact," "value," "good," and "ought" are all properties of the object. The differences lies in that "is" or "fact" is the factual property of the object independent of the needs, desires, and purposes of the subject; whereas "value, good, and ought" are the properties of the object which depend on the needs, desires and purposes of the subject, emerging only when "is" or "fact" is related to the needs, desires, and purposes of the subject. In the final analysis, they are the utility of "is" or "fact" of the object concerning the needs, desires, and purposes of the subject thus are the relational properties of the object: the factual property of the object is the source of the emergence of "value," "good," and "ought" and the substance of their existence, while the needs, desires, and purposes of the subject are the conditions for the emergence of "value," "good," and "ought" from the factual property of the object, and are the standard of measurement for the *value* or *good* of the factual property of the object.

Therefore, value, good and ought produce and are derived from "is" or "fact," but "is" or "fact" itself cannot produce value, good, and ought; consequently, it is impossible to deduce value, good, and ought purely from "is" or "fact." It can only occur when "is" or "fact" is related to the needs, desires, and purposes of the subject. In the final analysis, value, good, and ought are derived from "is" or "fact" through the needs, desires, and purposes of the subject: *positive value*, *good*, and *ought* are the utilities of "facts" that conform to the needs, desires, and purposes of the subject, while *negative value*, *bad*, and *ought-not* are the utilities of "facts" that do not conform to the needs, desires, and purposes of the subject.

For example, let's take humans as a subject and swallows as an object. People like swallows for many reasons but let's say that swallows have a

Deductive axioms and deductive postulates   143

positive value or are good because swallows eat insect pests: (1) swallows have a "positive value" or are "good" and (2) "swallows eat insects" are both properties of the swallow, but (2) "swallows eat insects" is the property of swallows alone; it is the factual property of swallows irrespective of whether it is related to human needs, desires, and purposes. Conversely, (1) the "positive value" or "good" of swallows is not the property of swallows alone, but the relational property of swallows when the factual property ("swallows eat insects") relates to human needs, desires, and purposes; it is the relational property of swallows, namely a "utility" that conforms to human needs, desires, and purposes. The factual property ("swallows eat insects") is the source of the emergence of the "positive value" or "good" attributed to swallows and the substance of the existence of the *value* or *good*, while human needs, desires, and purposes—concerning the eradication of insect pests more generally— are the conditions for the emergence and existence of the "positive value" or "good" from the factual property ("swallows eat insects"), and hence are the value standard of measurement for the goodness or badness of this factual property. In short, the consensus that swallows have positive value or are good emerges (and is derived) from the fact through the "human need to eradicate insects": the positive value or good is the utility of a fact that conforms to the "human needs, desires, and purposes" as demonstrated by the following reasoning:

> Premise 1: Swallows eat insects (the fact is what; substance of value).
> Premise 2: People need to eradicate insect pests (the needs, desires and
>   purposes of the subject are what; standard of value).
> Conclusion: Swallows have a positive value or are good (value).

> Thus, so-called value, good, and ought, in the final analysis, are the utilities of "is" or "facts" of the object concerning the needs, desires, and purposes of the subject and are therefore derived from the "is" or "facts" through the needs, desires and purposes of the subject: "positive value," good, and ought are the utilities of "facts" that conform to the needs, desires, and purposes of the subject, while "negative value," bad, and ought-not are the utilities of "facts" that do not conform to the needs, desires, and purposes of the subject.

In sum, this is the solution to "Hume's guillotine" and the process of the production and deduction of "value, good, and ought," the deductive method of "value, good, and ought," and the discovery and proof method of "value, good, and ought," which is "the deductive axiom of value in ethics." In a nutshell, the deductive axiom is universally applicable to all value sciences including specialist areas of study, for instance, stateology and Chinaology: "The deductive axiom of value in value science," "the deductive axiom of value in ethics," "the deductive axiom of value in stateology" and "the deductive axiom of value in Chinaology" share same concepts: fields

144 *The meta-ethical proof*

which more or less share revolve around similar value concepts are well served by the basic framework of this reasoning as demonstrated below:

Premise 1: the fact (substance of value).
Premise 2: the needs, desires and purposes of the subject (standard of value).
Conclusion: the ought (value).

4.1.3 The deductive postulate of moral value in ethics

We have established that the deductive axiom of value in ethics is a deductive method for all *ought*, *good*, and *value*, which is universally applicable to all value sciences. If the axiom was deduced to the fields of moral ought, moral good, and moral value, however, we will find the particular deductive method of moral ought, moral good, and moral values, that is, "the deductive postulate of moral value in ethics" which is only applicable to ethics. Then, what is it?

In the fields of moral ought, moral good, and moral value, it is that society is the agent that makes moral norms, and hence is a subject; the purpose for which it makes moral norms (namely the goal of morality) is the purpose of society's activities as a subject. The object therefore is all the actions in society that can be morally evaluated and regulated by morality. Thus, if the deductive axiom of value in ethics, which is universally applicable to all fields of ought, good, and value, is deduced to the fields of moral ought, moral good, and moral value, we can draw the following conclusion:

The moral value of the behavioral ought is the utility of the behavioral fact to the goal of morality. Therefore, the moral value of the behavioral ought emerges and is derived from the behavioral fact through the goal of morality: the behavioral ought is the utility of the behavioral fact that conforms to the goal of morality; the behavioral ought-not is the utility of the behavioral fact that does not conform to the goal of morality.

This is the basis for the process of the production and deduction of behavioral ought from the behavioral fact. It also is the basis for the particular deductive method of moral ought, moral good, and moral value, as well as the particular discovery method and proof method of moral ought, moral good and moral value. In short, it is "the deductive postulate of moral value," which is only applicable to ethics, as demonstrated here:

Premise 1: the behavioral fact (substance of moral value).
Premise 2: the goal of morality (standard of moral value).
Conclusion: the behavioral ought (moral value).

For example, "John ought not to kill" is the utility of the fact of John's killing to the goal of morality. Thus "John ought not to kill" is derived from

Deductive axioms and deductive postulates   145

the fact of John's killing through the goal of morality: "John ought not to kill" is the utility of the fact of John's killing not conforming to the goal of morality—i.e., to safeguard the existence and development of society and to promote everyone's interests. This can serve as a deductive postulate of moral value in ethics as shown below:

> Premise 1: John kills people (the behavioral fact; substance of moral value)
> Premise 2: the goal of morality is to safeguard the existence and development of society and to promote everyone's interests (the goal of morality; standard of moral value)
> Conclusion: John ought not to kill (the behavioral ought; moral value)

The earliest discoverer of this ethical postulate was neither Spinoza, who first constructed the axiomatic system in ethics, nor Rawls who advocated "ethical geometry," but was the great physicist Einstein. In his original *Laws of Science and Laws of Ethics* he demonstrated that all ethical propositions can be derived from several primitive propositions, which he termed "ethical axioms." He summed up these primitive propositions as "to safeguard social cooperation," "to protect people's life" and "pain and sadness shall be lessened as much as possible," which, in the final analysis, is the goal of morality, namely to safeguard the existence and development of society" and "to promote everyone's interests."

> As long as the initial premise is sufficiently precise, then other ethical propositions can be derived from them, which are the functions in ethics similar to axioms in mathematics. This is why we do not feel at all that it is meaningless to ask such questions as: "why we should not lie?" We feel that such questions are meaningful because in all discussions of this kind some ethical premises are tacitly taken for granted. We then feel satisfied when we succeed in tracing back the ethical rules in question to these basic premises. In the case of lying this might perhaps be done in some way such as this: Lying destroys confidence in the statements of other people. Without such confidence, social cooperation, which is essential to make human life possible and tolerable, is impossible or at least difficult. This means that the rule "Thou shalt not lie" has been traced back to the demands: "Human life shall be preserved" and "Pain and sadness shall be lessened as much as possible." But what is the origin of such ethical axioms?[7]

4.2 The deductive axiom of evaluation and deductive postulate of moral evaluation in ethics

4.2.1 The process of the production and deduction of value judgment

An examination of the process of the production and deduction of "value and ought" from "is" or "fact" makes it clear that value judgment emerges

146 *The meta-ethical proof*

and can be derived from factual judgment. This is because, by and large, factual judgment and factual cognition are the same concepts, both are human cognition concerning "is" or "fact," and are also mental reflections of "is" or "fact" in human mind. Conversely, value judgment, value cognition, and cognitive evaluation are generally the same concept, all of which are human cognition concerning "value," "good," and "ought" inasmuch as they are reflections of "value," "good," and "ought" in the human mind. In this way, since value, ought, and good can be derived from "is" or "fact," it follows that value judgment also undoubtedly can be derived from factual judgment.

However, Hare contends that value judgments cannot be derived from factual judgments, because in his view, value judgments can only be expressed through imperative sentences, while the logical rule of imperative sentences is that "No imperative conclusion can be validly drawn from a set of premises which does not contain at least one imperative."[8] Therefore, "from a series of indicative sentences about 'the character of any of its objects' no imperative sentence about what is to be done can be derived, and therefore no moral judgment can be derived from it either."[9] In this regard, John R. Searle gives a counter example:

(1) Jones uttered the words "I hereby promise to pay you, Smith, five dollars."
(2) Jones promised to pay Smith five dollars.
(3) Jones placed himself under (undertook) an obligation to pay Smith five dollars.
(4) Jones is under an obligation to pay Smith five dollars.
(5) Jones ought to pay Smith five dollars.[10]

This is a famous example which leads to many controversies in the field of meta-ethics. G. H. von Wright compresses it as follows:

> First premise: A promises to do p.
> Second premise: By promising to do p, A has placed himself under an obligation to do p.
> Conclusion: A ought to do p. [11]

Obviously, Numbers (1), (2), (3), and (4) of the first group of reasoning and premise 1 and premise 2 of the second group of reasoning are all declarative sentences, but the conclusions are imperative sentences, thus overthrowing the logic rule proposed by Hare that "imperative sentences cannot be derived from pure declarative sentences." However, these two groups of reasoning cannot overturn the idea of Hare that "value judgments cannot be derived from pure facts," because value judgments not only can be expressed through imperative sentences as Hare states, but can also be expressed through declarative sentences. Numbers (1) and (2) of the first group of reasoning and premise 1 of the second group of reasoning are declarative sentences, reflecting the commitment of Jones to pay Smith five dollars, hence are factual judgments.

Deductive axioms and deductive postulates   147

Numbers (3) and (4) of the first group of reasoning and premise 2 of the second group of reasoning are also declarative sentences, however they relay that Jones is obliged to pay Smith five dollars, hence are obligation judgments and value judgments, not factual judgments. Thus, although numbers (1), (2), (3), and (4) of the first group of reasoning and the two premises of the second group of reasoning are declarative sentences, not all of them are factual judgments, each group contains one value judgment at least. Therefore, these two groups of reasoning can only refute Hare's logic that imperative sentences cannot be derived from pure declarative sentences, but not his view that value judgments cannot be derived from pure facts. That is why G. H. Wright says that "Searle's argument would have no bearing at all on the Is–Ought issue, i.e., on the question whether normative conclusions can follow from (purely) factual premises."[12] Then, can we derive value judgment from pure factual judgment?

Toulmin's answer is yes. In his *The Place of Reason in Ethics* he discovers that moral value judgment is derived from the factual judgment through the judgment of the goal of morality which he calls the "function of morality." He emphasizes that "the analysis of what I have called the 'function' of ethics......as being to correlate our feelings and behaviour in such a way as to make the fulfillment of everyone's aims and desires as far as possible compatible."[13] Therefore, the moral judgment of whether a habit is right is derived from the factual judgment of whether the habit reduces conflict of interest and promotes happiness:

> Our discussion of the function of ethics led us on to a critique of moral judgment....Of course, "This practice would involve the least conflict of interests attainable under the circumstances" does not *mean* the same as "This would be the right practice"; nor does "This way of life would be more harmoniously satisfying" *mean* the same as "This would be better". But in each case, the first statement is *a good reason* for the second; the "ethically neutral" fact is *a good reason* for the "gerundive" moral judgment. If the adoption of the practice would genuinely reduce conflicts of interest, it is a practice *worthy of adoption*, and if the way of life would genuinely lead to deeper and more consistent happiness, it is one *worthy of pursuit*. And this seems so natural and intelligible, when one bears in mind the function of ethical judgments.[14]

How true this statement is! This is because both value judgment and factual judgment belong to the category of cognition, and are reflections of the properties of the object in the human mind, with the properties of the object as their object. The difference lies, first, in that the object of factual judgment is *is* or *fact*, which is the factual property of the object existing independently of the needs, desires, and purposes of the subject and, second, in that the objects of value judgment are "value," "good," and "ought," which are the relational properties of the object that emerge when the factual properties of

148 *The meta-ethical proof*

the object relate to the needs, desires, and purposes of the subject. While the object of factual judgment exists irrespective of subject, the objects of value judgment exist dependently on the subject as the utilities of the factual properties of the object to the needs, desires, and purposes of the subject.

Therefore, the value judgment emerges and is derived from the factual judgment. However, the factual judgment itself by no means can produce and deduce the value judgment; only when the factual judgment is related to the judgment concerning the needs, desires, and purposes of the subject can the factual judgment produce and deduce the value judgment. Put it another way, the value judgment is derived from the factual judgment through the judgment of the needs, desires, and purposes of the subject: positive value judgment equals the conformity of the factual judgment with the judgment concerning the needs, desires, and purposes of the subject, while negative value judgment equals the nonconformity of the factual judgment with the judgment of the needs, desires, and purposes of the subject.

For example, "John killed people" is a factual judgment, and the object it reflects is the behavioral fact that John killed people. It is the property of John's action of killing (the object) independent of society's purpose (the purpose of the subject) to establish the goal of morality. Conversely, "John ought not to kill people" is the moral value judgment, and the object it reflects is the moral value of John's killing which is a property not being alone of the action of John's killing. It is a relational property that emerges when the behavioral fact of John's killing relates to the goal of morality, which is the behavioral fact of "John's killing" not conforming to the goal of morality.

Therefore, the value judgment of "John ought not to kill" emerges and is derived from the factual judgment of "John kills people." But the moral value judgment of "John ought not to kill" cannot emerge and be derived alone from the factual judgment of "John kills people"; it is only when the factual judgment of "John kills people" is related to the judgment of the goal of morality that the moral value judgment of "John ought not to kill" can emerge and be derived from the factual judgment of "John kills people." In the final analysis, the moral value judgment of "John ought not to kill" emerges and is derived from the factual judgment of "John kills people" through the judgment of goal of morality: The value judgment of "John ought not to kill" equals the nonconformity of the factual judgment of "John kills people" with the judgment of the goal of morality.

> Therefore, the object that value judgment reflects is value, which, in the final analysis, is the utility of the factual properties of the object concerning the needs, desires, and purposes of the subject. Consequently, value judgment (cognitive evaluation) emerges and is derived from factual judgments through the judgment of the needs, desires, and purposes of the subject: positive value judgment is equal to the conformity of the factual judgment with the judgment of needs, desires, and purposes of the subject, while negative value judgment is equal to the nonconformity of

the factual judgment with the judgment of needs, desires, and purposes of the subject.

This is the process of the production and deduction of value judgment (cognitive evaluation), and the method of discovery and proof of value judgment, as well as the method of discovery, proof, and deduction of ought, good, and value in epistemology. It is the deductive formula of value judgment (cognitive evaluation) as presented below:

Premise 1: factual judgment
Premise 2: the judgment of the needs, desires, and purposes of the subject
Conclusion: value judgment (cognitive evaluation)

4.2.2 The deductive axiom of evaluation in Ethics

Can emotional evaluation, volitional evaluation and behavioral evaluation, like value judgment or cognitive evaluation, emerge and be derived from factual judgment through the judgment of the needs, desires and purposes of the subject? The answer is yes because modern psychology shows that cognition is the basis of emotion and volition, hence cognitive evaluation is the basis of emotional evaluation, volitional evaluation, and behavioral evaluation, all of which emerge and are derived from the cognitive evaluation or value judgment.

This is true because emotions undoubtedly occur with perceptual cognition, and there are obviously no emotions without perceptual cognition. A born blind person cannot visually appreciate the beauty of a sunset and a born deaf person cannot enjoy the rich sounds of Beethoven's symphonies. Before we have emotional, volitional, and behavioral evaluations for anything we must first know it, smell it, hear it, touch it, and feel it then understand it: we must first have cognition, cognitive evaluation, and value judgment before we have emotional, volitional, and behavioral evaluations.

Don't we first see the wolf and know that it can eat people, then based on such cognition and cognitive evaluation have the emotional evaluation of "fear" and the volitional evaluation of "deciding to run away," and then the behavioral evaluation of actually "escaping"? The saying that "a newly born calf is not afraid of a tiger" is precisely because it does not know the fierceness of a tiger. It is then quite clear that cognitive evaluation and value judgment are the basis of emotional evaluation, volitional evaluation, and behavioral evaluation. Hence emotional evaluation, volitional evaluation, and behavioral evaluation are consistent with value judgment and all are derived from value judgment or cognitive evaluation. Therefore, all evaluations, like value judgment, ultimately emerge and are derived from factual judgments through the judgment of the needs, desires, and purposes of the subject.

Let's think about flies. When we see a fly, why do we have a sense of disgust (emotional evaluation), decide to kill it (volitional evaluation), and finally kill

150 *The meta-ethical proof*

it (behavioral evaluation)? Isn't it because we know that health is the basic need of human beings (judgment of needs, desires, and purposes of the subject), and that because flies generally transmit bacteria (factual judgment) the fly in question does not meet the needs of human health, and is therefore bad (cognitive evaluation or value judgment). Therefore, all evaluations about flies ultimately emerge and are derived from the factual judgment that flies spread bacteria through the judgment of the needs, desires, and purpose of the subject.

Therefore, emotional evaluation, volitional evaluation, and behavioral evaluation all emerge and are derived from value judgment (cognitive evaluation), while the object of the reflection of value judgment is value, namely the utility of the factual properties of the object concerning the needs, desires, and purposes of the subject. Thus all evaluations ultimately emerge and are derived from factual judgments through the judgment of the needs, desires, and purposes of the subject: a positive evaluation is the conformity of the factual judgment with the judgment of the needs, desires, and purposes of the subject, while a negative evaluation is the nonconformity of the factual judgment with the judgment of the needs, desires, and purposes of the subject. This is the "process A" of the production and deduction of evaluation, the method A of the discovery and proof of evaluation, the method A of the discovery, proof, and deduction of ought, good, and value in the theory of evaluation. It can be termed "the deductive formula A of evaluation" as expressed below:

> Premise 1: Flies spread bacteria (factual judgment).
> Premise 2: Health is the basic need of human beings (judgment of the needs, desires, and purposes of the subject).
> Conclusion 1: Flies spread bacteria which does not conform to the needs of human health and is therefore bad (cognitive evaluation or value judgment).
> Conclusion 2: Seeing a fly could induce an aversive feeling (emotional evaluation), hence an intention to kill it (volitional evaluation), and finally the act of killing it (behavioral evaluation).

The reason that it is called "the deductive formula A of evaluation" instead of "the deductive formula of evaluation" is because the two premises of evaluation—about factual judgment and the judgment of the needs, desires, and purposes of the subject—are both non-value judgments or non-evaluation cognitions, which have been termed by some scholars as "cognition" opposite to evaluation. This is inappropriate because evaluation and cognition are not in an oppositional or contradictory relation but rather a "cross-conceptual" relation which can be analyzed from two perspectives. On the one hand, some cognitions are included in the extension of evaluation: cognitive evaluation, because, as mentioned above, evaluations are divided into "cognitive evaluation," "emotional evaluation," "volitional evaluation," and "behavioral

Deductive axioms and deductive postulates   151

evaluation." On the other hand, some evaluations also are included in the extension of cognition: evaluative cognition, because, as it is known, cognitions are also divided into evaluative cognition and non-evaluative cognition. For example, "the flower is beautiful" is an evaluative cognition, while "the flower is red" is a non-evaluative cognition.

It can be seen that evaluation and cognition are not in an oppositional or contradictory relation but rather a "cross-conceptual" relation. With the understanding that non-evaluative cognition or non-value judgment is not "cognition" in the sense it is opposite to evaluation, we ought to follow the Western meta-ethical terminology and term non-evaluative cognition "description" to distinguish it from evaluation. Thence so-called description is, on the one hand, a description of the fact of the object, namely factual judgment or factual cognition, which is a reflection of the facts of the object, and on the other hand is a description of the subject, namely the judgment of the subject or the cognition of the subject, which is also a reflection of the needs, desires, and purposes of the subject.

Thus, although evaluation cannot directly emerge and be derived from the factual judgment, it can directly emerge and be derived from description: an evaluation emerges and is derived from two descriptions, namely the description of the facts of the object and the description of the needs, desires, and purposes of the subject: a positive evaluation is equal to the conformity of the factual description with the description of the needs, desires, and purposes of the subject, while a negative evaluation is equal to the nonconformity of the factual description with the description of the needs, desires, and purposes of the subject. Description is process B of the production and deduction of evaluation, the deductive method B of evaluation, the method B of the discovery and proof of evaluation, and the discovery, proof, and deductive method B of ought, good, and value in the theory of evaluation. The deductive formula B of evaluation is as follows:

> Premise 1: flies spread bacteria (factual description).
> Premise 2: health is the basic need of human beings (description of needs, desires, and purposes of the subject).
> Conclusion 1: flies spread bacteria which does not meet human needs of health and is therefore bad (cognitive evaluation and value judgment).

Conclusion 2: seeing a fly could induce an aversive feeling (emotional evaluation), hence the intention to kill it (volitional evaluation), and finally the act of killing it (behavioral evaluation).

In summary, emotional evaluation, volitional evaluation, and behavioral evaluation emerge and are derived from value judgment (cognitive evaluations), while the object that value judgment reflects is value, namely the utility of the factual properties of the object concerning the needs, desires, and purposes of the subject. Consequently, all evaluations ultimately

152 *The meta-ethical proof*

emerge and are derived from factual judgment through the judgment of the needs, desires, and purposes of the subject: the positive evaluation is equal to the conformity of the factual judgment with the needs, desires, and purposes of the subject, while the negative evaluation is equal to the nonconformity of the factual judgment with the judgment of needs, desires, and purposes of the subject. In other words, a kind of evaluation emerges and is derived from two descriptions, namely the description of the facts of the object and the description of the needs, desires, and purposes of the subject: the positive evaluation is equal to the conformity of the factual description with the description of the needs, desires, and purposes of the subject, while the negative evaluation is equal to the nonconformity of the factual description with the description of the needs, desires, and purposes of the subject.

This is the process of the production and deduction of evaluation, the deductive method of evaluation, the method of the discovery and proof of evaluation, and the method of the discovery, proof, and deduction of ought, good, and value in the theory of evaluation. In the final analysis, it is the deductive axiom of evaluation, which is universally applicable to all value sciences, such as ethics and stateology and Chinaology: "the deductive axiom of evaluation in value sciences," "the deductive axiom of evaluation in ethics," "the deductive axiom of evaluation in stateology" and "the deductive axiom of evaluation in Chinaology" are the same concepts. The most essential arrangement of the two sets of reasoning for this axiom is as follows:

The deductive formula A of evaluation:

Premise 1: factual judgment
Premise 2: judgment of the needs, desires, and purposes of the subject
Conclusion 1: value judgment or cognitive evaluation
Conclusion 2: emotional, volitional, and behavioral evaluations

The deductive formula B of evaluation:

Premise1: fact description
Premise 2: descriptions of the needs, desires, and purposes of the subject
Conclusion 1: cognitive evaluation or value judgment
Conclusion 2: emotional, volitional, and behavioral evaluations

4.2.3 *The deductive postulate of moral evaluation in ethics*

In the field of moral value, society is the agent that makes moral norms, and hence is a subject; the purpose for which it makes moral norms (namely the goal of morality) is the purpose of the activities of society as a subject. The object therefore is all the actions in society that can be morally evaluated and regulated by morality. Thence, if the deductive axiom of evaluation in ethics, which is applicable to all fields of ought, good, and value, is deduced

Deductive axioms and deductive postulates   153

to the fields of moral ought, moral good, and moral value, we can draw the following conclusions:

> Emotional moral evaluation, volitional moral evaluation, and behavioral moral evaluation emerge and are derived from moral value judgment (cognitive moral evaluations), while the object that moral value judgment reflects is moral value, namely the utility of the behavioral fact conforms to the goal of morality. Consequently, all moral evaluations of the behavioral ought ultimately emerge and are derived from the judgment of the behavioral fact through the judgment of the goal of morality: a positive moral evaluation is equal to the conformity of the judgment of the behavioral fact with the judgment of the goal of morality, while a negative moral evaluation is equal to the nonconformity of the judgment of the behavioral fact with the judgment of the goal of morality. In other words, a kind of moral evaluation emerges and is derived from two descriptions, namely the description of the behavioral fact and the description of the goal of morality: the positive moral evaluation is equal to the conformity of the description of behavioral fact with the description of the goal of morality, while the negative moral evaluation is equal to the nonconformity of the description of the behavioral fact with the description of the goal of morality.

This is the process of the production and deduction of moral evaluation, the deductive method of moral evaluation, the method of the discovery and proof of moral evaluation, and the deductive postulate of moral evaluation. Only applicable to ethics the deductive formula is shown in the following formulas:
Deductive formula A of moral evaluation:

> Premise 1: judgment of behavioral fact
> Premise 2: judgment of goal of morality
> Conclusion 1: moral value judgment and cognitive moral evaluation
> Conclusion 2: emotional moral evaluation, volitional moral evaluation, and behavioral moral evaluation

Deductive formula B of moral evaluation

> Premise 1: description of behavioral facts
> Premise 2: description of goal of morality
> Conclusion 1: cognitive moral evaluation or moral value judgment
> Conclusion 2: emotional moral evaluation, volitional moral evaluation, and behavioral moral evaluation

For example, once we knew that John's abuse of his parents was indisputable (factual judgment or fact description), we had nothing but contempt for him (emotional moral evaluation) and decided to teach him a

154 *The meta-ethical proof*

lesson (volitional moral evaluation), so John was appropriately punished (behavioral moral evaluation). Why? This is because the goal of morality is to safeguard the existence and development of society and promote everyone's interests (judgment of the goal of morality or description of the goal of morality). The abuse of parents is against the goal of morality, hence is immoral, wicked or evil (cognitive moral evaluation or moral value judgment). Therefore, all these moral evaluations emerge and are derived from the factual judgment of John's abuse of his parents through the judgment of the goal of morality:

> Premise 1: John abuses parents (factual judgment or fact description).
> Premise 2: The goal of morality is to safeguard the existence and development of society and to promote everyone's interests (judgment of the goal of morality or description of the goal of morality).
> Conclusion 1: John's abuse of parents violates the goal of morality and is evil or immoral (cognitive moral evaluation or moral value judgment).
> Conclusion 2: Seeing John's abuse of his parents incited feelings of contempt (emotional moral evaluation) and the desire to teach him a lesson (volitional moral evaluation) lead to John's eventual punishment (behavioral moral evaluation).

4.3 The deductive axiom of the truth and falsehood and right and wrong of evaluation, and the deductive postulate of the truth and falsehood and right and wrong of moral evaluation in ethics

The study of "evaluation" in Chapter 1 on the category of meta-ethics shows that in the evaluation distinguishes between truth and falsehood and right and wrong. On the one hand, cognitive evaluation or value judgment can be true or false: it is true when it is consistent with the object it reflects, and false when it is not consistent with object it reflects. On the other hand, since emotional evaluation, volitional evaluation, and behavioral evaluation only have the utility, they do not have the issue of being true and false but only the issue of being right and wrong, and good and bad: the utility which satisfies the needs of the subject can be called right, good, and ought; the utility which does not satisfies the needs of the subject can be called wrong, bad, and ought-not. "Right and wrong," "good and bad," and "ought and ought-not" are the same concepts.

Then, how can the evaluation be true and right rather than false and wrong? In other words, how can we prove the truth or falsehood and right or wrong of evaluation? Or, moreover, what is the process for arriving at the truth or falsehood and right or wrong of evaluation? The answers to these problems constitute the axiom on the truth or falsehood and right or wrong of evaluation, and the postulate on the truth or falsehood and right or wrong of moral evaluation in ethics, which is undoubtedly a specific case of the axiom

Deductive axioms and deductive postulates 155

of evaluation and the postulate of the moral evaluation in ethics, and can be deduced from them easily. Therefore, let's start from the axiom of evaluation and the postulate of moral evaluation, first to deduce the truth or falsehood of cognitive evaluation or value judgment, and then to deduce the process of the production and deduction of the truth or falsehood and right or wrong of all evaluations.

4.3.1 The process of the production and deduction of the truth of value judgment

For the proof of the truth and falsehood of value judgment, Hare provided a profound argument through the example of how to judge and justify whether a strawberry is a good one. He points out:

> If we knew all the descriptive properties which a particular strawberry had (knew, of every descriptive sentence relating to the strawberry, whether it was true or false), and if we knew also the meaning of the word "good," then what else should we require to know, in order to be able to tell whether a strawberry was a good one? Once the question is put in this way, the answer should be apparent. We should require to know, what are the criteria in virtue of which a strawberry is to be called a good one, or what are the characteristics that make a strawberry a good one, or what is the standard of goodness in strawberries.[15]

That is to say, the proof that a strawberry is a good one requires knowledge in three aspects: the first is the description of the fact of the strawberry; the second is the meaning of the "good" of a good strawberry, and the third is the standard for the measurement of goodness or badness of the strawberry. To be more exact, to justify the truth or falsehood of value judgment that a strawberry is a good one, we must settle three problems. Firstly, whether the value judgment of the goodness or badness of the "strawberry" conforms to the value of the "strawberry"; secondly, whether the factual judgment of the "strawberry" is true or false; thirdly, whether the judgment of the standard of the goodness or badness of the strawberry, namely the judgment concerning the needs, desires, and purposes of the subject, is true or false.

How true Hare's argument is! As mentioned earlier, value is the utility of the fact of the object to the needs, desires, and purpose of the subject, so it follows that value judgment is the judgment concerning "the utility of the fact of the object to the needs, desires and purpose of the subject," and that value judgment emerges and is derived from "factual judgment" through the judgment of "the needs, desires, and purposes of the subject": the positive value judgment is equal to the conformity of the factual judgment with the judgment of needs, desires, and purposes of the subject, while negative value judgment is equal to the nonconformity of the factual judgment with the judgment of the needs, desires of the subject.

156 *The meta-ethical proof*

> Therefore, "the truth or falsehood of value judgment" depends directly on whether "value judgment" conforms to "value," and fundamentally speaking, on the one hand, depends on the truth or falsehood of the "factual judgment," and on the other hand, on the truth or falsehood of "the judgment of the needs, desires, and purposes of the subject": if both of them are true, the "value judgment" logically derived from the two certainly is true; if the "value judgment" is false, the "factual judgment" and the "judgment of the needs, desires, and purposes of the subject" certainly is false: either one or both of them are false.

For example, the value judgment that "eggs are nutritious" is true, generally speaking, because it conforms to the general value of the eggs, and fundamentally speaking, because, on the one hand, the factual judgment that egg has protein is true and on the other hand, the judgment concerning the needs of the subject that the "human body needs protein" is also true, hence the value judgment that "eggs are nutritious" is certainly true for it is derived from both. Conversely, if the value judgment of eggs is false (i.e., eggs have no nutritional value), the value judgment does not conform to the general value of eggs because either the "factual judgment" or the value judgment concerning the subject's needs is false (i.e., mistakenly believing that eggs have no protein or that the human body does not need protein), or both judgments are false.

This is the process of the production and deduction of truth or falsehood the judgment of ought, good, and value, the deductive method of the truth of value judgment or cognitive evaluation, the method of the discovery and proof of the truth of value judgment or cognitive evaluation, the method of the discovery, proof, and deduction of ought, good, and value in the theory of truth. The deductive formula is as follows:

> Premise 1: the factual judgment is true or false.
> Premise 2: the judgment of needs, desires, and purposes of the subject is true or false.
> Conclusion: the value judgment is true or false.

The process of the production and deduction of the truth or falsehood of value judgment shows that a value judgment or cognitive evaluation reflects three objects: it directly reflects the utility of the fact of the object of evaluation to the subject's needs, namely the *value* and *ought* of the object of evaluation; fundamentally speaking, it reflects, on the one hand, the fact of the object of evaluation, and on the other hand the needs, desires, emotions, and purposes of the subject. Therefore, Hare's revision of Stevenson's theory that value judgments have both emotional and descriptive meanings, namely that any value judgment has both meanings of evaluation and description,[16] is a big step forward, but it is not quite enough. More exactly speaking, any value judgment has one kind of evaluative meaning, which is the cognitive

Deductive axioms and deductive postulates 157

evaluation of the value and ought of the object of evaluation, and two kinds of descriptive meanings, which are the descriptions of the facts of the object of evaluation and of the needs, desires, emotions, and purposes of the subject.

Therefore, the science concerning "value," "ought," and "good" is much more complicated than the science concerning "is" and "fact." Factual science only has one research object, that is, fact, while value science has three research objects: value, fact, and subject's needs. Theoretical disagreement in factual science is only disagreement about facts, whereas there are three main kinds of theoretical disagreement in value science: generally, there is disagreement about *value*; but, precisely, there is disagreement about *facts* or disagreement about *the needs, emotions, and purposes of the subject*, or disagreement over the combination of the two. Thence Stevenson's statement that the disagreement over ethical problems has the duality of belief (cognition of fact) and attitudes (the cognition of needs and emotions of the subject) is not exact. More accurately, ethical disagreements have ternary properties: generally there is disagreement about moral value judgment concerning the behavioral ought; but, more precisely, the disagreement is over description: namely over the description of the behavioral facts or the description of the goal of morality, or disagreement over the combination of both.

4.3.2 The deductive axiom of truth and falsehood and right and wrong of evaluation

Emotional evaluation, volitional evaluation, and behavioral evaluation, as discussed earlier, are consistent with cognitive evaluation or value judgment, which emerges and is derived from cognitive evaluation or value judgment. Therefore, the right or wrong of emotional evaluation, volitional evaluation, and behavioral evaluation is determined by the truth or falsehood of value judgment or cognitive evaluation, and certainly is consistent with value judgment or cognitive evaluation: if value judgment or cognitive evaluation is true (i.e., conforms to the value), emotional evaluation, volitional evaluation, and behavioral evaluations certainly are right (i.e., certainly beneficial to satisfy the needs, desires, and purposes of the subject); if the value judgment or cognitive evaluation is false (i.e., does not conform to the value), emotional evaluation, volitional evaluation, and behavioral evaluation certainly are wrong (i.e., certainly an impediment to satisfy the needs, desires, and purposes of the subject).

Therefore, the truth or falsehood and right or wrong of all evaluations depend on the truth or falsehood of value judgment, and ultimately on the truth or falsehood of factual judgment and the judgment of the needs, desires, and purposes of the subject: if both are true, the value judgment or cognitive evaluation, which logically emerges and is derived from the two, certainly is true (i.e., certainly conforms to the value), and emotional evaluations, volitional evaluations, and behavioral evaluations certainly are

158 *The meta-ethical proof*

right (i.e., certainly is beneficial to satisfy the needs, desires, and purposes of the subject); if value judgment or cognitive evaluation is false (i.e., does not conform to the value), and emotional evaluation, volitional evaluation, and behavioral evaluation are wrong (i.e., are an impediment to satisfy the needs, desires, and purposes of the subject), the factual judgment and the judgment of the needs, desires, and purposes of the subject from which they are derived certainly are false: either one or both of them are false.

This is the deductive method of the truth or falsehood and right or wrong of evaluation, the method of the discovery and proof of the truth or falsehood and right or wrong of evaluation, the method of the discovery, proof, and deduction of the truth or falsehood and right or wrong of the evaluation of ought, good, and value, and the deductive axiom of the truth or falsehood and right or wrong of evaluation in ethics. In the final analysis, it is the deductive axiom of the truth or falsehood and right or wrong of the evaluation, which is universally applicable to all value science (e.g., ethics, stateology, Chinaology). The deductive axiom is as follows:

Premise 1: the factual judgment is true or false.
Premise 2: the judgment of subject's needs is true or false.
Conclusion 1: the value judgment or the cognitive evaluation is true or false.
Conclusion 2: the emotional evaluation, volitional evaluation and behavioral evaluation are right or wrong.

For example, if, on the one hand, our factual judgment on a certain food is true (i.e., conforms to the fact of the food), and, on the other hand, the subjective judgment concerning human's needs is true (i.e., conforms to human needs), then the value judgment *whether the food is good for health*, which is derived from the two judgments, must also be true (i.e., conforms to the value of the food); consequently the preference for or aversion to the food (emotional evaluation), the intention to eat it often or the refusal to eat it (volitional evaluation), and eating it frequently or not eating it (behavioral evaluation) certainly are right (i.e., certainly is beneficial to satisfy the needs of human health, irrespective of a subject's preferences).

By contrast, let's consider the falsehood of evaluation by taking the example of a briber who fails to bribe an official. Seeking favors the briber thinks that a certain gift will satisfy an official (i.e., the value judgment or cognitive evaluation is false). Enticed by the value of the gift (i.e., the emotional evaluation is wrong), he is intent on buying it to bribe the official (i.e., the volitional evaluation is wrong). He buys the gift and presents it to the official (i.e., the behavioral evaluation was wrong). The official informs the briber that he doesn't accept bribes. The briber had completely overestimated the value of the gift or rather bribe in terms of its value to the official. Isn't this because

Deductive axioms and deductive postulates   159

"the judgment of the subject" was false? Let's revisit as our next example the case of Zhu Geliang and Ma Su in Chapter 1. Zhu Geliang's value judgment that "Ma Su has the talent of a great general" was false, so his favor to Ma Su (emotional evaluation), his intention to utilize his talent (volitional evaluation) and entrust him with responsibility (behavioral evaluation) were all wrong because his "factual judgment" of Ma Su's ability was false.

4.3.3 The deductive postulate of the truth and falsehood and right and wrong of moral evaluation

In the field of moral value, society is the agent that makes moral norms, and hence is a subject; the purpose for which it makes moral norms (namely the goal of morality) is the purpose of the activities of society as a subject. The object therefore is all the actions in society that can be morally evaluated and regulated by morality. Thence, if "the deductive axiom of the truth or falsehood and right or wrong of evaluation," which is universally applicable to all fields of value, is deduced to the fields of moral value, we can draw the following conclusions:

> **Emotional moral evaluation, volitional moral evaluation and behavioral moral evaluation emerge and are derived from moral value judgment (cognitive moral evaluations). Therefore, the truth or falsehood and right or wrong of all moral evaluations depend on the truth or falsehood of moral value judgment, and ultimately on the truth or falsehood of the judgment of behavioral fact and the judgment of the goal of morality: if both are true, the moral value judgment or cognitive moral evaluation, which emerges and is derived from the two, certainly is true (i.e., certainly conforms to the moral value), and the emotional moral evaluations, volitional moral evaluations, and behavioral moral evaluations certainly are right, good or correct (i.e., certainly conform to the goal of morality); if moral value judgment is false (i.e., does not conform to moral value), and emotional moral evaluations, volitional moral evaluations, and behavioral moral evaluations are wrong, bad, or incorrect (i.e., do not conform to the goal of morality), the judgment of the behavioral fact and the judgment of the goal of morality from which they are derived certainly are false: either one or both of them are false.**

This is the process of the production and deduction of the truth or falsehood and right or wrong of moral evaluation, the deductive method of the truth or falsehood and right or wrong of moral evaluation, the method of the discovery and proof of the truth or falsehood and right or wrong of moral evaluation, the method of the discovery, proof and deduction of the truth or falsehood and right or wrong of evaluation of the moral ought, moral good, and moral value, and is "the deductive postulate of the truth or falsehood and right or wrong of the moral evaluation in ethics" presented as follows:

160   *The meta-ethical proof*

Premise 1: The judgment of behavioral fact is true or false.
Premise 2: The judgment of the goal of morality is true or false.
Conclusion 1: The judgment of moral value or cognitive moral evaluation is true or false.
Conclusion 2: The emotional moral evaluation, volitional moral evaluation, and behavioral moral evaluation are right or wrong.

This postulate, for example, has considerable relevance for disproving and dispelling the reasoning (and also contempt) that altruists such as Confucians, Kant, F. H. Bradley, and Christian ethicists have for the concept of "self-interest": first, they declare contempt for the notion (i.e., their emotional moral evaluation is wrong), feel they ought to criticize it (i.e., their volitional moral evaluation is wrong), and frequently do criticize it (i.e., their behavioral moral evaluation is wrong); second, they mistakenly assume that any "action in one's self-interest" is a negative moral value (i.e., their moral value judgment or cognitive moral evaluation is wrong). On this second point, ethicists ignore key logical considerations on both a general and more technical level: first, generally speaking, they neglect the fact that self-interest can benefit others, hence their moral value judgment on "self-interest" does not conform to the actual moral value of *"benefiting others out of one's self-interest"*; second, technically speaking, they mistakenly believe that the goal of morality is for the perfection of everyone's virtue, that is, that morality is for itself or "Morality is for its own sake"[17](i.e., their judgment of the goal of morality is wrong), and they one-sidedly hold that *"benefiting oneself"* is bound to harm others (i.e., their judgment of behavioral fact is wrong).

In contrast to altruists, rational egoists such as Laozi, Han Fei, Helvetius, and d'Holbach's assertion of the moral value judgment that *"benefiting others out of self-interest* is the greatest moral good" is true because it generally conforms to the moral value of *benefiting others out of self-interest* (the positive moral value of which is far greater than that of any action); and, more specifically, because, the judgment of the behavioral fact that benefiting others out of self-interest "maximizes the interests of everyone in the whole society" is true, and because, the judgment of the goal of morality that "the goal of morality is to promote everyone's interests" is also true. Both are true, so the judgment of moral value derived from the two, namely "benefiting others out of self-interest mostly conforms to the goal of morality, and is the greatest positive moral value," is certainly true. How can we therefore criticize or scorn the action of *benefiting others out of self-interest*? Like the rational egoists mentioned, we are bound to respect the essential principle of "self-interest" that benefits others (which is the correct moral emotional evaluation), to have the volition to restore the merit and reputation of the principle (which is the correct volitional moral evaluation), and hence effectively argue the principle (which is the correct behavioral moral evaluation).

4.4 The deductive axiom of excellent norms and deductive postulate of excellent moral norms in ethics

4.4.1 An analysis of the concepts of "norm," "value," and "value judgment"

"The deductive axiom of the truth or falsehood and right or wrong of evaluation" and "the deductive postulate of the truth or falsehood and right or wrong of moral evaluation" in ethics are the methods for justifying the truth of moral value judgment, and thus appear to be the ultimate ethical axiom and postulate. However, this is in fact not the case because ethics is a science concerning excellent morality: it explores the truth of moral value judgment and aims at making excellent moral norms, and it explores the "deductive axiom of the truth or falsehood and right or wrong of evaluation" and the "deductive postulate of the truth or falsehood and right or wrong of moral evaluation," with the aim of justifying "the deductive axiom of excellent norms" and "the deductive postulate of excellent moral norms."

It turns out that the making of excellent norms involves three inseparable but fundamentally different concepts, namely "norm," "value," and "value judgment." However, throughout history, most ethicists have not made a distinction between "norm" and "value," and mostly have regarded "morality" and "moral value" as the same concept. In fact, value is fundamentally different from norms. As mentioned at the outset of this volume, "morality" belongs to the category of "norms," thus "morality" and "moral norms" are essentially the same concept. Furthermore, norms are made or agreed upon by people but value is not. Put simply, people do not make the nutritional value of corn, wheat, and soybean. So, one might ask, what exactly is the relationship between value and norm?

It is not difficult to see that value is the basis for making norms and that norms are made or agreed upon based on value. Why is it that health experts, for instance, take "one ought to eat one egg every day" as the behavioral norm for how to eat eggs? Isn't it because, in their opinion, eating just one egg every day has positive nutritional value, and that eating more than one egg every day has negative nutritional value? It follows that the moral norms of behavioral ought are made or agreed upon based on the moral value of behaviors.

Why is it that rational egoists such as Laozi, Han Fei, Helvetius, and d'Holbach take *benefiting others out of one's self-interest* as a moral norm? Isn't it because, in their opinion, it has positive moral value in that it ultimately benefits others? Conversely, the reason that Confucius, Mozi, Kant, and Christian ethicists are strongly against *benefiting others out of one's self-interest* as a moral norm is because, in their opinion, it has negative moral value and in the end is harmful to oneself and others or so-called public interests.

Therefore, norms, like value judgments, take the value as its content, object and copies, and are the expressions of value. The difference is that value judgment is the reflection of value in mind, hence is the thought form

162   *The meta-ethical proof*

of value, while norm is the reflection of value in actions, hence is the normative form of value. Thus, there is a distinction between truth and falsehood in value judgment: the judgment that conforms to the value is true, while the judgment that does not conform to the value is false. Norms have no distinction of truth and falsehood but only right and wrong or good and bad: the norm that conforms to the value is excellent, good, right, or correct, while the norm that does not conform to the value is inferior, bad, wrong, or incorrect.

For example, if "one ought to eat an egg every day" has positive nutritional value just like the health experts advocate, then, on the one hand, their value judgment of "one ought to eat an egg every day" is true because it conforms to the nutritional value of eggs; on the hand, their taking "one ought to eat an egg every day" as the behavioral norm for how to eat eggs also conforms to the nutritional value of eggs, so it is an excellent behavioral norm.

If *benefiting others out of one's self-interest* indeed has negative moral value as Confucians declare, then, on the one hand, the Legalists'[18] moral value judgment that "one ought to benefit others out of one's self-interest" was false because it did not conform to the moral value of benefiting others for one's self-interest; on the other hand, the Legalists' taking *benefiting others out of one's self-interest* as a moral norm also did not conform to the moral value of benefiting others for one's self-interest, so it was a bad moral norm.

However, how can we make excellent or good norms that conform to value? It is undoubtedly that the making of any norm is under the guidance of certain value judgment, so it is obvious that only the norms that are made under the condition that the value judgment is true conform to value, hence can be excellent, good, right, or correct norms; conversely, if the value judgment is false, the norms made under its guidance certainly do not conform to the value, hence are inferior, bad, wrong or incorrect.

For example: if eating ten eggs every day has a positive nutritional value, the value judgment of "one ought to eat ten eggs every day" is true, then taking "one ought to eat ten eggs every day" as a behavioral norm for eating eggs conforms to the nutritional value of eating ten eggs every day, hence is an excellent or good moral norm. Conversely, if the value judgment of "one ought to eat ten eggs every day" is false, eating ten eggs every day has a negative nutritional value, then taking it as a behavioral norm for eating eggs does not conform to the nutritional value of eating ten eggs every day, hence is an inferior or bad norm.

If the moral value judgment that "benefiting others out of one's self-interest" has positive moral value" is true, then either Laozi's or Han Fei's taking it as a moral norm of behavioral ought conforms to its moral value, hence can be an excellent or good moral norm. Conversely, if the moral value judgment that "benefiting others for one's self-interest has positive moral value" is false and has negative value, then either Laozi's or Han Fei's taking it as a moral norm of behavioral ought does not conform to its moral value, and hence can be an inferior or bad moral norm.

Deductive axioms and deductive postulates 163

Thus, the truth of a value judgment is the means for achieving the goal of making excellent norms, which is also the necessary and sufficient condition for making excellent norms: if and only if our value judgment is the truth, we can make excellent, good, right, or correct norms that conform to the value, and avoid making inferior, bad, wrong, or incorrect norms that do not conform to the value. Similarly, if and only if our *moral* value judgment is the truth, we can make excellent, good, right, or correct moral norms that conform to the *moral* value, and avoid the making of inferior, bad, wrong, or incorrect morality that does not conform to the moral value.

4.4.2 The deductive axiom of excellent norm in ethics

To sum up, first of all, excellent, good, right, or correct behavioral norm is the one that conforms to the behavioral value, while the inferior, bad, wrong, or incorrect behavioral norm is the behavioral norm that does not conform to the behavioral value. Secondly, the truth of a value judgment is the means for achieving the goal of making excellent norms, and is the necessary and sufficient condition for making excellent norms; and finally, the deductive axiom of the truth and falsehood and right and wrong of evaluation in ethics indicates that the "truth or falsehood of value judgment" directly depends on whether "the value judgment" conforms to "the value," which, fundamentally speaking, depends on both the truth or falsehood of the "factual judgment" and truth or falsehood of the "judgment of the needs, desires, and purposes of the subject." In a nutshell, we can draw the following conclusions:

The excellent, good, right, or correct behavioral norm is the behavioral norm that conforms to the behavioral value, while the inferior, bad, wrong, or incorrect behavioral norm is the behavioral norm that does not conform to the behavioral value. Therefore, though the norms of behavioral ought are made and agreed upon by people, only the inferior, bad, wrong, or incorrect behavioral norms are arbitrary. The good, right, or correct behavioral norms by contrast are based on "the behavioral value," namely the utility of "the behavioral facts" to "the needs, desires, and purposes of the subject," which, in the final analysis is derived and made from "the behavioral facts" through "the needs, desires and purposes of the subject." Therefore, the excellence or inferiority of the behavioral norms, directly depends on the truth or falsehood of the "value judgment" of the behavioral ought, and, fundamentally speaking, depends on both the truth or falsehood of "the factual judgment" of the behavioral norm and the truth or falsehood of "the judgment of the needs, desires, and purposes of the subject": if both are true, the value judgment logically derived from the two certainly is true, hence the behavioral norms made under their guidance certainly conform to the behavioral value, and certainly are excellent behavioral norms; if the behavioral norms do not conform to the behavioral value, that is, are inferior behavioral norms, then "the value

164 *The meta-ethical proof*

judgment" of the behavioral ought certainly is false, hence either "the factual judgment" of the behavioral fact or the judgment of the "value standard" of the needs of the subject is certainly false or both are false.

For example, the reason why the behavioral norm that "one ought to eat an egg every day" is an excellent norm is because it depends directly on the truth of the value judgment that "one ought to eat an egg every day"; fundamentally speaking, on the one hand, it depends on the truth of the "factual judgment" that "an egg contains X amount of protein," and, on the other hand, on the truth of the judgment of the subject's needs that the "human body needs X amount of protein every day": if both are true, the value judgment logically derived from the two that "one ought to eat an egg every day" certainly is true, hence the behavioral norm that "one ought to eat an egg everyday" made under its guidance certainly conforms to the behavioral value that "one ought to eat an egg every day," and is therefore an excellent norm.

In contrast to this, in my childhood, my father taught me the behavioral norm of "one ought to eat as many eggs as possible every day." This was misguided advice reflecting a bad norm: bad because it directly depended on the falsehood of the value judgment that "the more eggs one eats every day the better," which, fundamentally speaking, depended on the falsehood of the "factual judgment" of eggs and "the judgment of what the human body needs": either one was false (the mistaken belief that an egg has a protein far less than X amount, or that the human body needs much more protein than X amount every day), or both were false (the mistaken belief that an egg has far less protein than X amount and that the human body needs much more protein than the X amount every day).

This is basic example reflects the process of the deduction and making of "excellent norms" based directly on the truth of "value judgment" and ultimately based on the truth of "factual judgments" and of "judgments of the subject's needs." It is a reflection of the method of deduction and making of excellent norms, the method of the discovery and proof of excellent norms, the method of the discovery, proof, and deduction of the ought, good and value in normative theory, the deductive axiom of the excellent norms in ethics, and the deductive axiom of the excellent norms in all value sciences such as stateology (the value science concerned with goodness and badness of state institutions), and Chinaology (the value science concerned with goodness and badness of China's state institutions). The deductive axiom is presented below:

Premise 1: The factual judgment is true or false.
Premise 2: The judgment of the needs, desires, and purposes of the subject is true or false.
Conclusion 1: The value judgment of ought is true or false.
Conclusion 2: The norm is good or bad (whether the norm conforms to the value or not).

Deductive axioms and deductive postulates 165

The formula can be further simplified as follows:

Premise 1: The fact (substance of value).
Premise 2: The needs, desires and purposes of the subject (standard of value).
Conclusion 1: The ought (value).
Conclusion 2: The norms is good or bad (whether the norm conforms to the value or not).

4.4.3 The deductive postulates of excellent moral norm

In the field of moral norms, society is the agent that makes moral norms, and hence is a subject; the purpose for which it makes moral norms (namely the goal of morality) is the purpose of the activities of society as a subject. The object therefore is all the actions in society that can be morally evaluated and regulated by morality: moral value is the utility of the behavioral facts to the goal of morality. Thence, if the "deductive axiom of excellent norms," which is universally applicable to all fields of norms, is deduced to the field of moral norms, we can draw the following conclusions:

The excellent, good, right, or correct moral norm is the moral norm that conforms to the moral value, while the inferior, bad, wrong, or incorrect moral norm is the moral norm that does not conform to the moral value. Therefore, though the moral norms are made and agreed upon by people, only inferior, bad, wrong or incorrect moral norms are arbitrary. On the contrary, excellent, good, right, or correct moral norms are based on "the moral value of the behavioral ought," namely the utility of "the behavioral facts" to "the goal of morality," which, in the final analysis, can only be derived and made from "behavioral facts" through the goal of morality. Therefore, the excellence or inferiority of the moral norms of the behavioral ought, depends directly on the truth or falsehood of "the judgment of moral value," which, fundamentally speaking, on the one hand, depends on the truth or falsehood of "the factual judgment" of the behavior, on the other hand, depends on the truth or falsehood of "the judgment of the goal of morality": If both are true, the moral value judgment logically derived from the two must be true, and the moral norms of the behavioral ought made under their guidance certainly are excellent; if the moral norms of the behavioral ought made are inferior, then the judgment of moral value of the behavioral ought certainly is false, hence the factual judgment and the judgment of the goal of morality from which it is derived certainly are false: either one or both of them are false.

For example, the reason why the principle that "one ought to benefit others for one's self-interest" advocated by the rational egoists (Laozi, Hanfei,

166 *The meta-ethical proof*

Helvetius, and d'Holbach) is an excellent moral norm is that it depends directly on the truth of the moral value judgment that "benefiting others for one's self-interest has positive moral value," which, fundamentally speaking, depends on both the truth of the factual judgment that "benefiting others for one's self-interest factually benefits both oneself and others" and the truth of the judgment of the value standard that "the goal of morality is to promote everyone's interests": if both are true, then the moral value judgment that "benefiting others promotes everyone's interests" conforms to the goal of morality, hence has "positive moral value," which derived from the two, certainly is true; thus the moral norm that "one ought to benefit others for one's self-interest," made under its guidance, certainly is an excellent moral norm. On the contrary, the moral norm advocated by altruist (the Confucians, the Mohists, Kant, and the Christian ethicists), that *"benefiting others for one's self-interest is ought not,"* is a bad one because it depends directly on the falsehood of the moral value judgment that "benefiting others for one's self-interest has negative moral value," and fundamentally speaking, and on both the falsehood of the factual judgment about benefiting others for one's self-interest and the falsehood of the judgment of the goal of morality: either of them is false (mistakenly believing that benefiting others for one's self-interest will lead to *harming others to benefit oneself*, or mistakenly believing that the goal of morality is to perfect everyone's moral character, so that benefiting others for one's self-interest is seen not to conform to the goal of morality or both are false (mistakenly believing that benefiting others for one's self-interest will lead to *harming others to benefit oneself* and that the goal of morality is to perfect everyone's moral character).

This is the process of the deduction and making of excellent moral norms based directly on the truth of moral value judgment, and is ultimately based on the truth of the judgment of behavioral fact and the judgment of the goal of morality. It is the method of the deduction and making of excellent moral norms, the method of the discovery and proof of excellent moral norms, the method of the discovery, proof, and deduction of the moral ought, moral good, and moral value in normative theory, and the deductive postulate of excellent moral norms which is only applicable to ethics. This postulate is illustrated as below:

> Premise 1: The judgment of behavioral facts is true or false.
> Premise 2: The judgment of the goal of morality is true or false.
> Conclusion 1: The judgment of the behavioral ought is true or false.
> Conclusion 2: The moral norm is good or bad (whether the moral norm conforms to the moral value).

The formula can be simplified as follows:

> Premise 1: The behavioral fact is what (substance of moral value).
> Premise 2: The goal of morality is what (standard of moral value).

Conclusion 1: The behavioral ought is what (moral value).
Conclusion 2: The moral norm is good or bad (whether the moral norm conforms to the moral value).

4.5 Theories on deductive axioms and deductive postulates in ethics

4.5.1 Conclusion: Four deductive axioms and four deductive postulates in ethics

To sum up, the "deductive axiom and deductive postulate in ethics" can be shown in the following eight "primitive propositions" or "axioms and postulates":

4.5.1.1 The deductive axiom of value in ethics

"Value, good, and ought" are the utility of "is" or "fact" to the needs, desires, and purposes of the subject. Therefore, "value, good, and ought" emerge and are derived from "is" or "fact" through the needs, desires, and purposes of the subject: "Good, ought and positive value" are the utility of "facts" that conform to the needs, desires and purposes of the subject, while "bad, ought-not, and negative value" are the utility of "facts" that do not conform to the needs, desires and purposes of the subject. Formula:

Premise 1: The fact (substance of value).
Premise 2: The needs, desires, and purposes of the subject (standard of value).
Conclusion: Ought (value).

4.5.1.2 The deductive axiom of evaluation in ethics

Emotional evaluation, volitional evaluation, and behavioral evaluation emerge and are derived from value judgment (cognitive evaluations), while the object that value judgment reflects is value, namely the utility of the factual property of the object concerning the needs, desires, and purposes of the subject. Consequently, all evaluations ultimately emerge and are derived from the factual judgment through the judgment of the needs, desires, and purposes of the subject: in the final analysis, the positive evaluation is equal to the conformity of the factual judgment with the needs, desires, and purposes of the subject, while the negative evaluation is equal to the nonconformity of the factual judgment with the judgment of needs, desires, and purposes of the subject. In other words, a kind of evaluation emerges and is derived from two descriptions, namely the description of the facts of the object and the description of the needs, desires, and purposes of the subject: the positive evaluation equals the conformity of factual description with the description of the needs, desires, and purposes of the subject, while the negative evaluation equals the

168 *The meta-ethical proof*

nonconformity of the factual description with the description of the needs, desires, and purposes of the subject. Formula:

The deductive formula A of evaluation:

Premise 1: The factual judgment
Premise 2: The judgment of the needs, desires, and purposes of the subject
Conclusion 1: The value judgment or cognitive evaluation
Conclusion 2: The emotional evaluation, volitional evaluation, and behavioral evaluations

The deductive formula B of evaluation:

Premise 1: description of the facts of the subject
Premise 2: description of the needs, desires, and purposes of the subject
Conclusion 1: value judgment or cognitive evaluation
Conclusion 2: emotional evaluation, volitional evaluation, and behavioral evaluations

4.5.1.3 The deductive axiom of the truth or falsehood and right or wrong of evaluation

Emotional evaluation, volitional moral evaluation, and behavioral moral evaluation emerge and are derived from moral value judgment (cognitive evaluations). Therefore, the truth or falsehood and right or wrong of all evaluations depend on the truth or falsehood of value judgment, and ultimately on the truth or falsehood of the factual judgment and of the judgment of the needs of the subject: if both are true, the value judgment or cognitive evaluation logically emerge and are derived from the two, certainly are true (i.e., certainly conforms to the value), and emotional moral evaluations, volitional moral evaluations, and behavioral moral evaluations certainly are right (i.e., certainly beneficial to satisfy the needs, desires, and purposes of the subject); if the value judgment is false (i.e., does not conform to the value), and emotional moral evaluation, volitional moral evaluation, and behavioral moral evaluation certainly are wrong (i.e., certainly an impediment to satisfy the needs, desires, and purposes of the subject), hence the factual judgment and the judgment of the needs of the subject from which they are derived certainly are false: Either one or both of them are false. Formula:

Premise 1: The factual judgment is true or false.
Premise 2: The judgment of the needs of the subject is true or false.
Conclusion 1: The value judgment or cognitive evaluation is true or false.
Conclusion 2: The emotional moral evaluation, volitional moral evaluation, and behavioral evaluation are right or wrong.

Deductive axioms and deductive postulates   169

4.5.1.4 The deductive axiom of excellent norm in ethics

The excellent "behavioral norm" is the behavioral norm that conforms to the behavioral value, while the inferior "behavioral norm" is the behavioral norm that does not conform to the "behavioral value." Therefore, excellent behavioral norms by no means can be arbitrary; these norms are based on the "behavioral fact," namely the utility of "the behavioral facts" to "the needs, desires, and purposes of the subject," which, in the final analysis, only can be derived from "the behavioral facts" through "the needs, desires, and purposes of the subject." Therefore, the excellence or inferiority of the behavioral norms, depends directly on the truth or falsehood of the value judgment of the behavioral ought; fundamentally speaking, on the one hand, it depends on the truth or falsehood of the factual judgment of the behavioral facts, and, on the other hand on the truth or falsehood of the judgment of the needs, desires, and purposes of the subject: if both are true, the value judgment logically derived from the two certainly are true, hence the behavioral norms made under their guidance certainly conform to the behavioral value, and certainly are excellent behavioral norms; if the behavioral norms made do not conform to the behavioral value, and are inferior behavioral norms, then the value judgment of the behavioral ought certainly is false, hence the factual judgment of the behavior, and the judgment of the needs of the subject from which they are derived certainly are false: either one or both of them are false. Formula:

Premise 1: The judgment of the facts is true or false.
Premise 2: The judgment of the needs, desires, and purposes of the subject is true or false.
Conclusion 1: The value judgment of ought is true or false.
Conclusion 2: The norms are good or bad (whether the moral norms conform to moral value).

4.5.1.5 The deductive postulate of moral value in ethics

The moral value of the behavioral ought is the utility of the behavioral fact to the goal of morality; therefore, the moral value of the behavioral ought emerges and is derived from the behavioral fact through the goal of morality: while the behavioral ought is the utility of the behavioral fact that conforms to the goal of morality, the behavioral ought-not is the behavioral fact that does not conform to the goal of morality. Formula:

Premise 1: the behavioral fact (substance of moral value).
Premise 2: the goal of morality (standard of moral value).
Conclusion: the behavioral ought (moral value).

4.5.1.6 The deductive postulate of moral evaluation in ethics

Emotional evaluation, volitional evaluation, and behavioral evaluation emerge and are derived from moral value judgment (cognitive moral

170 *The meta-ethical proof*

evaluations), while the object that moral value judgment reflects is moral value, namely whether the facts of the behavior conform to the goal of morality. Consequently, all moral evaluations of the behavioral ought ultimately emerge and are derived from the judgment of the behavioral fact through the judgment of the goal of morality: the positive moral evaluation is equal to the conformity of the judgment of the behavioral fact with the judgment of the goal of morality, while the negative moral evaluation is equal to the nonconformity of the judgment of the behavioral fact with the judgment of the goal of morality. In other words, a kind of moral evaluation emerges and is derived from two descriptions, namely the description of the behavioral fact and the description of the goal of morality: the positive moral evaluation is equal to the conformity of the description of behavioral fact with the description of the goal of morality, while the negative moral evaluation is equal to the nonconformity of the description of behavioral fact with the description of the goal of morality. This is the process of the emergence and deduction of moral evaluation, the deductive method of moral evaluation, the discovery and proof method of moral evaluation, and the deductive postulate of moral evaluation that is only applicable to ethics, which can be summed up as two formulas:

Deductive formula A of moral evaluation:

Premise 1: Judgment of behavioral fact
Premise 2: Judgment of goal of morality
Conclusion 1: Moral value judgment or cognitive moral evaluation
Conclusion 2: Emotional moral evaluation, volitional moral evaluation, and behavioral moral evaluation

Deductive formula B of moral evaluation:

Premise 1: Description of the behavioral fact
Premise 2: Description of the goal of morality
Conclusion 1: Cognitive moral evaluation or moral value judgment
Conclusion 2: Emotional moral evaluation, volitional moral evaluation, and behavioral moral evaluation

4.5.1.7 The deductive postulate of the truth or falsehood and right or wrong of moral evaluation in ethics

Emotional moral evaluation, volitional moral evaluation, and behavioral moral evaluation emerge and are derived from moral value judgment (cognitive moral evaluations). Therefore, the truth or falsehood and right or wrong of all moral evaluations depend on the truth or falsehood of moral value judgment, and ultimately on the truth or falsehood of the judgment of behavioral fact and the judgment of the goal of morality: if both are true, then the moral value judgment that logically emerges and is derived from the two certainly is true (i.e., certainly conforms to the moral value), and the emotional moral evaluations, volitional moral evaluations, and behavioral moral evaluations certainly are right, good, or correct (i.e., certainly conform to the goal of morality); if the moral value judgment is false (i.e., does not conform to moral value), the emotional moral evaluations, volitional moral evaluations, and behavioral moral evaluations certainly are wrong, bad, or incorrect (i.e., do not conform to the goal of morality), and the judgment of the behavioral fact and the judgment of the goal of morality from which they are derived certainly are false: either one or both of them are false. Formula:

Premise 1: The judgment of the behavioral fact is true or false.
Premise 2: The judgment of the goal of morality is true or false.
Conclusion 1: The moral value judgment or cognitive moral evaluation is true or false.
Conclusion 2: The emotional moral evaluation, volitional moral evaluation, and behavioral moral evaluation are right or wrong.

4.5.1.8 *The deductive postulate of excellent moral norms in ethics*

The excellent "moral norm" is the moral norm that conforms to the "moral value," while the inferior moral norm is the moral norm that does not conform to the moral value. Excellent moral norms are based on "the moral value of the behavioral ought," namely the utility of "the behavioral facts" to "the goal of morality," which, in the final analysis, is derived and made from "the fact of ethical behavior" through the goal of morality. Therefore, the excellence or inferiority of the moral norm of the behavioral ought directly depends on the truth or falsehood of the judgment of moral value and fundamentally depends, on the one hand, on the truth or falsehood of the factual judgment of the objective nature of behavioral facts and on the other, on the truth or falsehood of the judgment of the goal of morality of the subject: if both are true, the moral value judgment logically derived from the two certainly is true, hence the moral norms of the behavioral ought made under their guidance certainly are excellent; if the moral norm of the behavioral ought made is inferior, then the judgment of moral value of the behavioral ought certainly is false, hence the judgment of the behavioral fact and the judgment of the goal of morality from which it is derived certainly are false: either one or both of them are false. Formula:

Premise 1: The judgment of behavioral fact is true or false.
Premise 2: The judgment of the goal of morality is true or false.
Conclusion 1: The judgment of the behavioral ought is true or false.
Conclusion 2: The moral norm is good or bad (whether the moral norm conforms to the moral value).

172   *The meta-ethical proof*

4.5.2 *Relationship between ethical axioms and ethical postulates and its implications*

It is easy to see that the deductive axiom of the excellent norm and deductive postulate of the excellent moral norm in ethics is the ultimate goal of "the system of ethical axioms and postulates." This is because ethics is a science concerned with excellent morality, which explores the truth of moral value judgment, aiming at making and realizing excellent morality that conforms to moral values. However, we must also use the deductive axiom of the truth or falsehood and right or wrong of evaluation and deductive postulate of the truth or falsehood and right or wrong of moral evaluation in ethics to obtain and justify the truth of moral value judgment. In order to obtain the deductive axiom of the truth or falsehood and right or wrong of evaluation and deductive postulate of the truth or falsehood and right or wrong of moral evaluation in ethics, we obviously must obtain the deductive axiom of evaluation and deductive postulate of moral evaluation in ethics and deductive axiom of value and deductive postulate of moral value in ethics. This is why there are as many as eight deductive axioms and postulates in ethics.

Furthermore, in order to discover the deductive axiom of value and the deductive postulate of moral value in ethics, it is obvious that we must know where ought, good, and value exist, so we must find this through the axioms of the existence of value and postulates of the existence of moral value. As described in Chapter 3, there are six in total. Adding the six existent axioms and postulates to eight deductive axioms and postulates makes a total of 14 ethical axioms and postulates. The kinds of deductive relationships that make up the 14 types of ethical axioms and postulates, have the ultimate goal to make and realize excellent moral norms, while the ultimate goal of the axiom system itself in ethics is the deductive axiom of the excellent norm and the deductive postulate of the excellent moral norm.

Then, is there a means–end relationship between "the deductive axiom of excellent norms" and "the deductive postulate of excellent moral norms"? The answer is yes because the ultimate goal of ethics is not to make excellent norms, but to make excellent moral norms: making excellent norms is only a method for making excellent moral norms. Therefore, the system of ethical axioms and postulates, namely the entire meta-ethics, can ultimately be summed up as the "deductive postulate of the excellent moral norm." We can call the system of axioms and postulates in ethics meta-ethics (and refer to its 14 axioms and postulates as axioms and postulates) because, as demonstrated in the *Introduction,* all the objects, contents, and propositions of ethics can be derived from the "deductive postulate of the excellent moral norm."

The scientific value of the 14 ethical axioms and postulates lies in obtaining the seven ethical postulates from the seven ethical axioms and finally from the deductive postulate of the excellent moral norm. In this way, the axiomatic system of ethics is as objective, inevitable, precise, and operational as physics.

Deductive axioms and deductive postulates 173

For example, all the objects, contents and propositions of my work the *New Ethics* (2008), are derived from this postulate.

Furthermore, the seven ethical axioms are applicable to all value sciences. Two such value sciences, which I have noted elsewhere, are stateology and Chinaology: stateology is the value science of the goodness and badness of state institutions and Chinaology the value science of the goodness and badness of Chinese state institutions. From the seven axioms we can deduce the deductive postulates of stateology and Chinaology and from these derive all the objects, contents, and propositions of each. Thus, demonstrating, as we do in ethics, that the axiom system in each is as objective, inevitable, precise, and operational as physics.

For example, from the seven ethical axioms we can derive "the deductive postulate of excellent state institutions":

Premise 1: The facts of the state (substance of value).
Premise 2: The goal of state (standard of value).
Conclusion 1: The ought of the state (value).
Conclusion 2: The state institution is good or bad (whether the institutions conform to the value).

These four propositions formed the basis of my work titled *Stateology* (2012). All the objects, contents, and propositions in that work were derived from a close study of the above.

Likewise, from the seven ethical axioms, we can also derive the "deductive postulate of the excellent Chinese state institution":

Premise 1: The facts of the Chinese state institution (the substance of value).
Premise 2: The goal of the state (the standard of value).
Conclusion 1: The oughts of the Chinese state institution (value).
Conclusion 2: The Chinese state institution is good or bad (whether the state institution conforms to the value).

As with the study of stateology, all the objects, contents, and propositions of Chinaology can be derived from the four propositions. (Naturally, with my interests in the Chinese state and as a follow-up to my work on stateology, I am nearing the completion of a new work titled *Chinaology* based on these propositions.)

Of all the value sciences, however, ethics is the most complicated. Though we simplify the ethical axioms and postulates, there is no way of avoiding their complexity—ethics is as complex as it is profound. Thence, on the one hand, as mentioned above, meta-ethicists' studies of what here are called "the axiom of existence of value and postulate of existence of moral value in ethics" lead to the four proof theories, namely the theories of objectivism, realism, subjectivism, and object–subject relationship, and, on the other hand, to five schools

174   *The meta-ethical proof*

(which we examine below), namely naturalism, intuitionism, emotionalism, prescriptivism, and descriptivism, all of which are proof theories of meta-ethics on the production and deduction of ought, good and value, which, in the final analysis, are proof theories concerning the deductive axioms and deductive postulates in ethics. Obviously, if we do not further analyze these theories and point out their merits and demerits, our studies on deductive axioms and postulates in ethics would be inadequate and incomplete.

4.5.3 Naturalism

What is naturalism? W. D. Hudson takes naturalism as a meta-ethics theory that uses the natural (factual) property to define the value concepts such as "good" and "right."[19] Beauchamp believes that naturalism is a meta-ethical method of deduction or proof that uses factual judgment to justify value judgment: "According to this theory, value judgments can be justified through a factual method (sometimes called the 'rational method' by naturalists)— one that parallels methods of historical and scientific proof."[20]

The combination of the two can be the definition of naturalism, because naturalism certainly is a theory of proof of meta-ethics, and to be more precise, it is a theory of proof of the process of emergence and deduction of "ought," a theory of proof about how "ought" emerges and is derived from "is," which, in the final analysis, is a theory of proof of the "deductive axioms and postulates in ethics." The features of this theory, as Moore, the coiner of the term "naturalism," pointed out (later summed up by Hudson and Beauchamp), are that, on the one hand, it uses the concept of "fact" to define the value concepts such as "good," for instance, "good is pleasure," and, on the other hand, it uses factual judgment to prove value judgments, such as "I ought to want something because I factually want something."[21] In sum, naturalism mistakenly equates "value" or "ought" with "facts" or "nature," hence can be called the "naturalistic fallacy."

The "naturalistic fallacy" is undoubtedly a great discovery of Moore, because, on the one hand, many great thinkers do use the natural or factual concepts to define the value concept, hence have the "naturalistic fallacy" of equating the value concepts such as "good" with the factual concepts such as "pleasure" or "the things that can bring pleasure." That is why Locke wrote that good and bad are nothing but pleasure and pain, or things that cause or elevate pleasure and pain in our bodies.[22] Spinoza also said: "whenever we feel anything that makes us happy or sad, we call it good or bad."[23] But in fact, "good" is fundamentally different from "pleasure" or "the things that can bring pleasure" for "good" is the utility of "pleasure" or "the things that can bring pleasure" to satisfy the needs of the subject, belonging to category of "value," while "pleasure and the things that bring pleasure" are substances of "good" belonging to the category of "fact." Therefore, the naturalistic fallacy lies in the equation of "value" with "fact," "value" with "substance of value," and "good" with "substance of good."

Deductive axioms and deductive postulates 175

On the other hand, the naturalistic fallacy, as Moore discovered, not only exists in the definition of good but also in the proof of the definition of good; not only in one judgment but also in the deduction that consists of several judgments. The naturalistic fallacy mainly is a wrong proof theory in meta-ethics that derives ought (value) solely from fact (nature) hence equating ought (value) with fact (nature). Mill, as Moore stated, is a representative of this fallacy, for Mill wrote in his *Utilitarianism*:

> Pleasure and free from pain, are the only thing desirable as ends, and enjoying both in quality and quantity makes a pleasant life... This kind of life is the purpose of human's action in the view of utilitarianism, thus must be the standard of morality.[24]
>
> What ought to be required of this doctrine—what conditions is it requisite that the doctrine should fulfil—to make good its claim to be believed? The only proof capable of being given that an object is visible, is that people actually see it. The only proof that a sound is audible, is that people hear it: and so of the other sources of our experience. In like manner, I apprehend, the sole evidence it is possible to produce that anything is desirable, is that people do actually desire it....Happiness has made out its title as one of the ends of conduct, and consequently one of the criteria of morality.[25]

This proof, as Moore pointed out, is the "naturalistic fallacy": it derives behavioral ought directly from the behavioral facts (because happiness is in fact the purpose of human actions, so happiness ought to be the purpose of human actions; because people actually want something, so people ought to want something), and thus regards the *behavioral facts* as the *behavioral ought*. Many great thinkers made this naturalistic fallacy. For example, Maslow says, "Do you want to find out what you ought to be? Then find out who you are! 'Become what thou art!' The description of what one ought to be is almost the same as the description of what one deeply is."[26] "And yet, exactly the same statement about the way the world looks, is also a value statement."[27]

Although the naturalistic method of proof is untenable, it is not as completely wrong as Moore says, because "value, good, or ought" are the utility of "is" or "fact" to the subject's needs, hence are the relational properties that emerge and are derived from facts when "facts" relate to the needs of the subject. Therefore, the naturalists' claim that "ought exists, emerges and is derived from fact" is indeed a great truth, just as Maslow states, "Facts creates ought."[28]

> The best way for a person to discover what he ought to do is to find out who and what he is, because the path to ethical and value decisions, to wiser choices, to oughtness, is via "isness," via the discovery of facts, truth, reality, the nature of the particular person.[29]

176 *The meta-ethical proof*

How profound these statements are! The fallacy of naturalism lies in that it fails to see that only when facts are related to the needs of the subject can ought emerge and be derived from facts: "Facts" is the source and substance of the emergence of "ought," while the needs of the subject are the condition and standard of the emergence and deduction of "ought" from facts. Naturalism only sees that fact is the source of the emergence of ought, and fails to see that the needs of the subject is the condition of the emergence of ought, thus mistakenly believes that ought emerges and is derived from facts themselves, and mistakenly takes "facts" as "ought" and equates "fact" with "ought."

4.5.4 Meta-ethical intuitionism

In his argument against naturalism, Moore establishes a new meta-ethical proof theory: meta-ethics intuitionism. What is intuition? Sidgwick said:

> When he calls the judgment of rightness or wrongness of action as "intuitive," it is not pre-determining the final level of validity of this judgment from a philosophical point of view, but simply means that its authenticity is clearly recognized at the moment, not as a result of reasoning.[30]

Thus, intuition means that we can directly perceive the nature of some things without reasoning. So intuitionism, just as Walter Sinnott-Armstrong says, is the theory holding that people can directly perceive the nature of some things without reasoning: "Intuitionism is the claim that some people are immediately or noninferentially justified in believing that some moral judgments are true."[31]

There are three kinds of the extension of intuitionism. The first is the universal and general intuitionism represented by Descartes, Spinoza, Leibniz, Bergson, and so on, which can be called philosophical intuitionism. It holds that people do not need to reason to directly perceive the nature of some things such as "the straight line is the shortest between two points." The second is the ethical intuitionism represented by Shaftesbury, Hutcheson, Butler, Price, and Sidgwick, who hold that people can directly perceive the truth of moral judgments such as "one ought not to steal" without reasoning. The third is the meta-ethical intuitionism represented by Moore, Pritchard, Ross, and Ewing, which holds that people can directly perceive the nature of meta-ethics such as "what is *good*" without reasoning.

What we examine undoubtedly is only meta-ethical intuitionism, which regards certain meta-ethical concepts such as *good, ought, right*, and *obligation* as simple, self-evident, undefined, or reasoned, hence is also a proof theory of the deductive axiom and deductive postulate in ethics. Just as Moore points out,

> good is a simple notion, just as "yellow" is a simple notion; that, just as you cannot, by any manner of means, explain to anyone who does not already know it, what yellow is, so you cannot explain what good is.[32]

Ross also says:

> Moral rightness is an indefinable characteristic, and even if it be a species of a wider relation, such as suitability, its difference cannot be stated except by repeating the phrase "morally right" or a synonym; just as, while red is a species of colour, what distinguishes it from other colours can be indicated only by saying that it is the colour that is red.[33]

Since good and right and so on are simple, self-evident, undefined, or reasoned, we can then perceive their nature only through intuition, just as we intuitively perceive mathematical axioms. As Ross continues: "If we now turn to ask how we come to know these fundamental moral principles, the answer seems to be.... as in mathematics, it is by intuitive induction that we grasp the general truths."[34] For the intuitive understanding of the basic ethical principles of "right" and so on, Pritchard also explains:

> This kind of understanding is direct. The so-called direct understanding, precisely speaking, is the direct understanding shown in mathematics, like the direct understanding that "the triangle must have three corners because it has three sides." The two understandings are direct in this sense: the two insights into the nature of the subjects make us directly understand that the subjects have the nature of the predicates; and this is only an indication—from the aspect of the object of understanding—that in both situations, the facts that are directly understood are self-evident.[35]

What, then, is the nature of *good* and *right* we directly perceive? Moore holds that "good" is the same as "yellow" in the sense that both are properties of the object, and that they are also different in the sense that "yellow" is a natural property of the object while "good" is an unnatural property of the object: "For I do not deny that good is a property of certain natural objects: certain of them, I think, *are* good; and yet I have said that good itself is not a natural property."[36] Ross also shares this view and points out that there is a causal link between the non-natural properties of the object, such as right and good, and the natural properties or factual properties of the object:

> Rightness is always a resultant attribute, an attribute that an act has because it has another attribute....It is only by knowing or thinking my act to have a particular character, out of the many that it in fact has, that I know or think it to be right....I think that it is right because it is the relieving of a human being from distress.[37]

This is to say, the same action has two properties at the same time, one is behavioral facts (the relieving of a human being from distress), which is perceptible; while the other is *behavioral ought* (i.e., *right*), which can only

178 *The meta-ethical proof*

be intuited: the *behavioral right* that can only be intuited, emerges from the behavioral facts that can be perceived.

It can be seen that, fundamentally, meta-ethical intuitionism is consistent with the naturalism it opposes: Both correctly believe that *right* or *good* is the property of the object, and that right or good emerges from fact, hence both are termed objectivism. The difference is that naturalism mistakenly holds that *right* can directly emerge and be derived from fact itself, thus mistakenly equates *fact* with *right*, while meta-ethics intuitionism holds that only through the intermediary of intuition can *right* emerge from *fact*, and thus distinguishes *fact* from *right*. Then, is this viewpoint of meta-ethical intuitionism which is different from naturalism the truth?

We must not assert in general terms whether intuitionism is the truth because the fundamental feature of intuitionism is that it holds that people can directly perceive the nature of some things without reasoning: not the nature of everything but of something. Therefore, whether intuitionism is the truth depends entirely on what things it considers can be perceived intuitively. If these things are intuitively perceivable, then the intuitionism holding that these things can be intuitively perceived is true. If these things are not intuitively perceivable, then the intuitionism holding that these things can be intuitively perceived is false. For example, the intuitionism contending that one can directly know some mathematical axioms without resorting to theoretical proofs is the truth, because some mathematical axioms indeed cannot be proved but only be intuited. Similarly, intuitionism holding that certain moral judgments can be directly perceived without theoretical reasoning may also be truth because certain moral judgments, such as "one ought to help the blind people across the street" and "one ought not to lie," as listed by Ross, are indeed intuitively perceivable without reasoning. Therefore, some philosophical intuitionism and ethical intuitionism might be true. Then, may meta-ethical intuitionism also be true?

No. It is not possible to understand meta-ethical concepts, whether "good," "right" or "ought," by intuition, so any kind of meta-ethical intuitionism is wrong. The reason Moore believes that "good" can be known by intuition is that "good" is the purest and simplest concept, hence is a thing that is self-explanatory and cannot be analyzed. Indeed, a pure or self-evident thing such as the simplest mathematical axiom can only be known through intuition. However, is "good" the same kind of thing? Moore's argument is not convincing. If it is self-evident, it is absurd that thinkers have debated it for more than two thousand years.

The evidence Pritchard uses to show that the nature of "obligation" and "good" is self-evident and intuitively perceivable is mainly the self-evident nature of mathematical propositions such as $7 \times 4 = 28$.[38] The evidence Ross uses to show that the nature of "right," "obligation," or "ought" is self-evident and intuitive is mainly based on the self-evident nature of moral judgment such as "one ought to help blind people cross the street" and "one ought not lie" etc.[39] The evidence Ewing uses to show that the nature of "ought," "right." or "good" is self-evident and intuitive is that if intuition is not resorted to, arguments from one judgment to the next would be endless.[40] It is easy to see that all three of them made the logical mistakes of "taking one part for the whole" and of "failing to derive." Mathematical propositions such as $7 \times 4 = 28$ and moral judgments that one "ought to help blind people across the street" are indeed self-explanatory: if intuition is not resorted to such arguments are futile. Obviously, however, we cannot derive from these premises that all moral concepts (e.g., right and good) and judgments are self-evident.

To sum up, meta-ethical intuitionism, just like naturalism, is also a proof theory of meta-ethics about the process of the emergence and deduction of ought, good, and value, and is a proof theory of meta-ethics about whether "ought" can emerge and be derived from "is," which is closer to the truth than naturalism. This is because, on the one hand, it correctly perceives the error of naturalism's deduction of "ought" directly from "fact," and thus equates "ought" with "fact": on the other hand, it correctly points out that only through an intermediary can "ought" emerge from "fact," hence distinguishes "ought" from "fact." However, meta-ethical intuitionism fails to discover that this intermediary is "the needs, desires, and purposes of the subject" and mistakes it as "intuition," thus wrongly holds that ought, right, and good emerge from "facts" through "intuition."

4.5.5 Emotivism

As we can see from above, meta-ethical intuitionism is not so much a rival but rather a cousin of naturalism: they both belong to the big family of meta-ethical objectivism that holds "good and value exist in the object." Their common adversary is meta-ethical subjectivism believing that "good and value exist in the subject," namely emotivism, which, as J. O. Urmson says, is a meta-ethical proof theory holding that the essence of value judgment is the expression of the emotions of the subject rather than the description of the facts of the object:

> Negatively, what these theories have in common is a denial that the primary function of evaluative utterances is to convey true or false information about any aspect of the world. Positively, while differing in detail, they claim that evaluative utterances have the primary function of expressing the speaker's emotions and/or attitudes, and/or of eliciting certain emotions and/or attitudes in others.[41]

The representatives of emotivism are Russell, Wittgenstein, Carnap, Ayer, and Stevenson. However, just as Richard A. Spinello rightly points out, the real founder of emotivism is Hume.[42]

Emotivists, such as Hume, perceive that, on the one hand, the facts themselves do not have the issue of "ought," and that the existence of ought

180 *The meta-ethical proof*

depends on the subject; and, on the other hand, that "ought" must be consistent with the subject and is often contrary to facts. As a result, they conclude that "ought" exists in the subject and is the emotions, volition, and attitude of the subject, and is the property of the subject instead of the factual property of the object:

> Take any action allow'd to be inferior: Wilful murder, for instance. Examine it in all lights, and see if you can find that matter of fact, or real existence, which you call vice. In which-ever way you take it, you find only certain passions, motives, volitions and thoughts. There is no other matter of fact in the case. The vice entirely escapes you, as long as you consider the object. You never can find it, till you turn your reflexion into your own breast, and find a sentiment of disapprobation, which arises in you, towards this action. Here is a matter of fact; but tis the object of feeling, not of reason. It lies in your- distinction self, not in the object. So that when you pronounce any action or character to be inferior, you mean nothing, but that from the constitution of your nature you have a feeling or sentiment of blame from the contemplation of it.[43]

Therefore, Russell adds, "The question of 'value' is entirely outside the scope of knowledge... that is, when we assert that this or that has 'value,' we are expressing our own emotions, not the reliable fact despite that our personal emotions are different."[44] Ayer also writes: "The function of the relevant ethical word is purely 'emotive.' It is used to express feeling about certain objects, but not to make any assertion about them."[45] Although Stevenson admits that ethical words have the dual meaning of describing facts and expressing emotions, he believes that emotional meanings are primary, complete, and independent, while descriptive meanings are used to serve emotional meaning, and therefore are not complete and independent, as he says:

> Doubtless there is always *some* element of description in ethical judgments, but this is by no means all. Their major use is not to indicate facts but to *create an influence*. Instead of merely describing people's interests they *change* or *intensify* them. They *recommend* an interest in an object, rather than state that the interest already exists.[46]

Since good and ought are merely or mainly the emotions and properties of the subject rather than the properties of the object and the fact, it is clear that good and ought can only be derived from the subject but not from the fact. Therefore, after it was clarified that ought is the emotion of the subject instead of the factual property of the object, Hume put forward the famous thesis which later became the cornerstone of meta-ethics: ought cannot be derived from "is" and that there is a logical gap between "ought" and "is." Stevenson also concludes that "empirical facts are not inductive grounds from which the ethical judgment problematically follows."[47]

Deductive axioms and deductive postulates   181

Since ethical judgments are merely expressions of the emotions of the subject instead of the statements of the factual properties, and cannot be derived from the factual judgment, ethical judgments have no issue of being true or false, thus are non-cognitive. Therefore Russell said, "Strictly speaking, I don't think there is such a thing as moral knowledge."[48] Carnap says: "A value judgment is neither true nor false. It does not assert anything, and it can neither be proved nor disproved."[49] Ayer repeatedly states that sentences which only express moral judgments do not state anything. They are purely emotional expressions, and therefore cannot fall into the category of truth or falsehood.[50]

Stevenson holds that the emotional meaning of moral judgment has no truth or falsehood, but admits that its descriptive meaning has truth or falsehood. However, since he holds that emotional meaning plays a dominant role, he also believes that ethical judgments—mainly speaking—have no truth or falsehood and are non-cognitive, and that they merely depend on knowledge to some extent, though in themselves are not knowledge: "Ethical issues involve personal and social decisions about what is to be approved, and that these decisions, they vitally depend on knowledge, do not themselves constitute knowledge."[51] Therefore, like Russell, Wittgenstein, and Carnap, he also believes that normative ethics is not a science:

> I conclude, therefore, that scientific methods cannot be guaranteed the definite role in the so-called normative sciences that they may have in the natural sciences......that normative ethics is not a branch of any science......it draws from all the sciences; but a moralist's peculiar aim-that of redirecting attitudes-is a type of activity, rather than knowledge, and falls within no science.[52]

Therefore, just like the naturalism and meta-ethical intuitionism, emotivism is also a proof theory of meta-ethics about the process of the emergence and deduction of "ought," namely the proof theory of meta-ethics about whether "ought" can emerge and be derived from "is," which, in the final analysis, is also the proof theory about the deductive axiom and deductive postulate in ethics. However, emotivism is undoubtedly further away from the truth than intuitionism and naturalism.

First of all, emotivism mistakenly believes that "ought" is the emotional property of the subject rather than the factual property of the object, hence can only be derived from the subject rather than the facts. The mistake based on that, on the one hand, is that the fact itself does not have the issue of "ought": the existence of ought depends on the subject; on the other hand, it is also that "ought" must be consistent with the subject but is often contrary to the fact. Can these grounds be established? The existence of "ought," as the emotivists contend, is indeed dependent on the subject: there is no "ought" without the subject and there is "ought" as long as the subject exists. However, it can only be said that the subject is the condition for the existence of "ought";

182   *The meta-ethical proof*

one cannot say that the subject is the source of the existence of "ought." So, where the emotivists assert that "ought" must be consistent with the subject it can only be said that the subject is the standard of "ought," not the source of "ought." Because, as mentioned earlier, "ought" is the utility of the facts of the object to the needs of the subject, and is a property that emerges from the fact but not from the needs of the subject when facts are related to the needs of the subject, the needs of the subject are just the conditions for the emergence of "ought" from facts and the standard for the measurement of whether the fact is "ought"; it is the fact that is the carrier and substance of the emergence and existence of "ought." The error of emotivism is that it mistakes the conditions and standard for the emergence and existence of "ought"—the needs, desires, and emotions of the subject—as the source of the emergence and existence of "ought," thus mistakenly holds that "ought" exists in the needs, desires, and emotions of the subject, and is their property, and thus only can be derived from the needs, desires, and emotions of the subject instead of from the fact.

Secondly, the mistake of emotivism lies in the belief that value judgment is merely or mainly an expression of the emotions of the subject. Because, as mentioned above, a value judgment certainly reflects three objects, thus having one evaluative meaning and two descriptive meanings: generally speaking, it has an evaluative meaning which expresses the utility of the facts of the object of the evaluation to the needs of the subject, namely the value and ought of the object of the evaluation; fundamentally speaking, it has two descriptive meanings, on the one hand, it expresses the facts of the object of the evaluation, and, on the other hand, it expresses the needs, desires, and emotions of the subject. In view of this, Russell, Wittgenstein, Carnap, and Ayer believe that the value judgment is only the expression of the emotions of the subject, the mistake of which obviously lies in that they obliterate the reflection of the value judgment of the factual property of the object and that of the value property of the object, instead only seeing the value judgment as the reflection of the emotion of the subject. Stevenson acknowledges that value judgment has dual meanings of emotions and descriptions, but his mistake is to obliterate the evaluative meaning of value judgment, exaggerate the meaning of emotional description of value judgment, and to reduce the meaning of the factual description of value judgment.

Finally, the error of emotivism lies in its further assertion that value judgment is completely or mainly non-cognitive hence has no truth or falsehood from the partial statement that "value judgment is the expression of emotions." But in fact, even if it is true that "value judgment is the expression of emotions," it does not lead to the conclusion that "value judgment has no truth or falsehood" because it is only "emotions" that have no truth or falsehood, that is, "the expression of emotions," such as the *cognitive expression of emotions*, has truth or falsehood. Then, how do the emotivists draw the conclusion that value judgment has no truth or falsehood from the statement that "value judgment is the expression of emotions"? It turns out that when emotivism asserts that "value judgment is the expression of emotions," the error is much more serious than the surface meaning of this sentence because the "expression of emotions" undoubtedly includes two aspects: one is the "cognitive expression of emotions," such as I make the judgment that "John is really painful," which belongs to the category of cognition and thus has the distinction of being true or false; the other is the "non-cognitive expression of emotions," such as "moaning" or "yelling," which mainly belong to the category of actions, and thus are neither true nor false. Then, what kind of emotional expression does the statement that "value judgment is the expression of emotions" refer to? Undoubtedly, it is the cognitive expression of emotions rather than the non-cognitive expression of emotions because value judgment belongs to the category of judgment and therefore belongs to the category of cognition. However, emotivists hold that the assertion of value judgment—the "cognitive expression of emotions"—is the "assertion of feelings." This is wrong; it is the viewpoint of orthodox subjectivism. According to the definition of emotivists, the so-called emotional expression is definitely not the "assertion of feelings" or the cognitive expression of emotions, but the non-cognitive expression of emotions. Discussing this kind of distinction between the "expression of emotions" and "assertions of feelings," Ayer says: "subjectivists believe that ethical statements actually determine the existence of certain emotions; and we believe that ethical statements are expressions and stimuli of emotions, and such expressions and stimuli need not involve any assertion."[53] It can be seen that the mistake of emotivism lies in its denial that the "expression of emotions" can be the "cognitive expression of emotions." Its one-sided definition that the "expression of emotions" is the "non-cognitive expression of emotions," mistakenly equates the statement, "value judgment is the expression of emotions," with the statement, "value judgment is the non-cognitive expression of emotions," hence wrongly draws the non-cognitivism conclusion that value judgment has no truth or falsehood.

4.5.6 Prescriptivism

Although Hare sees that value judgment has double meanings of evaluation and description, as W. D. Hudson points out, Hare believes that in fact, the most important usage of moral language is prescriptive.[54] This is true, as in the opening of his *The Language of Morals*, Hare clearly points out that the nature of moral language lies in its *prescriptivity*.[55] In his *Essays in Ethical Theory*, Hare further clarified that moral judgment has two kinds of "Logical Features":

> The first is sometimes called the *prescriptivity* of moral judgment....The second feature... is usually called *universalizability*. Universalizability means that, by saying "I ought", he commits himself to agreeing that *anybody* ought who is in just those circumstances.[56]

184 *The meta-ethical proof*

Obviously, universalizability is a modification of prescriptivity: moral language is a prescriptive language with universal prescriptivity. Therefore, the logical features of moral language and moral judgment can also be summed up as the universal prescriptivity. Consequently, Hare's theory of ethics is termed "prescriptivism," which Hare himself calls "Universal Prescriptivism," that is, the combination of universalizability (holding that moral judgment is universalizable) and prescriptivism (holding that moral judgment is prescriptive in all typical situations).[57]

Obviously, prescriptivism is the theory contending that "the nature of moral language and moral judgment lies in the prescriptivity."[58] Since the nature of moral judgments is prescription, then moral judgments have no truth or falsehood, and are non-cognitive. This is because, just as G. H. Wright says, "prescriptions are neither true nor false."[59] Similarly, John Roth says: "prescriptivism implies that there is no ethical knowledge.... [b]ecause command is different from description and *has no truth or falsehood.*" [60] Thus prescriptivism still belongs to non-cognitivism and emotivism, and, in the final analysis, is a proof theory of the deductive axioms and postulates in ethics. For the similarity and difference between Hare's theory and his emotivism predecessors, Louis P. Pojman has a very good explanation:

> He agrees with the emotivists that we cannot ascribe true or falsity to moral statements and that moral judgments are attitudinal, he changes the emphasis regarding moral terms from the feelings of approval (or disapproval) to certain types of judgment that includes a universalizability feature and a prescriptive element.[61]

Therefore, fundamentally speaking, the mistake of prescriptivism and emotivism are the same: their understanding of the expression of value judgment on the subject's needs, feelings, and commands is one-sided. Hare's "new contribution" to the errors of emotivism is that he equates the nature of "prescription"(has no truth or falsehood, and is non-cognitive) with the nature of "the judgments of prescription" (has truth or falsehood and is cognitive), and equates the nature of "morality (i.e., moral norms)" (has no truth or falsehood, and is non-cognitive) with the nature of "moral judgment" (has truth or falsehood and is cognitive), asserting that the nature of prescribed language and moral language is the prescription that is neither true nor false nor cognitive.

4.5.7 Descriptivism

The fallacy of non-cognitive theories means that cognitive theory is the truth because so-called cognitive theory, as mentioned earlier, is the theory holding that all value judgment belongs to the category of cognition and thus has truth or falsehood. However, people tend to exaggerate the truth of cognitivism, asserting that all evaluations have the distinction of truth or falsehood

Deductive axioms and deductive postulates 185

and, from that, all value judgments have truth or falsehood. Just as Li Lianke states:

> Value evaluation is actually a reflection of value, which is the relationship between the object and the needs of the subject in consciousness, and is a subjective judgment to value, an emotional experience, and a guarantee of volition and their synthesis. As a reflection in the consciousness, value evaluation certainly has subjective arbitrariness, hence has truth or falsehood.[62]

However, value judgment and evaluation are not the same concept. Value judgments are undoubtedly evaluations, but evaluations are not all value judgments because evaluation, as Li Lianke says, is a kind of psychology and consciousness, belonging to the category of psychology and consciousness, while psychology and consciousness are divided into three parts, namely "cognition," "emotions," and "volition." Therefore, the evaluation can be divided into three, namely "cognitive evaluation," "emotional evaluation," and "volitional evaluation."

Evaluation and value consciousness obviously are the same concept with broad extension, which includes all psychological activities of cognition, emotion, and volition towards value, while value judgment, value recognition, and value cognition are generally the same concept with narrow extension, which only refer to the cognition activities towards value. The crux of the problem lies in the fact that, as mentioned earlier, only cognition has truth or falsehood, while emotions and volitions can only be right or wrong. Therefore, only some evaluations, namely value judgment or value cognition, has truth or falsehood; while other evaluations, namely value emotions and value volitions, can only be right or wrong. Who can say, for instance, that A's love of B is true or false. Isn't it that one can only say that A's love of B is right or wrong?

The fact that non-cognitive theory is false while cognitive theory is true does not imply that doctrines supporting cognitive theory or against non-cognitive theory are all true. Both naturalism and intuitionism oppose non-cognitive theory but support cognitive theory, but as mentioned earlier, they are not the completely true. Then, is descriptivism that is against non-cognitive theory—particularly prescriptivism—true?

What is descriptivism? Lawrence C. Becker says, "according to descriptivism, moral words like "good" and "wrong" resemble ordinary descriptive words like 'red' and 'rectangle' in that their meaning and their application-conditions are firmly linked."[63] Indeed, the famous figures of descriptivism, Philippa Foot, after arguing how value words such as rightness, obligation, goodness, duty, and virtue are similar and related to descriptive words such as harm, advantage, benefit, importance,[64] draws the conclusion that:

> When people argue about what is right, good, or obligatory, or whether a certain character trait is or is not a virtue, they do not confine their

186 *The meta-ethical proof*

remarks to the adducing of facts which can be established by simple observation, or by some clear-cut technique…. in this sort of discussion as in others, in the field of literary criticism for instance, or the discussion of character, much depends on experience and imagination.[65]

This means that moral argument, like descriptive reasoning, depends on facts, experience, and imagination. In other words, the reasoning logic of evaluation is the same as the reasoning logic of description, and it is wrong to categorize them into two logic types with different functions. Thus, the reasoning logic from description to evaluation and from description to description are the same, so just as description can be directly derived from description, evaluation can also be derived directly from factual description, or value can be directly derived from fact: there is no logical gap between evaluation and description, between value and fact. Foot gives an example that "Someone is offensive" is the factual judgment and factual description, and from this judgment we can derive the evaluation and value judgment that "the person is rude":

whether a man is speaking of behaviour as rude or not rude, he must use the same criteria as anyone else, and that since the criteria are satisfied if O is true, it is impossible for him to assert O while denying R. It follows that if it is a sufficient condition of P's entailing Q that the assertion of P is inconsistent with the denial of Q, we have here an example of a non-evaluative premise from which an evaluative conclusion can be deduced.[66]

Obviously, descriptivism is a meta-ethical proof theory that equates evaluation logic with description logic, holding that there is no difference in reasoning logic between evaluation and description, hence that evaluation can be directly derived from factual description (or value can be directly derived from fact). In the final analysis it is a naturalistic epistemology of meta-ethic because the so-called naturalism is a proof theory of meta-ethics holding that ought (value) can be directly derived from facts (nature). Therefore descriptivism is a fallacy like naturalism. Then, where are the errors of descriptivism?

It is not difficult to see that the mistakes of descriptivism mainly lie in its equation of evaluative logic with descriptive logic, namely the equation of the logic of factual judgment with the logic of value judgment. The description logic obviously is that from a description or factual judgment one can directly derive another description or factual judgment. For example, from the description that "it rains" one can directly derive that "the ground is wet." On the contrary, the evaluation logic is that there are at least two descriptions—a description of the fact and a description of the needs of the subject—so one can derive an evaluation or value judgment. To be more precise, the logic of evaluation is that an evaluation or value judgment is derived indirectly from the descriptive judgment of the fact through the descriptive judgment of the needs of the subject.

Deductive axioms and deductive postulates   187

It is true that from "someone is offensive" we can directly derive "the person is impolite." However, after a careful consideration we can see that only "the person ought not to be impolite" is an evaluation or value judgment, while "the person is impolite," just like the premise that "someone is offensive," is a description or factual judgment. Therefore, Foot derives a descriptive conclusion directly from a descriptive premise instead of directly deriving an evaluative conclusion from a non-evaluative premise.

Obviously, the mistake of descriptivism, like that of naturalism, lies in that it fails to understand that although evaluation and value judgment indeed emerge and are derived from descriptions and factual judgments, only when the factual description is related to the description of the needs of the subject, can the evaluation and value judgment emerge and be derived from the factual description—without the description of the subject and the relationship with the description of the needs of the subject, evaluation and value judgment cannot emerge and be derived from factual judgment itself: factual description is the source and basis of the emergence and existence of evaluation, while the description of the needs of the subject are the conditions and standard of the emergence and deduction of evaluation or value judgment. Like naturalism, descriptivism only sees that factual description is the source and basis of the emergence of value judgment; it fails to see that the description of the needs of the subject is the condition and standard of the value judgment, hence mistakenly believes that value judgment can emerge and be derived directly from the factual judgment alone, and that an evaluation can be derived directly from a description. Consequently, it wrongly equates the reasoning logic of evaluation with the reasoning logic of description.

By analyzing naturalism, intuitionism, emotivism, prescriptivism, and descriptivism, we can see that all five theories are one-sided and wrong proof theories about the deductive axioms and deductive postulate in ethics, because they are all one-sided and wrong proof theories about the process of emergence and deduction of *ought*, *good*, and *value*, as well as one-sided and wrong proof theories about whether "ought" can be derived from "is":

Emotivism and prescriptivism regard the condition and standard of the emergence and existence of "ought"—the needs, desires, and emotions of the subject—as the source and substance of the emergence and existence of "ought," mistakenly holding that "ought" exists in and is property of the needs, desires, and emotions of the subject, and thus can only be derived from the needs, desires, and emotions of the subject rather than from the facts. On the contrary, naturalism, and descriptivism fail to see that the needs, desires, and purposes of the subject are the conditions and standard of the emergence and existence of "ought"; instead, these theories regard "facts" as the only source and substance of the emergence and existence of "ought," mistakenly believing that "ought" can directly emerge and be derived from the facts themselves, and consequently equating facts with "ought." Intuitionism correctly sees that only through an intermediary can "ought" emerge from

188 *The meta-ethical proof*

"facts," but fails to recognize that such an intermediary is the needs, desires, and purposes of the subject, mistakenly holding that it is intuition, hence that "ought" emerges from "facts" through intuition. In sum, the one-sidedness of these theories further validates the process of the production and deduction of *ought*, *good*, and *value* that we have revealed:

Value, good, and ought are the utilities of "is" or "facts" to the needs, desires and purposes of the subject: factual properties of object are the source and substance of the production and existence of value, good, and ought, while the needs, desires, and purposes of the subject are the conditions and standard of the production of value, good, and ought from the factual properties of the object. Therefore, value, good, and ought emerge and are derived from "is" or "facts" through the needs, desires, and purposes of the subject: good, ought, and "positive value" are the utilities of "facts" that conform to the needs, desires, and purposes of the subject, while bad, ought-not, and "negative value" are the utilities of "facts" that do not conform to the needs, desires, and purpose of the subject.

This is the real process of the production and deduction of *value, good,* and *ought* that the naturalism, intuitionism, emotionalism, prescriptivism, and descriptivism have been painstakingly seeking, which is also the answer to Hume's guillotine. Furthermore, it is the ethical axiom that can derive all propositions of ethics, which has been the concern of the ethicists from Spinoza to Rawls; in the final analysis, it is the ethical axiom that can derive all the propositions in value sciences (e.g., ethics, stateology, and Chinaology).

Premise 1: The fact (substance of value)
Premise 2: The need, desire, and purpose of the subject (standard of value)
Conclusion: The ought (value)

Notes

1 David Hume: *A Treatise of Human Nature*. Clarendon Press, Oxford, 1960, pp. 469–470.
2 W. D. Hudson: *The Is–Ought Question: A Collection of Papers on the Central Problem in Moral Philosophy,* St. Martin's Press, New York, 1969, p. 11.
3 See W. D. Hudson: *The Is–Ought Question*, pp. 41, 227, 102; J. L. Mackie: *Ethics: Inventing Right and Wrong*, Richard Clay Ptd Ltd, Singapore, 1977, p. 66; George Sher: *Moral Philosophy: Selected Readings*, Harcourt Brace Jovanovich, New York, 1987, p. 329.
4 W. D. Hudson: *The Is–Ought Question: A Collection of Papers on the Central Problem in Moral Philosophy*, St. Martin's Press, New York, 1969, p. 102.
5 W. D. Hudson: *The Is–Ought Question: A Collection of Papers on the Central Problem in Moral Philosophy,* St. Martin's Press, New York, 1969, p. 106.
6 W. D. Hudson: *The Is–Ought Question: A Collection of Papers on the Central Problem in Moral Philosophy,* St. Martin's Press, New York, 1969, p. 111.
7 Albert Einstein: *Works of Einstein*. vol. 3, Commercial Press, Beijing, 1976, p. 280.
8 R. M. Hare: *The Language of Morals*, Oxford University Press, London, 1964, p. 30.

Deductive axioms and deductive postulates   189

9 R. M. Hare: *The Language of Morals*, Oxford University Press, London, 1964, p. 28.

10 W. D. Hudson: *The Is–Ought Question: A Collection of Papers on the Central Problem in Moral Philosophy,* St. Martin's Press, New York, 1969, p. 121

11 M. C. Doeser and J. N. Kraay: *Facts and Values*, Martinus Nijhoff, Boston, 1986, p. 33.

12 M. C. Doeser and J. N. Kraay: *Facts and Values*, Martinus Nijhoff, Boston, 1986, p. 41.

13 Stephen Edelston Toulmin: *The Place of Reason in Ethics*, The University of Chicago Press, 1986, p. 137.

14 Stephen Edelston Toulmin, *The Place of Reason in Ethics,* The University of Chicago Press, 1986, pp. 223–224.

15 R. M. Hare: *The Language of Morals*, Oxford University Press, London, 1964, p. 111.

16 See R. M. Hare: *Essays on the Moral Concepts*, University of California Press Berkeley and Los Angeles, 1973, pp. 57–59.

17 F. H. Bradley: *Ethical Studies*, Part 1, the Republic of China Commercial Press, Beijing, 1944, p. 84. If the goal of morality is exactly what Bradley and other altruists assert, for morality itself, which is to perfect everyone's moral character, then benefiting others for self-interest, of course, does not conform to the goal of morality for it is not the perfect state of virtue and morality, thus is immoral with negative moral value.

18 A school of thought in the Spring and Autumn and Warring States Periods in China, 770–221 BC.

19 Lawrence C. Becker: *Encyclopedia of Ethics*, Volume II, Garland Publishing, New York, 1992, p. 1007.

20 Tom L. Beauchamp: *Philosophical Ethics,* McGraw-Hill, New York, 1982, p. 339.

21 Also see Lawrence C. Becker: *Encyclopedia of Ethics*, Volume II, Garland Publishing, New York, 1992, p. 1007; Tom L. Beauchamp: *Philosophical Ethics*, McGraw-Hill, New York, 1982, p. 339.

22 Henry Sidgwick: *The Methods of Ethics*, China Social Sciences Press, 1993, p. 225.

23 Baruch Spinoza: *Ethics*, Commercial Press, Beijing, 1962, p. 165.

24 J. S. Mill: *Utilitarianism*, China Social Sciences Publishing House, Chengcheng Books, Ltd, pp. 10–12.

25 J. S. Mill: *Utilitarianism*, China Social Sciences Publishing House, Chengcheng Books, Ltd, pp. 52–53.

26 Abraham H. Maslow: *The Farther Reaches of Human Nature*, Yunnan Press, 1987, Penguin Books Ltd, 1993, p. 108.

27 Abraham H. Maslow: *The Farther Reaches of Human Nature*, 1987, Penguin Books Ltd, 1993, p. 105.

28 Abraham H. Maslow: *The Farther Reaches of Human Nature*, Penguin Books Ltd, 1993, p. 115

29 Abraham H. Maslow: *The Farther Reaches of Human Nature*, Penguin Books Ltd, 1993, pp. 106–107.

30 Henry Sidgwick: *The Methods of Ethics*, Chinese Social Science Publishing House, 1993, p. 231.

31 Lawrence C. Becker: *Encyclopedia of Ethics*, Volume II, Garland Publishing, Inc. New York, 1992, p. 628.

32 G. E. Moore: *Principia of Ethic*, China Social Science Publishing House, Chengcheng Books Ltd, p. 69.

190 *The meta-ethical proof*

33 W. D. Ross: *Foundation of Ethics,* Clarendon Press, Oxford, 1939, p. 316.

34 W. D. Ross: *Foundation of Ethics,* Clarendon Press, Oxford, 1939, p. 320.

35 A. I. Melden: *Ethical Theories: A Book of Readings,* Prentice-Hall, Inc, Englewood Cliffs, N.J., 1967, p. 531.

36 G. E. Moore: *Principia of Ethic,* China Social Science Publishing House, Chengcheng Books Ltd, p. 93.

37 W. D. Ross: *Foundation of Ethics,* Clarendon Press, Oxford, 1939, p. 168.

38 A. I. Melden: *Ethical Theories: A Book of Readings,* Prentice-Hall, Inc, Englewood Cliffs, N.J., 1967, p. 537.

39 W. D. Ross: *Foundation of Ethics,* Clarendon Press, Oxford, 1939, p. 316.

40 A. C. Ewing: *The Definition of Good,* Hyperion Press, Westport, CN, pp. 25–26.

41 Lawrence C. Becker: *Encyclopedia of Ethics,* Volume II, Garland Publishing, New York, 1992, pp. 304–305.

42 John K. Roth: *International Encyclopedia of Ethics,* Braun-Brumfield Inc, U.C., 1995, p. 258.

43 David Hume: *A Treatise of Human Nature.* Clarendon Press, Oxford, 1960, pp. 468–469.

44 Bertrand Russell: *Religion and Science.* Commercial Press, Beijing, 1982, p. 123.

45 Louis P. Pojman: *Ethical Theory: Classical and Contemporary Readings,* Wadsworth Publishing Company, 1995, p. 415.

46 Charles L. Stevenson: *Facts and Values: Studies in Ethical Analysis,* Yale University Press, New Haven and London, 1963, p. 16.

47 Charles L. Stevenson: *Facts and Values: Studies in Ethical Analysis,* Yale University Press, New Haven and London, 1963, p. 28.

48 Bertrand Russell: *Why I Am Not a Christian,* Commercial Press, Beijing, 1982, p. 55.

49 Rudolf Carnap: *Philosophy and Logic Syntax.* Shanghai People's Press, 1962, p. 9.

50 Charles L. Stevenson: *Facts and Values: Studies in Ethical Analysis,* Yale University Press, New Haven and London, 1963, p. 415.

51 Charles L. Stevenson: *Ethics and Language.* China Social Sciences Publishing, 1991, p. 4.

52 Charles L. Stevenson: *Facts and Values: Studies in Ethical Analysis,* Yale University Press, New Haven and London, 1963, p. 8.

53 Charles L. Stevenson: *Facts and Values: Studies in Ethical Analysis,* Yale University Press, New Haven and London, 1963, p. 416.

54 W. D. Hudson: *Modern Moral Philosophy,* The Macmillan Press Ltd, London, 1983, p. 203.

55 R. M. Hare: *The Language of Morals,* Oxford University Press, London, 1964, p. 2.

56 R. M. Hare: *Essays in Ethical Theory,* Clarendon Press, Oxford, 1989, p. 179.

57 R. M. Hare: *Freedom and Reason,* Clarendon Press Oxford, 1963, p. 16.

58 John K. Roth: *International Encyclopedia of Ethics,* Braun-Brumfield Inc., U.C., 1995, p. 693.

59 M. C. Doeser and J. N. Kraay: *Facts and Values,* Martinus Nijhoff, Boston, 1986, p. 36.

60 John K. Roth: *International Encyclopedia of Ethics,* Braun-Brumfield Inc., U.C., 1995, p. 693.

61 Louis P. Pojman: *Ethical Theory: Classical and Contemporary Readings,* Wadsworth Publishing Company, 1995, p. 428.

62 Li Lianke: *The Significance of the World—Axiology*. People's Publishing House, 1985, p. 106.
63 Lawrence C. Becker: *Encyclopedia of Ethics* Volume II, Garland Publishing, Inc., New York, 1992. p. 1007.
64 Philippa Foot: *Virtues and Vices and Other Essays in Moral Philosophy,* University of California Press Berkeley and Los Angeles, 1978, p. 109.
65 Philippa Foot: *Virtues and Vices and Other Essays in Moral Philosophy,* University of California Press Berkeley and Los Angeles, 1978, p. 106.
66 Philippa Foot: *Virtues and Vices and Other Essays in Moral Philosophy,* University of California Press Berkeley and Los Angeles, 1978, p. 104.

Appendix
Contents of *The Principles of Ethics*

Endorsement
Author's Preface

Introduction to *The Principles of New Ethics*

0.1 Definition of ethics
    0.1.1 Ethics: Science concerning morality
    0.1.2 Ethics: Science concerning excellent morality
    0.1.3 Ethics: Science concerning moral value
0.2 The objects of ethics
    0.2.1 Axiomatic method: The scientific method for determining the objects of ethics
    0.2.2 Ethical axioms and postulates: Deduction of the objects of ethics
    0.2.3 Axiom system of ethics: Its history and current situation
0.3 The system structure and discipline classification of ethics: The studies and controversies in contemporary western academia
    0.3.1 The misconception of two disciplines: Meta-ethics and normative ethics
    0.3.2 Two modes of studying the same object: Normative ethics and virtue ethics
    0.3.3 The central discipline of ethics: Moral-centrism and virtue-centrism
0.4 The position of ethics in sciences
    0.4.1 Theoretical status: The most complicated science
    0.4.2 Practical status: The most valuable science

VOLUME 1 META-ETHICS

Introduction: Definition and objects of meta-ethics

I.1 Ethics: Etymology and definition
I.2 Meta-ethics and the sciences of meta-ethics: Etymology and definition
I.3 Objects of meta-ethics

Appendix 193

Part I Categories of Meta-ethics

1 Categories of meta-ethics: The starting concept of ethics

1.1 The concept of value: Utility theory of value
    1.1.1 Subject and object: Subjectivity is also autonomy
    1.1.2 Value: The utility of the object to the need of the subject
    1.1.3 Value: Can only be defined by "object" and "subject"
1.2 The concept of value: The theory of marginal utility and labor theory of value
    1.2.1 Value of commodity: The utility of commodity to human needs
    1.2.2 The solution of the "paradox of value": Use value is the marginal utility of commodity
    1.2.3 The misunderstanding of "paradox of value": Commodity value is the congealed human labor in commodity
1.3 Reaction of value: The concept of evaluation
    1.3.1 Reflection and reaction: Truth and falsehood and right and wrong
    1.3.2 Definition of evaluation: Reaction of value
    1.3.3 Types of evaluation: Cognitive, emotional, volitional and behavioral evaluations

2 The categories of meta-ethics: Primitive concepts of ethics

2.1 Good
    2.1.1 The definition of good: The satisfaction of desire is good
    2.1.2 Types of good: Intrinsic good, instrumental good and ultimate good
    2.1.3 Types of bad: Pure bad and necessary bad
2.2 Ought and right
    2.2.1 Ought: The good of action
    2.2.2 Right: Moral good of action
    2.2.3 Right and ought: The universalizability of the moral ought
2.3 Fact and is
    2.3.1 Facts: The concept of fact in a broad sense
    2.3.2 Is: The concept of fact in a narrow sense
    2.3.3 Conclusion: Two concepts of fact

Part II The meta-ethical proof

3 The meta-ethical proof: The axiom of the existence of value and the postulate of the existence of moral value in ethics

3.1 The axiom of essence of the existence of value and the postulate of the essence of the existence of moral value in ethics
    3.1.1 The essence of the existence of value: The property of object

194 *Appendix*

 3.1.2 The essence of the existence of value: The relational property and tertiary qualities of the object

 3.1.3 Conclusion: The axiom of essence of the existence of value and the postulate of essence of the existence of moral value

3.2 The axiom of structure of the existence of value and the postulate of the structure of the existence of moral value in ethics

 3.2.1 Substance and standard: The structure of the existence of value

 3.2.2 Reality and potentiality: The duality of the structure of the existence of value

 3.2.3 Conclusion: The axiom of structure of the existence of value and the postulate of structure of the existence of moral value

3.3 The axiom of nature of the existence of value and the postulate of the nature of the existence of moral value in ethics

 3.3.1 The nature of the existence of value: Particularity and universality

 3.3.2 The nature of the existence of value: Relativity and absoluteness

 3.3.3 The nature of the existence of value: Subjectivity and objectivity

 3.3.4 The axiom of the nature of the existence of value and the postulate of the nature of the existence of moral value in ethics

3.4 Theories about the axiom of the existence of value and the postulate of the existence of moral value in ethics

 3.4.1 Conclusion: Three axioms of the existence of the existence of value and three postulates of the existence of moral value of ethics

 3.4.2 Objectivism and realism

 3.4.3 Types of theory of realism

 3.4.4 Subjectivism

 3.4.5 Theory of relationship

4 The meta-ethical proof: The deductive axiom and deductive postulates in ethics

4.1 The deductive axiom of value and deductive postulate of moral value of ethics

 4.1.1 The answer to is-ought problem

 4.1.2 Proof of the answer to is-ought problem: The deductive axiom of value in ethics

 4.1.3 The deductive postulate of moral value in ethics

4.2 The deductive axiom of evaluation of ethics and deductive postulate of moral evaluation of ethics

 4.2.1 The process of emergence and deduction of value judgment

 4.2.2 The deductive axiom of evaluation of ethics

 4.2.3 The deductive postulate of moral evaluation of ethics

4.3 The deductive axiom of the truth and falsehood and right and wrong of evaluation, and the deductive postulate of the truth and falsehood and right and wrong of moral evaluation in ethics

Appendix 195

4.3.1 The process of production and deduction of the truth of value judgment
4.3.2 The deductive axiom of the truth and falsehood and right and wrong of evaluation
4.3.3 The deductive postulate of the truth and falsehood and right and wrong of moral evaluation
4.4 The deductive axiom of excellent norms and deductive postulate of excellent moral norms in ethics
  4.4.1 An analysis of the concepts of "norm", "value" and "value judgment": conceptual analysis
  4.4.2 The deductive axiom of excellent norms
  4.4.3 The deductive postulate of excellent moral norms
4.5 Theories on the deductive axiom and deductive postulate of ethics
  4.5.1 Conclusion: Four deductive axioms and four deductive postulates of ethics
  4.5.2 Relationship between ethical axioms and ethical postulates and its implications
  4.5.3 Naturalism
  4.5.4 Meta-ethical Intuitionism
  4.5.5 Emotivism
  4.5.6 Prescriptivism
  4.5.7 Descriptivism

VOLUME 2 NORMATIVE ETHICS I

Part I The standard of moral value: The goal of morality

1 The concept of morality

1.1 1 The definition of morality
  1.1.1 Morality and ethics
  1.1.2 Morality and ought
  1.1.3 Morality and law
1.2 The structure of morality
  1.2.1 The basic structure of morality: Moral norms and moral value
  1.2.2 The complete structure of morality: Moral values, moral value judgments and moral norms
  1.2.3 The deep structure of morality: Behavioral fact and goal of morality
1.3 Types of morality
  1.3.1 The universality and particularity of morality: Universal morality and particular morality
  1.3.2 The relativity and absoluteness of morality: The absolute morality and relative morality
  1.3.3 The subjectivity and objectivity of morality, as well as the excellence and inferiority of morality: Excellent morality and inferior morality

196   *Appendix*

1.4 Theories on the concept of morality
    1.4.1 Ethical relativism
    1.4.2 Ethical absolutism: Situation ethics
    1.4.3 Moral subjectivism and moral nihilism/skepticism
    1.4.4 Moral objectivism and moral realism

2 The origin and goal of morality

2.1 The origin and goal of morality: From the point of view of moral community
    2.1.1 The concept of moral community: Moral agent and moral patient
    2.1.2 Boundary of moral community: The living beings that are beneficial to human beings
    2.1.3 The origin and goal of morality: Safeguarding the interest community and promoting human Interests
2.2 Origin and goal of morality: From the point of view of the social moral needs
    2.2.1 The social moral needs: The origin and goal of morality
    2.2.2 All sources and goals of morality
    2.2.3 The social nature of the origin and goal of morality
2.3 The origin and goal of morality: From the point of view of personal moral needs
    2.3.1 Personal moral needs: The ways and means for the actualization of morality
    2.3.2 Morality and virtue: A kind of necessary bad
    2.3.3 The nature of heteronomy of the origin and goal of morality
2.4 Theories on origins and goals of morality
    2.4.1 Anthropocentrism and anti-anthropocentrism
    2.4.2 Theories of moral heteronomy and moral autonomy

3 The ultimate standard of morality: The ultimate value standards of the state institutions

3.1 The system of ultimate standard of morality
    3.1.1 Increasing or decreasing everyone's quantum of interests: The ultimate general standard of morality and the ultimate general value standard of the state institutions
    3.1.2 The net balance of the maximum interests: The ultimate standard for interests conflicts
    3.1.3 The greatest interests for the greatest number: Precedence over the standard of net balance of maximum interests
    3.1.4 Increasing quantum of interests without negatively affecting anyone: The ultimate standard under the circumstance that the interests are not in conflict

Appendix 197

3.2 The theories on the ultimate standard of morality
    3.2.1 Deontology and utilitarianism
    3.2.2 The truth and fallacy of utilitarianism and deontology
    3.2.3 The previous utilitarianism: The shortcomings and reproaches

Part II The substance of moral value: Facts of ethical behavior

4 Human nature

4.1 The concept of human nature
    4.1.1 The definition of human nature: The universal nature that is inherent
    4.1.2 The structure of human nature: The substance and utility of human nature
    4.1.3 Types of human nature: Human characteristics and human animality
4.2 The concept of ethical behavior: The concept of human nature in ethics
    4.2.1 The definition of ethical behavior
    4.2.2 The structure of ethical behavior
    4.2.3 Types of ethical behavior
4.3 The law of the ultimate motivation of ethical behavior: Qualitative analysis of human nature
    4.3.1 Introduction: The ultimate motivation of ethical behavior—love and hatred, personal pain and pleasure, as well as the desires of self-interest
    4.3.2 Love and hatred: The ultimate motivation of ethical behaviors
    4.3.3 Loving others, compassion and gratitude: The ultimate motivation of benefiting others as an end
    4.3.4 Hating others, envy, and vengeance: The ultimate motivation of harming others as an end
    4.3.5 Self-hatred, the sense of guilty and inferiority complex: The ultimate motivation of self-harming as an end
    4.3.6 Self-love, desires to live and self-respect: The ultimate motivation of self-interest as an end
    4.3.7 Conclusion: The law of the ultimate motivation of ethical behavior
4.4 Law of relative quantity of ends of ethical behavior: Quantitative analysis of human nature
    4.4.1 Degrees of love: The most profound law of human nature
    4.4.2 Law of relative quantity of the ends of ethical behavior: The deduction of the law of human nature of the degrees of love
    4.4.3 The significance of the law of human nature of the degrees of love
4.5 Law of relative quantity of means of ethical behavior: Quantitative analysis of human nature
    4.5.1 Non-statistical law of relative quantity of means of ethical behavior

198 *Appendix*

4.5.2 Statistical law of relative quantity of means of ethical behavior
4.5.3 The significance of statistical law of relative quantity of means of ethical behavior
4.6 Law of relative quantity of types of ethical behavior: Quantitative analysis of human nature
4.6.1 Non-statistical law of relative quantity of types of ethical behavior
4.6.2 The statistical laws of relative quantity of types of ethical behavior

Part III Moral value and the standard of morality: Excellent morality that conforms to moral value

5 Good: General principles of morality

5.1 Good and evil
5.1.1 Good and evil of human nature: The moral value of 16 types of ethical behavior
5.1.2 The establishment of six principles of good and evil
5.1.3 The scope of application of six principles of good and evil
5.1.4 General principles of morality: Two principles of good and evil, as well as six principles of good and evil
5.2 Theories on the good and evil of human nature
5.2.1 The theory of human nature without good or evil
5.2.2 The theory of the good of human nature
5.2.3 The theory of the evil of human nature
5.2.4 The theory of the good and evil of human nature
5.3 Theories on general moral principle
5.3.1 Altruism
5.3.2 Egoism: Rational egoism and individualism
5.3.3 Egoism: Psychological egoism and ethical egoism
5.3.4 The doctrine of benefiting both self-other interests: The unity of altruism and egoism
5.3.5 The comparison of truth and falsehood as well as the excellence and inferiority of altruism, egoism, and the doctrine of benefiting self-other interests

6 Justice and equality: Fundamental value standard of State Institutions

6.1 The exchange of equal interests or harms: The general principle of justice
6.1.1 The definition of justice: The exchange of equal interests or harms
6.1.2 Justice, Fairness, and evenhandedness: The same concept
6.1.3 Types of justice: Distributive justice and retributive justice

Appendix 199

6.1.4 Types of justice: Procedural justice and substantive justice
6.1.5 The principle of justice: The fundamental value standard of state institutions
6.2 Equality between rights and duties: Fundamental principle of justice
    6.2.1 Definition of right and duty
    6.2.2 Types of rights and duties: Moral rights and duties, statutory rights and duties, and natural rights and duties
    6.2.3 Types of rights and duties: Rights and duties between human and non-human beings
    6.2.4 The relationship between rights and duties: The fundamental principle of justice
6.3 Principle of contribution: Fundamental principle of social justice
    6.3.1 Distribution of rights according to contribution: The principle of contribution
    6.3.2 Distribution of rights according to virtue and talents: The potential principle of contribution
6.4 Equality: The most important justice
    6.4.1 The concept of equality
    6.4.2 The principle of full equality
    6.4.3 The principle of proportional equality
    6.4.4 The relationship between full equality and proportional equality: The general principle of equality
    6.4.5 Theories on general principle of equality: The contribution and imperfections of Rawls' *A Theory of Justice*
6.5 Specific principles of equality
    6.5.1 The principle of political equality
    6.5.2 The principle of economic equality
    6.5.3 The principle of equality of opportunity
6.6 Theories on social justice
    6.6.1 The theory of contribution
    6.6.2 The theory of need
    6.6.3 The theory of liberty-justice
    6.6.4 Egalitarianism

VOLUME 3 NORMATIVE ETHICS II

1 Humanity and liberty: The supreme value standards of state institutions

1.1 Humanity
    1.1.1 Humanism: A social and thought system that regards humans as the highest value
    1.1.2 Humanism: A social and thought system that regards humans' creative potential as the highest value
    1.1.3 Humanity: A supreme value standard of state institutions

200 *Appendix*

1.2 Liberty: The most fundamental humanity
    1.2.1 Concept of liberty: Liberty and the ability to exercise liberty
    1.2.2 Two concepts of liberty: Liberty as self-restraint
    1.2.3 Values of liberty: liberty as the most fundamental necessary condition for achieving the creative potential of individuals
1.3 Principles of liberty: General principles of liberty
    1.3.1 The rule-of-law principle of liberty
    1.3.2 The equality principle of liberty
    1.3.3 The limit principle of liberty
1.4 Specific principles of liberty
    1.4.1 Principle of political liberty
    1.4.2 Principle of freedom of thought
    1.4.3 Principle of economic freedom
1.5 Liberalism: A state institution and thought system that regards liberty as the supreme value
    1.5.1 Liberalism: Definition and objects
    1.5.2 The theoretical system of liberalism: Theory of value of liberty, theory of principle of liberty, and theory of constitutional democracy
    1.5.3 Theoretical categorization of liberalism: The most fundamental humanism
1.6 Alienation: The most fundamental non-humanity
    1.6.1 The concept of alienation
    1.6.2 The value of alienation
    1.6.3 Economic alienation
    1.6.4 Political alienation
    1.6.5 Social alienation
    1.6.6 Religious alienation

2 Justice, humanity, and increasing or reducing the quantum of interests of everyone: The system of value standards of state institutions

2.1 26 Value standards: System of value standards for measuring state institutions
    2.1.1 Justice, humanity, and increasing or decreasing the quantum of interests of everyone
    2.1.2 System of value standards for state institutions
2.2 Trade-off principles for conflicts among value standards of state institutions
    2.2.1 Justice takes precedence over humanity and liberty
    2.2.2 Equality takes precedence over liberty
    2.2.3 The ultimate value standards of state institutions take precedence over all other value standards including justice

Appendix   201

2.3

    2.3.1 Despotism: A state institution and a theoretical system that is extremely inhumane, unfree, unjust, unequal, and harmful to the interests of the largest majority

    2.3.2 The concept of despotism

    2.3.3 The origin and nature of despotism: The fundamental problem of despotism

    2.3.4 Value of despotism: The fallacies of despotism

    2.3.5 Theoretical basis of despotism

3 Happiness: The moral principle of self-regarding

3.1 Concept of happiness

    3.1.1 Definition of happiness: Psychological experience of the realization of the great needs, desires, and purposes of life

    3.1.2 Structure of happiness: The subjective form of happiness, the objective standard of happiness, and the objective essence of happiness

    3.1.3 Types of happiness

    3.1.4 Two concepts of happiness: The pleasure theory and the perfection theory

3.2 Value of happiness

    3.2.1 Pleasure: Good

    3.2.2 Happiness: The ultimate good

    3.2.3 Purpose of life

    3.2.4 Value of life and the meaning of life

    3.2.5 Hedonism

3.3 Nature of happiness

    3.3.1 Subjectivity and objectivity of happiness

    3.3.2 Authenticity and illusion of happiness

    3.3.3 Relativity and absoluteness of happiness

    3.3.4 Two theories on the nature of happiness: Subjectivism and objectivism

3.4 Laws of happiness

    3.4.1 Laws of fact of happiness

    3.4.2 Laws of value of happiness

    3.4.3 Laws of the realization of happiness

3.5 Principles of happiness

    3.5.1 Principle of cognition: Make one's cognition of happiness consistent with the objective nature of happiness

    3.5.2 Principle of choice: Make choice of happiness consistent with one's talent, effort, destiny, and virtue

    3.5.3 Principle of action: Align the effort to pursue happiness with the cultivation of one's virtue

202 *Appendix*

4 System of moral rules

4.1 Honesty
    4.1.1 Concept of honesty
    4.1.2 Moral value of honesty
    4.1.3 Scope of application of honesty
4.2 Cherishing-life
    4.2.1 Concept of cherishing-life
    4.2.2 Value of cherishing-life
    4.2.3 Approaches to cherishing-life
4.3 Self-respect
    4.3.1 Concept of self-respect
    4.3.2 Value of self-respect
    4.3.3 Principles of self-respect
4.4 Modesty
    4.4.1 Definitions of modesty
    4.4.2 Value of modesty
    4.4.3 Cultivation of modesty
4.5 Wisdom
    4.5.1 Concept of wisdom
    4.5.2 Laws of wisdom
    4.5.3 Acquisition of wisdom
4.6 Continence
    4.6.1 Concept of continence
    4.6.2 Value of continence
    4.6.3 Principles of continence
4.7 Courage
    4.7.1 Definition of courage
    4.7.2 Classification of courage
    4.7.3 Value of courage
4.8 The doctrine of the mean
    4.8.1 Concept of the doctrine of the mean
    4.8.2 Value of the doctrine of the mean
    4.8.3 Method of the doctrine of the mean

VOLUME 4 VIRTUE ETHICS

1 Conscience and reputation: Ways for the realization of excellent morality

1.1 Concepts of conscience and reputation
    1.1.1 Specific moral evaluation: Conscience and reputation
    1.1.2 Conscience: Definition, structure and types
    1.1.3 Reputation: Definition, structure and types

Appendix 203

1.2 Objective nature of conscience and reputation
    1.2.1 Origin of conscience: The goal and motivation of conscience
    1.2.2 Origin of reputation: External source and internal source
    1.2.3 Function of conscience
    1.2.4 Function of reputation
    1.2.5 A comparison of functions between conscience and reputation
1.3 Subjective evaluation of consciences and reputation
    1.3.1 Motivation and effect of concepts
    1.3.2 Behavior itself and the agent's moral character: "The theory of motivation and effect should be examined separately"
    1.3.3 Theories on evaluation of conscience and reputation: Motivationism, consequentialism, and the theory on unity of motivation and consequence
1.4 The truth and falsehood and right and wrong of conscience and reputation
    1.4.1 Concepts of the truth and falsehood and right and wrong of conscience and reputation
    1.4.2 Proof of the truth and falsehood and right and wrong of conscience and reputation
    1.4.3 Significance of the truth and falsehood and right and wrong of conscience and reputation

2 Virtue: The realization of excellent morality

2.1 Concept of virtue
    2.1.1 Definition of virtue
    2.1.2 Structure of virtue
    2.1.3 Types of virtue
2.2 Nature of virtue
    2.2.1 Value of moral character: Utility of virtue and vice
    2.2.2 Reasons of moral character: Why would a person moral?
    2.2.3 Realms of moral character: Realm of immorality, realm of virtue, and realm of vice
2.3 Laws of moral character
    2.3.1 The law of virtue and wealth: The relationship between national moral character and economy
    2.3.2 The law of virtue and happiness: The relationship between national moral character and politics
    2.3.3 The law of virtue and knowledge: The relationship between national moral character and culture
    2.3.4 The law of virtue and morality: The relationship between national moral character and morality
    2.3.5 The four laws of moral character: The statistical law of moral character changes of the majority of people

204 *Appendix*

2.4 Cultivation of moral character: Institutional construction
  2.4.1 The market economy system without government control: The basic method in cultivating elements of moral character and emotion of the Chinese people's constitutional democracy: The main method in cultivating elements of moral character and emotion of the people
  2.4.2 Freedom of thought: The basic method in cultivating elements of moral character and knowledge of the Chinese people
  2.4.3 Moral norms system of liberalism and egalitarianism: The compound method in cultivating elements of moral character, moral emotion and moral will of people
  2.4.4 Institutional construction: Relationships amongst the four methods in cultivating overall moral characters of people
2.5 The cultivation of moral character: Moral upbringing
  2.5.1 Moral upbringing: Moral education and moral self-cultivation
  2.5.2 Moral education: The external means in cultivating individual moral cultivation of people
  2.5.3 Moral self-cultivation: The internal means in cultivating individual moral cultivation of people
  2.5.4 Relationship between two ways of moral cultivation—moral upbringing and institutional construction

Index

absoluteness: of moral values and norms 126–7; and objectivity 124; relativity and 118–21
aesthetics 2, 17, 25, 34, 130
Analects of Confucius 36
Anderson, R. M. 102
Anscombe, G. E. M. 23
anthropology 2, 17
Aquinas, Thomas 24, 128
Aristotle 3, 7, 20, 24, 31, 36, 41, 51, 59, 66, 75, 80, 101, 109, 128
Ashley-Cooper, Anthony 128
autonomy(ous) 52; agent 92; properties 53
axiomatic deduction of objects of ethics 19
axiomatic systems of ethics 6–10, 17–19; completeness 9–10; conditions for 8–9; consistency 9; elements of 7; of geometry 16; independence 9; meta-ethics 11, 15–16, 19–23; primitive and derived parts 7; propositions of 9
axiomatic systems: of geometry 16–17; of mathematics 17
axiomatization 5–6, 16–17, 19
axioms 8, 18; *see also* deductive axioms
axioms of existence of value: essence of the existence of value in ethics 126; nature of the existence of value in ethics 110–16, 126–7; postulate of essence of the existence of moral value in ethics 101–10, 127; postulate of nature of existence of moral value in ethics 116, 127–8; structure of the existence of value in ethics 126; *see also* deductive axioms
Ayer, M. J. 17, 19–20, 179

bad/badness 3; necessary bad 80–3; pure bad 80–3; types of 80–3; *see also* good/goodness
bad-in-result 81
Barbon, Nicholas 59
Beauchamp, Tom L. 174
Becker, Lawrence C. 185
Beethoven's symphonies 149
behavioral evaluation 149–52, 157
behavioral facts 14–15; laws of 14; types of 14
behavioral moral evaluation 153–4, 168, 170
behavioral norms 4, 11–12
behavioral oughts 14, 15, 177
behavioral values 11–12
beneficence 27, 35
benevolence 3, 35, 79
Bergson, Henri 176
beyond-ethics 43–4
Blocker, H. Gene 1, 3
Boehm-Bawerk, Eugen von 61
Bond, E. J. 102, 122, 128
Bradley, F. H. 160
Braybrooke, David 77
Brink, David O. 128
Brink, Max 140–1
Broad, C. D. 104
Burke, Edmund 128

Capital (Marx) 6
Carnap, Rudolf 19–20, 179
Chen Duxiu 37
Chen Huaxing 103
cherishing life 14
Chinaology 12, 109, 114, 143, 152, 158, 164, 173, 188
Christian ethicists 160–1, 166

206 *Index*

Christianity 30
chrysanthemums 116–17
Chuang Tzu 1, 30, 36
Cicero 2, 41
cognitions 69, 151
cognitive evaluation 70–2, 149, 185
cognitive expression of emotions 182
cognitive theories 184
commodities 6, 55, 59; exchange value of 60–1; marginal utility of 60; use value 60
common sense 55
Commons, John R. 26
completeness 8–10
Comte, Auguste 30
condition of non- contradiction 9
conformity 55
Confucius 30, 35–6, 160
conscience 15
consciousness 69
consistency 9, 55
Constitution and Confucianism (Chen Duxiu) 37
continence 2, 14, 22
Copp, David 20
Cooper, David E. 43–4
courage 2, 14
cross-conceptual relation 151

Darwin, Charles 69
Darwin's natural selection 52
deciding to run away, volitional evaluation of 149
deductive axioms 11, 139; evaluation in ethics 149–52, 167–8; excellent norm in ethics 12–13, 163–5, 169; is-ought problem 142–4; truth and/or falsehood and right and/or wrong of evaluation 157–9, 168; value in ethics 167
deductive method 5–7; excellent moral norms 13, 17; excellent norms 12; moral value 15; value 12; *see also* axiomatic systems of ethics
deductive postulates 13–16, 139; excellent moral norms in ethics 165–7, 171; is-ought problem 144–5; moral evaluation in ethics 152–4, 169–70; moral value in ethics 169; truth and/or falsehood and right and/or wrong of moral evaluation 159–60, 170–1
Deng Xiaoping 27
Descartes, Rene 5, 17, 19, 176

description 151
descriptivism 184–8
d'Holbach, Baron 160–161
Diary of a Madman (Lu Xun) 3
doctrine of the mean 14
dress codes of women 2
Dukas, paul 134

Earl of Shaftesbury, 3rd 128
economic philosophy 2
Einstein, Albert 9, 11, 17–18, 93
Elements (Euclid) 6
elimination of alienation 14
elimination of alienation and happiness 35
emotion 69
emotional evaluation 71–2, 149–52, 157, 168, 185
emotional moral evaluation 153–4, 170
emotivism 179–83, 187
emotivists 179
Engels, F. 52
Epicurus 2
equality 2, 14, 35
essence of existence of value 101, 108–10, 126; property of object 101–04; relational property and tertiary qualities of object 104–8
ethical absolutism 35
ethical axioms 15, 18
ethical axioms and ethical postulates 172–4
ethical intuitionism 176
ethical postulates 15, 18
ethical relativism 35
ethical terms 11
ethics 91; applied ethics 19–20; axiomatic system 11, 17–19; axiomatization 5; defined 1–5, 41–3; etymology 41–3; excellent morality 2–3; meta-ethics and normative ethics 19–23; moral-centrism and virtue-centrism 26–33; morality 1–2; moral value 4–5; normative ethics and virtue ethics 23–5; objects of 5–19, 16; postulates of 11; primitive concepts of 11; purpose 3; science, position in 33–8; scientification 5; system structure and discipline classification 19–33; terminology 45; theoretical ethics 19–20
Ethics (Frankena) 23
Ethics (Spinoza) 18

Euclid 6–7, 109
evaluation: classification of 70–1;
    cognitive 71; deductive axioms
    149–52, 167–8; emotional 71;
    volitional 71
Ewing, A. C. 11, 78–9, 84, 178
excellent moral norms in ethics 5, 13–15;
    deductive axioms 12–13, 163–5, 169;
    deductive postulates 165–7, 171
excellent norms 12
exchange needs 62
exchange value 61
extrinsically good 79

fact: in broad sense 90–2; in narrow
    sense 92–5
factual judgments 12, 15, 146, 156, 159,
    162, 164
factual laws 42
factual property: of commodity 114; of
    object 105–6; of relation 106
factual relational properties 107
factual science 155
falsehood 67; *see also* wrongness
fear, emotional evaluation of 149
Feng Youlan 75
Feuerbach, Ludwig 30
Foot, Philippa 24, 140
Frankena, William K. 2, 20–1, 46, 85–6

Gautier, David 56
Geach, Peter 24
Geivett, R. Douglas 20–2
geometrization of ethics 17
Gert, Bernard 82
Gewirth, Alan 140
goal of morality 13, 169
Goethe 128
Gong Sunlongwere 36
good/goodness 2–3, 14, 35, 83, 109;
    definition 75–8; in meta-ethics 75;
    types of 78–80; *see also* bad/badness
good-in-itself 79
guillotine 46, 91, 139

Han Fei 160, 162
Han Feizi 36
happiness 2, 14
Hare, R. M. 11, 19, 84, 155, 183
Hege, Georg Wilhelm Friedrich 128
Helvétius, Claude Adrien 19, 30, 160
Hester, Joseph P. 20
Hobbes, Thomas 5, 17, 19

honesty 2, 14
Hong Shaoguang 4
Horbach, 30
Huang Jianzhong 41
Hudson, W. D. 94, 140, 174, 183
human body 85
humanity 2, 14, 35
human nature 14
Hume, David 3, 12, 17, 19, 21, 93–4, 111,
    139, 179–80
Hume's guillotine 12, 43, 91, 94, 111,
    139–40, 142, 188
Hutcheson, Francis 128

independence 9
independent system 10
ineffective needs 113–14
inferior morality 3–4
instrumental good 78–80
instrumentally good 80
interest 54, 77
interpersonal relationships 41; factual
    laws 42; kinds of 42; norms of 42
intrinsically bad 80
intrinsically good 78–80
intrinsic properties 104, 106
intuitionism 187
is-ought problem 139–42; deductive
    axiom of value in ethics 142–4;
    deductive postulate of moral value in
    ethics 144–5

Jellinek, Georg 27
Joad, C. E. M. 128
Johnson, Oliver A. 22
justice 2, 14, 35

Kahane, Howard 7–9, 17
Kant, Immanuel 24, 30–1, 84, 90,
    128, 160
Kollar, Nathan R. 24
Kong Ming 70

labor and land 63
labor theory of value 58, 63–4
Lai Jinliang 56
Language of Morals, The (Hare) 183
Laozi 36, 160, 162
Laws of Science and Ethics, The
    (Einstein) 11
legal philosophy 2
Leibniz, Gottfried Wilhelm 176
liberty 2, 14, 35

208   *Index*

Li Deshun 53, 55, 135
Li Jianfeng 56
Li Lianke 55, 185
Locke, John 107
logic 2
logic of deduction 139
lún lǐ (Chinese term for ethics) 41
Lu Xun: criticism of Confucian morality 3; inferior morality 3

MacIntyre, Alasdair 23–4, 26, 140
Mackie, J. L. 11, 85, 88, 140
MacKinnon, Barbara 24
Makiguchi, Tsunesaburo 58, 71
marginal utility 59–61
Marx, Karl 52, 54–5, 59, 62–6, 105, 114, 123
Maslow, Abraham H. 175
Ma Su 70, 159
mathematical transformations 8
May Fourth Movement 52
Meek, Ronald L. 63
Meilaender, Gilbert C. 26
Mencius 20, 36, 75
meta-ethical intuitionism 176–9
meta-ethical method 174
meta-ethical objectivism 128
meta-ethical proof theory 186
meta-ethical subjectivism 179
meta-ethics 11, 15–16, 19–23, 78, 80, 101; beyond-ethics 43–4; categories 46; defined 21–2; etymology 43–5; objects of 19–21, 45–7; *see also* specific entries
Mill, John Stuart 31, 66, 175
Mill's ethics of utilitarianism 31
modesty 2, 14
monarch–subject relationship 41
Moore, G. E. 11, 17–19, 22, 31, 46, 75, 83, 105, 128, 140, 174–5, 178
moral bad 84, 86
moral bad actions 86
moral-centrism 26–33
moral evaluation in ethics, deductive postulates 152–4, 169–70
moral facts 131
moral good 84, 86, 144
morality 1, 4, 33; badness 3–5; behavioral norms 4; of culture 2; defined 3, 43; excellent morality 5; goals of 14, 88; goodness 3–5; minimum of 27
moral judgments 21–2
moral language 22

morally good 78
moral norms 2–3, 33, 166; violation of 30
moral objectivism 35
moral ought 88–9, 144; ought-not 88–9; universalizability of 88–90
moral philosophy 1–2; *see also* ethics
moral principle 4–5
moral realism 35
moral skepticism 35
moral standard 33
moral subjectivism 35
moral terms 11, 45
moral values in ethics 4, 13; behavioral facts 12; behavioral ought 144; deductive postulates 169; judgment 4–5, 13, 15
Mozi 30, 36, 77

naturalism 174–6, 187
naturalistic fallacy 140, 174–5
natural sciences 25
nature of the existence of value 116; moral value in ethics 124–6; particularity and universality 116–18; relativity and absoluteness 118–21; subjectivity and objectivity 121–4
necessary bad 80–3
needs 57
negative value *see* bad
Nicomachean Ethics (Aristotle) 83
Nietzsche, Friedrich 30
non-cognitive expression of emotions 183
non-cognitive theories 184
non-Euclidean geometry 8
non-evaluative cognition 151
non-fact 90, 96
non-independent axioms 9
non- interpersonal behavior 42
non-moral bad 86, 89
non-moral good 86–7, 89
non-moral ought 88–90
non-power norms 27
non-value fact 92
non-value judgment 151
non-value sciences 92, 94, 96
Nordhaus, William D. 59–60
normative ethics 14–15, 19–25
normative science 31
norm, value, and value judgment 161–3

Index 209

object 53, 57; utility to need of subject 53–6
objectivism 128–30
object of value 51
objects of ethics 16; axiomatic system of ethics 17–19; deduction of 10–17; scientific method for determining 5–10
ought 83–4, 88–90, 103, 109
ought judgment 103
ought-not 83

paradox of value 61–6
Perry, Ralph Barton 53; concept of interest 54; theory of interest 54
Philosophical Ethics (Beauchamp) 23
philosophical intuitionism 176
philosophy 25, 34
Place of Reason in Ethics, The (Toulmin) 104
Plato 36, 128
Pojman, Louis P. 51
political economy 61
political philosophy 2
Popper, Karl 8, 18
Porter, Burton F. 88
positive moral values 13
positive value *see* good
postulates systems 7–18
potential needs and desires 113
power norms 27
prescriptivism 183–4, 187
primary quality 107–8, 110
primitive concepts 11
primitive inference rules 11
primitive propositions 11
Principia Ethica (Moore) 20, 25
principle of economic freedom 28–9
principle of freedom of thought 29
principle of political liberty 28
principles of self-regarding 14
Pritchard, H. A. 18, 20, 178
pro attitude 80
production and deduction of truth of value judgment 154–5; deductive axiom of truth and falsehood and right and wrong of evaluation 157–9; deductive postulate of the truth and falsehood and right and wrong of moral evaluation 159–60; process 155–7
production and deduction of value judgment: deductive axiom of evaluation in ethics 149–52; deductive

postulate of moral evaluation in ethics 152–4; process 145–9
property, categories of 106–7, 107
property of factual relation 106
property of object 101–4
property of value relation 106
Protagoras 36, 112
proximity 55
psychology 69
pure bad 80–3
purposelessness. 84

Rachel, James 32
Rawls, John 5, 18–19, 26, 36, 188
reaction 67
reaction of value 69–71
realism 128, 136; subjectivism 133–5; theory of relationship 135–6; types of theory of 130–3
real substance of value 112
reflection 67–8
reflection of value mistakes 70
Reichenbach, Hans 10, 17, 19
Reid, Charles L. 46
relational property 105
relationship, 134
relativity: and absoluteness 118–21; of existence of ought 121
reputation 15
Ricardo, Smith 58–60, 62–3, 66
Rickert, Heinrich 101
right 78, 84–90
Right and the Good, The (Ross) 46
righteousness 42
rightness 177
right or wrong utility 68
Rolston III, Holmes 128
Ross, W. D. 18, 20, 26, 46, 78–9, 83–84, 86, 178
Russell, Bertrand 11, 18, 20, 35, 75, 84, 91, 179–81

Saburo, Makiguchi 54
Samuelson, Paul A. 59–60
Santas, Gerasimos X 32
Sartre, Jean-Paul 30
Schlick, Moritz 18, 20, 84, 86
Schumpeter, Joseph A. 66
science, ethics of: excellent morality 2–3; morality 1–2; moral values 4–5; practical status 35–8; theoretical status 33–5
scientification 5–6

210 *Index*

scientific axioms 11
Searle, John R. 146
secondary qualities 107–8, 110
self-interest 160, 166
self-knowledge 53
selflessly benefiting others 27, 88
self-preservation 76, 89
self-respect 2, 14
self-sacrifice 30, 76–7, 89
self-transformation 53
Shu Hong 56
Shuo Wen Jie Zie 41, 75
simplicity 9
Sinnott-Armstrong, Walter 176
Skousen, Mark 66
Slote, Michael 24
Smith, Adam 61–3, 66
Smith, Michael 22, 59
social sciences 25
Socrates 35–6
Spinello, Richard A. 179
Spinoza, Baruch 5, 17–20, 116, 176, 188;
   axioms 18; postulates 18
standard of the peony's beauty 111
stateology 114, 143, 173
Statman, Daniel 32
Stegmüller, Wolfgang 75
Stevenson, Charles L. 11, 19–20, 46,
   179, 181
Stevenson's theory 156
subject 71
subjective judgments 12, 15
subjective needs 121
subjectivism 133–4, 136
subjectivity 51–3, 92
subject–object relationship 56, 136
substance and standard 110–16, 126;
   duality of the structure of existence of
   value 112–13; structure of existence of
   value 110–12
substance of value 112
suicide 1–2; behavioral ought 2; cultural
   moral norm 2
system of mutually independent
   axioms 10
system of scientific theory 9

Tarski, Alfred 9
Taylor, Richard 24, 85
tertiary qualities 108
theoretical system 8
theory of human nature 14
theory of interest 54

Theory of Justice, A (Rawls) 18, 23
theory of marginal utility 58, 62
theory of meaning 56
theory of property 56
theory of realism 123–7
theory of relationship 55
Timmons, Mark 20
Toulmin, Stephen Edelston 19–20, 104–5
Treatise of Human Nature, A
   (Hume) 139
Trianosky, Gregory Velazco Y. 23–4, 32
truth 67
truth and/or falsehood and right and/
   or wrong of evaluation: deductive
   axioms 157–9, 168
truth and/or falsehood and right and/or
   wrong of moral evaluation: deductive
   postulates 159–60, 170–1

Ukraintseff, Украинцев, БС 68
Ultimate Consciousness of Our Youth
   (Chen Duxiu) 37
ultimate goal of morality 15
ultimately bad 80
ultimately good 78–80
unconsciousness 84
universalizability 90
universal moral norms 2
universal needs of subject 116
Urmson, J. O. 179
utilitarianism 175
utility 54
utility of "surplus needs" 60
utility theory of value 51, 55–63, 66

value, concept of 54, 58, 65, 109;
   commodity 58–61; defined 58–9;
   paradox of value 61–6
value, duality of the structure of the
   existence of 112
value, reaction of: cognitive, emotional,
   volitional, and behavioral evaluations
   71–2; definition of evaluation 69–71;
   reflection and reaction 66–9
value sciences 91, 95, 95
values: of commodity 61; in ethics,
   deductive axioms 167; fact 92–3;
   judgments 12, 84, 103, 149, 164;
   relation 56; structure of the existence
   of 110–12
value terms 11, 45
value, utility theory of 51, 61–2; object
   and subject 56–8; subject and object

Index   211

51–3; utility of the object to need of subject 53–6
virtue-centrism 26–33
virtue ethics 15, 19, 23–5
volcanoes 52
volition 69
volitional evaluation 71–2, 149–52, 157
volitional moral evaluation 153–4, 168, 170

Wang Xianjun 6
Watson, Gary 24, 32
Western ethics 23
Wicksell, Knut 58
Wilsons, Bryan 51
Windelband, Wilhelm 134
wisdom 2, 14
Wittgenstein, Ludwig 18, 20, 179
Wright, G. H. von 146, 184

wrongness 1, 3, 8, 31, 80; of actions 31; of emotional evaluation 157; moral bad 84–6; moral evaluation in ethics 154–5; morality 3; normative theories 20; reflection and reaction 66–9; utility 68
Wu Changde 7
Wundt, Wilhelm 43

Xianjun Wang 10
Xia Zhentao 68

Yang Zhu 30
Yan Zhijie 59, 65
Yuan Guiren 56, 103

Zhu Di 128–9
Zhu Geliang 159
Zhu Guangqian 102, 134–5